GUITAR

MUSIC · HISTORY · PLAYERS

GUITAR

MUSIC · HISTORY · PLAYERS

RICHARD CHAPMAN
FOREWORD BY ERIC CLAPTON

LONDON, NEW YORK, MUNICH,
MELBOURNE, DELHI

Editorial: Cover (2) Cover a.t.e.

Design: Tim Foster

Managing Editor: Susannah Marriott

Art Director: Anne-Marie Bulat

Production Controller: Martin Croshaw

First published in Great Britain in 2000
First paperback edition in 2003
by Dorling Kindersley Limited
80 Strand, London WC2R ORL

Dates

Dates have been checked to be as accurate as possible.
Recordings are dated by the year of their release.
For classical works, dates of first performances are
given where relevant.
Life dates are given wherever possible. All efforts
have been made to find the life dates of all
guitarists featuring in the book but in some instances
the information has been impossible to find.

A CIP catalogue record for this book is available from
the British Library

ISBN 1 4053 0190 2

Text film output by Brightside Partnership
Reproduced in Singapore by Colourscan
Printed and bound by L. Rex Printing
Company Limited, China.

see our complete
catalogue at

www.dk.com

CONTENTS

FOREWORD

Music has always been the most essential part of my life. Ever since I first heard the guitar introduction to Buddy Holly's "That'll Be The Day", listening to, and eventually making, music has been a very serious business to me. I love, and have loved, all kinds of music, from the ragas of Bismullah Khan to the second-line shuffles of Prof. Longhair, but I have been drawn most of all to the music of the guitar. There are countless reasons for this, but in hindsight perhaps the most significant is that, at its best, it represents the human voice in an almost anonymous, spiritual way, bypassing the intellect and coming straight from the heart. There are many other instruments that, in the right hands, are also able to achieve this phenomenon, most notably the Shehnai and the Sitar, but for me the guitar has offered the most accessible route.

Then, of course, there is the visual history, a whole other journey, taking us through the evolution of design, from the 'ud to the Strat, with eroticism always lurking just beneath the surface, and I'm sure this book will offer a very enlightened view on these matters. In my experience, the guitar has transcended all these things, it has become a friend, and we have had a deep relationship that has lasted over 40 years. These days, I never like to be without a guitar somewhere near me; it has enhanced my life, and healed me in ways that are beyond words. I hope in this book you will find something of that which has nurtured me so well for so long.

Eric Clapton

INTRODUCTION

As far as I am aware, this is the first attempt to cover all the main areas of guitar music in one volume. For many years I have felt strongly that something needed to be written about a phenomenon that plays a part in almost every musical genre and many cultures throughout the world. This book is my attempt to fill the gap; it is predominantly the story of individuals whose creativity and self-expression has produced music that is central to people's lives.

In a way, this project also completes part of my own personal history. I was irresistibly drawn to the guitar as a child in the 1960s and, looking back, I realize that this was partly because the guitar was going through one of its golden periods, with great music of all types evolving almost daily. However, the jazz musicians I admired played other instruments, and my favourite composers did not write for guitar, so I felt the need to search for interesting guitarists who were working in areas to do with creative improvisation and unusual harmonies – this also led me to feel that, for me as a player, the instrument was undeveloped and could be a vehicle for some of the incredible ideas that had emerged in other areas of music.

Coming from a village in Kent that was a cultural wasteland, a school I detested, and a family in which music-making was seen as dangerous and subversive, this was not easy, and I have to thank my brother Mick for helping me initially. Eventually I managed to save up and buy a guitar, and found self-fulfilment through playing. When I was 14, all my music and instruments were destroyed and burnt by my father, but this only gave me a greater determination to succeed. On a long musical journey, I worked hard at playing the guitar and exploring music. I was continually surprised to discover that the guitar had produced an unrivalled variety of music, and I felt comforted that it had often been produced by people who had had a difficult time in the world.

This book is written to help and inspire people and, apart from charting the courses of those who are well known, to point to some of the more obscure and overlooked areas for the benefit of the mainstream reader. This has been a vast undertaking and my manuscript notes ran to many times the length of this book. The final selection of artists, instruments and material was difficult to make and is personal to a certain extent. I hope that readers will enjoy what I have chosen to include and that this book will do some good and play a small part in helping the guitar to continue to evolve.

Richard Chapman

CLASSICAL

THE GUITAR HAS A LONG AND MYSTERIOUS
HISTORY. EMERGING CLEARLY IN THE 16TH
CENTURY, IT IS PART OF A FAMILY OF
INSTRUMENTS THAT HAS BEEN IN EXISTENCE
FOR THOUSANDS OF YEARS. EARLY GUITAR
MUSIC LED TO CENTURIES OF MUSICAL
DEVELOPMENT THAT FORMS THE BASIS OF
THE CLASSICAL GUITAR REPERTOIRE.

ANDRÉS SEGOVIA *Represented here in an oil painting from c.1920 as a man of the arts,
Segovia brought the guitar into the mainstream as a concert instrument.*

EARLY HISTORY

Images of instruments resembling guitars date back over 3000 years. By the 13th century there are frequent depictions of a guitar-shaped instrument throughout Europe. References to playing occur in the 15th century, and guitar music appears from the 16th century.

CANTIGAS DE SANTA MARIA
These manuscripts of vocal works from c.1275 show the instrument, known in some sources as the guitarra latina, *being played with a plectrum in a court setting. The Latin guitar is a precursor of early guitars.*

Various early forms of instrument with strings running along a neck, which were stopped and plucked to form notes, and with a resonating sound chamber to increase the volume, undoubtedly existed in remote antiquity. An instrument with affinities with the guitar as we know it today appears on stone reliefs from an area of Asia Minor, now in modern Turkey, dating from as far back as 1350 BC. This instrument had a body with incurved sides, a neck with frets and a number of strings. This form of instrument was not depicted or described by the Greeks or Romans, but may have survived in the Near East until its descendant surfaced in Europe in the medieval period. An image in the Carolingian Psalters of the 9th century shows an instrument whose outline form has affinities with these ancient images. By the 13th century, church iconography and manuscripts show the precursors to renaissance and baroque guitars.

In 1349 Duke Jehan of Normandy employed musicians who played guitars known as *guiterre morische* (Moorish guitar) and *guitarra latina* (Latin guitar). The *guiterre morische* was not really a guitar but an early form of lute, which later developed into both the European lute and the modern Arabic 'ud, but the *guitarra latina* was the direct ancestor of the modern guitar. There is much confusion over the nomenclature of these early instruments, which appeared in various forms in Spain, Italy and Southern France, and names varied according to country, social class and repertoire as well as type of instrument.

Johannes Tinctoris, writing in 1487, describes two separate forms of instrument – one "invented by the Spanish which both they and the Italians call the *viola* [*vihuela* in Spanish, not be confused with the modern viola]...This *viola* differs from the lute in that the lute is much larger and tortoise shaped, while the *viola* is flat and curved inwards on each side"; and the other "the instrument invented by the Catalans, which some call the *guiterra* and others the *ghiterne*... the *guiterra* is used most rarely because of the thinness of its sound. When I heard it in Catalonia it was being used much more often by women to accompany love songs, than by men". In Italy these two instruments were known respectively as the *viola da mano* and *chitarra*. The *vihuela da mano* in Spain was predominantly an instrument with six pairs, or courses, of strings and its repertoire was quite sophisticated. It coexisted with the *guitarra,* which was a smaller and lighter instrument with only four courses, and a limited and simpler repertoire. The instruments had similarities and there were fingerstyle and plectrum techniques. Faxardo, writing in the 16th century, states that the *guitarra* "won't bear the fingers but must be touched with a fine quill to make it exert its harmony".

By the 16th century, the guitar had become widespread. In 1547, Henry VIII of England had 21 guitars among his large collection of musical instruments in Hampton Court Palace, and a writer in France in 1556 states that "in my earliest years we used to play the lute more than the guitar, but for twelve or fifteen years now everyone has been guitarring". Referring to the guitar, Tobias Stimmer (1539–84) wrote "one can tell by the looks of it that it served as an introduction to the lute, for accompanying old songs, for reciting old tales and a good many other things. We should preserve the tradition of our elders".

VIHUELA MUSIC

The earliest surviving music for the *vihuela* comes from early 16th-century Spain, and consists of courtly dances, sets of variations and song accompaniments written for the upper levels of society. Seven manuscripts of *vihuela* music have survived. These collections of pieces acted as both entertainment and instruction, and the music was written using a diagrammatic notation called tablature, with numbers representing fret positions on each string and notes above showing the time values. The *vihuela* was originally tuned similarly to the lute, but specific *vihuela* tunings evolved. The composer Luis Narvaez (fl.1530–50), in 1538 mentions tunings at different registers with bottom strings ranging from A down to D, and Juan Bermudo (c.1510–65) gives tunings for the six courses of ADGBEA and GCFADG in 1555.

VIOLA DA MANO
This engraving from 1510 by Marcantonio Raimondi shows the Bolognese Giovanni Filoteo Achillini (1466–1538) playing fingerstyle on a five-course viola de mano. He was an improvisatore, a singing poet who composed words and music and accompanied himself on what is in effect an early guitar.

El Maestro (1535) by the Spaniard Luis Milan (1500–1561) contains the earliest known *vihuela* music with pieces of varying degrees of technical difficulty, including six courtly dances known as pavanes. Alonso Mudarra's (1508–80) *Tres Libros de Musica en Cifra para Vihuela* (1546) contains a sophisticated *Fantasia,* a freely composed piece based on material found throughout Europe, later appearing under the name *La Folia* (The Folly). The *Fantasia* includes sections based on a recurrent theme known as a ground bass, and the style is modelled on the playing of the contemporary harpist Ludovico. Syncopation gives it an energetic feel, and the style ranges from simple chords to complex counterpoint, and adventurous harmonies with some clashing discords.

GUITAR MUSIC

With a more limited range than the *vihuela,* repertoire for the four-course guitar was less sophisticated. Mudarra's *Tres Libros* also contain some of the first music for the guitar. There are four fantasias, a courtly pavane and a version of *O guardame les vacas* (Mind the cows for me) based on the traditional Romanesca ground bass.

During the 1550s, a number of books of music specifically for the guitar existed in France, where the instrument was widely played and well established. Collections by Guillaume De Morlaye, Simon Gorlier, Adrian Le Roy and others contain adaptations of lute pieces, arrangements and compositions including fantasias and courtly dances such as the pavane and galliard, and there are also song accompaniments and consort music including melodic parts for the guitar.

The *vihuela de cinco ordines,* a five-course guitar, also appeared around this time. The first music for this instrument was included in the 16th-century composer Miguel de Fuenllana's *Orphenica Lyra* (1554), which included fantasias, transcribed excerpts from a mass and a *villancico* love song.

Vihuela

El Maestro
First published in Valencia in 1535, Luis Milan's Libro de Musica de Vihuela de Mano *has a frontispiece showing Orpheus serenading birds and animals. The term* da mano *refers to the right-hand playing technique with fingers which was standard practice, and there was a* vihuela de penola *played with a quill plectrum.*

Vihuela
This instrument in the Musée Jacquemart Andrée in Paris was made in the 1500s. It has six courses of strings and originally had ten gut frets tied at the back. It is stamped with the mark of the Spanish monastery of Guadalupe. Vihuelas were used on their own and in consorts.

GUITAR STRINGS & TUNINGS

Early guitars had gut strings placed in pairs, or courses, with a variety of tunings. Mudarra's four-course guitar, which had ten frets, was tuned to either FCEA or later GCEA, with the top three courses tuned in unison (the same note), and the bottom pair an octave apart, known as a *bordon*; but Bermudo states that the tuning of the four-course guitar is the same as the four middle strings of the *vihuela* — CFAD. There were also some "re-entrant" tunings, where the bottom course is tuned to a pitch higher than some of the other strings: for example the GDF♯B tuning, where the fourth course is tuned just above the second strings. French guitar books of the 1550s show guitars with a single top string, hence the Italian name *chitarra da sette corde* (7-string guitar), and there were also some five-course instruments.

This early guitar music was not played rigidly, and room was given for improvisation allowing for small variations and expressive ornamentation within the form.

Among early playing techniques were *inegale*, picking notes and melodies with the thumb and index finger, and *rasgueado* strumming, unfurling the fingers across the strings. There were many different levels of ability among guitarists, and pieces were aimed at different levels of society; depending on the skill of the player, techniques ranged from *punteado*, plucking harmonies and florid single-note passages and counterpoint, to simple strumming.

The fashion in the late 16th century for rather basic styles and a use of rigid chord patterns for strumming prompted some criticism. The popularity of the guitar among ordinary people was lamented by the inquisitor Covarrubias writing in 1611, who complained: "but now the guitar is no more than a cowbell, so easy to play, especially *rasgueado*, that there is not a stable lad who is not a musician on the guitar".

FIVE-COURSE TUTOR
*Carlos y Amat's 1596
Guitarra Espanola y
Vandola self-instruction
book for five-course guitar
uses an ADGBE tuning and
shows pictures of twelve*

*major and twelve minor
chords. It advocates a
simple strumming style
that enables the guitarists
to play dances and songs
in different keys.*

BELCHIOR DIAS
*Being so fragile, no totally
authentic early guitars have
survived. This heavily
restored instrument has a
label indicating that it was
made by Belchior Dias in*

*Lisbon in 1581, and is one
of the only dated guitars
from the 16th century. It
has a small body, a vaulted
back, a string length of
just over 55.4cm (22in)
and five courses.*

MATTEO SELLAS
*This five-course instrument
was made by Matteo Sellas
in Venice in 1614. His
labels often state that he
was based at the "sign of
the star". It has foliate
decoration, a soundhole
with a parchment rosette
with an intricate pattern,
a vaulted back and a 71cm
(28in) string length with
nine frets made of gut and
tied around the neck.*

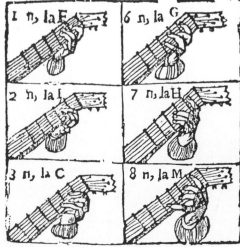

VOBOAM GUITAR
Made in 1641 in Paris by René Voboam, this instrument represents a period when the guitar was treated as a work of art, with its ebony and ivory edge-binding and inlays, decorated bridge and fingerboard and tortoiseshell back panels.

THE BAROQUE AGE

During the Baroque period, from roughly 1600 to the early 1700s, the five-course guitar effectively replaced the four-course guitar and the six-course *vihuela*, and a standard ADGBE began to predominate, with the two lowest courses often using bourdons and sometimes creating re-entrant tunings with high notes.

The first major figure is the Italian Giovanni Paolo Foscarini. Little is known about him, but published works from 1630 show that he was bringing a new level of sophistication with a mixture of strummed and plucked styles. After him, another Italian, Francesco Corbetta

LADY WITH A GUITAR
This painting by Dutch artist Johannes Vermeer from 1672 shows a five-course guitar not dissimilar in style to many French guitars from the 17th century. The guitar was played by both men and women, and was popular with wealthy families.

(c.1615–81), one of the foremost virtuosos of the period, travelled widely, becoming well known and highly influential. He wrote material which is often technically difficult, with complex invention and ornamentation including double trills. Among his most developed works are the chaconnes, courtly dances. Corbetta's *La Guitarre Royale* (1671) was dedicated to Charles II, who played the guitar.

Amusingly, the diarist Samuel Pepys wrote upon hearing Corbetta that he played admirably, yet "I was mightily troubled that so many pains were taken on so bad an instrument".

The Frenchman Robert de Visée (c.1660–1720) studied with Corbetta, and produced suites in his *Livre de Guitarre* (1682) and *Livre de Pieces* (1686).

The Spanish guitarist and composer Gaspar Sanz (1640–1710) was influenced by Italian music and thought Corbetta "the best of all". He published *Instruccion de Musica Sobra la Guitarra Espanola* (1674), and wrote passacalles, preludes, and pavannes; and among his works are the attractive Canarios melodies. During the 17th century, music with a continuo role for the guitar was in widespread use where the player has a bass part from which he can improvise voicings to lay down a harmonic part in songs and ensemble pieces.

Toward the end of the 17th century William Turner, writing in 1697, could say that "the fine easie ghittar, whose performance is soon gained, at least after the brushing way, hath at this time overtopt the nobler lute" and "nor is it to be denied that after the pinching way the ghittar makes some good work".

THE 1700s

In the 18th century, many changes took place with the invention of the piano and the advent of the classical era, and there are few serious written works. Paintings by French artist Antoine Watteau (1684–1721) reflect one aspect of the guitar in society as an instrument for the amorous or frivolous. A German writer in 1713 says "the flat guitar with its strum, strum we shall happily leave to the garlic-eating Spaniards". Yet the Italian composer Domenico Scarlatti (1685–1757), of whom it was said "surely no composer ever fell more deeply under its spell", has Spanish guitar influences reflected in his harpsichord compositions. The guitar was still popular and published works are often light song accompaniments. After the French Revolution of 1789, among the property confiscated from the aristocracy by the Committee for Public Safety were dozens of guitars.

THE GUITAR IN TRANSITION

During the mid 1700s, there was a gradual move to adding a lower string, tuned to E, to the five-course guitar, giving a standard tuning of EADGBE. Books started to appear for six-course instruments with this tuning, including Antonio Ballestero's *Obra para Guitarra de Seis Ordenes* (Works for the six-course guitar) in 1780. Modern stave notation started to replace the old tablature, and one of the first to use this exclusively was Michel Corrette's *Les Dons d'Apollon* (1763). Toward the end of the 18th century, the Spanish monk Padre Basilio in Madrid composed 6-string music for guitar and one of his pupils, Federico Moretti, wrote *The Principles of Playing the Guitar with Six Strings* (1799).

GUITAR DEVELOPMENTS

During the 1780s across Europe, there was a trend toward making guitars with six single strings led by the Italians and French with small pockets of change in other countries. Many Spanish makers, however, continued to produce six-course instruments, and this stringing system was not fully eclipsed by the six single strings until the 1830s. Music for six single strings was being produced by the 1790s. Ferdinando Carulli (1770–1841) was born in Naples and he developed his playing technique at a time when six-single-string instruments were firmly established in the city. He was one of the figures who played a part in the resurgence of the guitar, and developed his own approaches to technique that formed the basis of his studies and compositions, which he published a number of years later after he moved to Paris.

FABRICATORE
This instrument made by Giovanni Battista Fabricatore in Naples in 1793 has six single strings. He was consistently making instruments of this type from the 1780s onward; other Neapolitan makers were also producing instruments with six single strings.

THE 19th CENTURY

A new generation of Spanish and Italian guitarists took up the guitar with six single strings, composing and performing work to a high standard. Many were displaced by the Napoleonic wars and moved north to the musical centres of London, Paris and Vienna.

During the first half of the 19th century, there was a resurgence of interest in the guitar, and figures emerged with great ability as players, composers and teachers. Their music, together with the studies and methods they produced, helped to modernize the instrument. London, Paris and Vienna became major centres for the guitar, which once again became fashionable and popular. One of the key figures, Fernando Sor (1778–1839), was born in Barcelona and studied music in the monastery of Montserrat, where he was forbidden to use a guitar. After leaving the monastery, he was influenced by the work of Federico Moretti and left Spain in 1813, settling in Paris. An outstanding virtuoso, Sor built a tremendous reputation across Europe and his first book of *Studies* (Op.6) contains important material. Sor produced a large body of work, ranging from short minuets to sonatas, and among his chief characteristics is his gift for writing and arranging melodies. Among his best-known works are the Variations on a theme from Mozart's the *Magic Flute* (Op.9), based on the melody "Das Klingelt So Herrlich", the duo for two guitars, *L'Encouragement* (Op.34) and his highly creative *Fantasy* (Op.54). The sonata *Grand Solo* is an exceptional piece reflecting influences from the keyboard composer Domenico Scarlatti. Sor also wrote a *Method for the Guitar* (1830).

Another Spaniard, Dionisio Aguado (1784–1849), also wrote a *Method for Guitar* (1825), which contains complex studies to develop right-hand techniques, including harmonic control and rhythmic independence between thumb and fingers; he used right-hand nails in contrast to Fernando Sor. After moving to Paris in 1826, he became friends with Sor and wrote extensively for the guitar, producing works such as *Variations on the Fandango* (Op.16).

1836 PANORMO
Louis Panormo, who worked in London, considered that he made guitars in "The Spanish Way", partly referring to the use of internal fan bracing. His guitars have raised fingerboards and slotted headstocks.

1835 LACOTE
Rene Francois Lacote's (1785–1855) instruments were played by Aguado and recommended by Sor. This one has the older style fingerboard flush with the top, a string saddle on the bridge and a modern-style slotted headstock.

CARULLI & CARCASSI

Two Italians who settled in Paris early in the 19th century produced important guitar material. Ferdinando Carulli (1770–1841) wrote a *Method for Guitar* (Op.27) (1810) and *Le Harmonie Applique a la Guitare* (1825), which dealt with accompaniment and theory. He also wrote concerti, a sonata, trios for guitar, flute and violin, duos for guitar and piano and music for three guitars. Matteo Carcassi (1792–1853), whose outstanding *Etudes* (Op.60) are fine compositions, also made a major contribution.

MAURO GIULIANI

The Italian virtuoso Mauro Giuliani (1781–1829) settled in Vienna in 1806, where he made a tremendous impact. Vienna was one of the great musical centres and his concerts were attended by Ludwig Van Beethoven, who pronounced that "the guitar is an orchestra in itself". He played duos with the pianist Johann Nepomuk Hummel, and as a soloist toured throughout Europe to great acclaim. He used unusual techniques, such as using his thumb for bass notes. An important moment in the development of the guitar was his *Concerto No.1* in A major for guitar and orchestra, which he performed in 1808. This was the first modern concerto for the instrument. It has strong melodic themes that are developed in the first movement. The second movement is slower, with a siciliana rhythm, and the final movement is a lively polonaise. Themes and motifs are exchanged between the guitar and the orchestra. He also wrote two further concertos and fine sonatas, and 22 duos for guitar with flute or violin. His *Duo Concertant* (Op.25) for violin and guitar in E minor and *Gran Duetto Concertante* (Op.52) for flute and guitar in A major stand out. His six *Rossinianae* (Op.119–124), written during the 1820s, are based on themes by Rossini, and have a sophistication that marks the growing development of guitar music. Guiliani also wrote quartets with a *terz* guitar, which is tuned a third higher.

Great figures played the guitar, including the composer Schubert (1797–1828), who stated: "the guitar is a wonderful instrument understood by few", and wrote songs with guitar accompaniment, and the brilliant Italian violin virtuoso Nicolò Paganini (1782–1840), who played the guitar to a high standard and wrote solo and chamber works for it, including the *Grand Sonata* in A.

After the age of Sor and Giuliani, a younger generation of guitarists emerged who developed current trends and composed for guitar. Napoleon Coste (1806–83) wrote *Grand Duo* for two guitars and *La Source du Lyson*, and made arrangements of J. S. Bach. His music has a pianistic style, as does the work of Johann Kaspar Mertz (1806–56) – known as "the Liszt of the guitar" – whose *Bardenklange* pieces are dazzling and energetic.

The distinguished Italian Giulio Regondi (1822–72) wrote *Reverie*, an early tremolo piece, and flamboyant works, including *Introduction et Caprice* (Op.23), which has fast tempos, rapid scale passages and ornamentation conveying passionate intensity.

DIONISIO AGUADO
This illustration from 1843 shows Aguado supporting a French Laprevotte guitar on a stand called a tripodison.

This device was not adopted by guitarists, who used a range of postures to support the guitar on their left or right leg.

FERNANDO SOR
The most famous of the early 19th-century figures, Fernando Sor became established in the classical world through his compositions and concerts in cities ranging from Moscow to London.

THE GIULIANIAD
Such was Mauro Giuliani's fame that the first English guitar magazine published by Ferdinand Pelzer in London was launched in 1833 and called The Giulianiad. *It included reviews of performances as well as articles about guitar music.*

FRANCISCO TÁRREGA

The Spanish guitarist Francisco Tárrega (1852–1909) studied with Julian Arcas (1832–82) and made his debut at the age of eleven. He practised long hours, becoming a tremendous virtuoso, and he toured extensively, paving the way for the modern classical guitar

FRANCISCO TÁRREGA
Tárrega played without nails, and helped to standardize techniques and establish a posture with the guitar on the left leg with support from a footstool. Among his pupils were figures who later played a major part in developing the guitar in the 20th century, including Miguel Llobet and Emilio Pujol.

by adopting the new instruments built by Antonio De Torres and others. As an arranger, Tárrega made an important step in the evolution of the guitar repertoire by transcribing and arranging works originally written for other instruments by major composers such as J. S. Bach. Previously, very little serious music had been transcribed for guitar, and the repertoire was limited to works specifically composed for the instrument and some arrangements of popular and rather lightweight pieces. Tárrega made transcriptions of piano works by Chopin and contemporary Spanish composers Isaac Albeniz and Enrique Granados.

As a composer, Tárrega wrote *Capricho árabe* (1888), which has an atmospheric Moorish flavour and contrasting moods, ranging from dark colours using a sixth string dropped to D to brighter melodic sections. His well-known study *Recuerdos de la Alhambra* features a continuous rippling melody line, with the notes played with rapid tremolo with three fingers, supported by attractive arpeggios that are played with the thumb.

Tárrega was an extremely influential teacher and he built up a close circle of admirers and pupils.

1889 TORRES GUITAR

The key figure in the evolution of the modern classical guitar, Antonio de Torres (1817–92) built his first known instrument in Seville in 1854. His guitars have more volume and projection with a larger, deeper body, and Torres designed a new, aesthetically pleasing outline shape and bridge that became the template for the standard modern classical form. His major contribution is the improvement of a fan-bracing system which balances the instrument and enhances tone. Built in Almeria in 1889, with a spruce top and mahogany body, this instrument was later modified with slots cut for machine-heads.

MIGUEL LLOBET
A foremost Spanish guitarist, Llobet (1878–1938) studied with Tárrega and, in contrast to him, played with nails. After a triumphant recital in Paris in 1905, he became a major figure, prompting Manuel De Falla to write Homenaje Pour Le Tombeau De Claude Debussy in 1920. He recorded from 1925.

ANDRÉS SEGOVIA

A strong individualist, Andrés Segovia was a powerful performer whose magnetic charisma and authoritative stage presence gave the guitar a new stature. He worked hard to establish the guitar in the classical world and had a conservative approach to music, working within Spanish traditions.

played a *Gavotte* and *Rondeau* from Bach's solo violin *Partita* in E major BWV 1006, a Courante from the *Cello Suite* BWV 1009 and Sor's *Theme Varie*. His characterful interpretation of Bach is marked by strong, mannered accents and see-sawing tempos and dynamics. He plays Sor with a seductive charm and impish sparkle. In his 1928 adaptation of Bach's *Prelude* in D minor BWV 999, written for the lute, he transposes the piece up a tone from C minor to D minor, and makes a number of small alterations for the guitar. Segovia, in his own words, worked "deliriously" on Bach's *Chaconne* from the Second *Partita* in D minor for solo violin during the 1920s, and did not perform it until 1935 in Paris, where it was met with derision by those who thought it was inappropriate for the guitar. It was, in fact, a triumph, and was to became a staple of the

The great classical guitar figure of the 20th century, Andrés Segovia (1893–1987) was born in Linares in Spain. He was self taught, and although he did not study with Tárrega, developed within the framework established by him, playing a repertoire based around both guitar compositions and arrangements of works written for other instruments by major composers and lesser known figures. Segovia made his debut in Granada at the Centro Artistico in 1909, performed in Madrid in 1912 and, from 1916, toured South America. In 1924, Segovia made debuts in London and Paris. Segovia's repertoire consisted of a wide variety of works and he played with a lyrical musicality, using nails on gut strings.

Segovia made an effort to bring the work of the great composer J. S. Bach (1685–1750) to the guitar repertoire, transcribing and adapting pieces and arranging excerpts. On his first commercial recording date on 2 May 1927, he

I LOVE EVE
Pablo Picasso's oil painting
I Love Eve (at Sorgues
1912) is one of many
works featuring the guitar
and other instruments in a
Cubist style, and reflects the
instrument's growing re-
emergence and popularity
in the early 20th century.

GUITAR AMBASSADOR
In the 1920s, Segovia
travelled the world and was
starting to establish a
reputation as the
"ambassador of the guitar".
A masterful performer,
Segovia demanded silence
and concentration from his
audiences and drew them
with pieces that acted as
vehicles for his emotional
expressiveness.

instrument's repertoire. During the 1920s and 1930s Segovia recorded a wide range of material by figures ranging from Robert De Visée to Tárrega, and he continually enlarged his performing repertoire.

COMMISSIONING WORKS

Segovia wrote for the guitar himself but was particularly interested in encouraging composers who did not write for the instrument to start producing works. Great

changes had been taking place with the introduction of new ideas, such as the increasing abandonment of older forms and the use of dissonance and atonality. Segovia disliked this and had strong views on music, wanting material that was traditional and melodic, with a style harking back to earlier eras. Through his advocacy, the Spanish composers Joaquín Turina (1882–1949) and Federico Moreno Torroba (1891–1981) produced a number of works for guitar that often have strong Spanish characteristics

BACH'S CHACONNE

Segovia made his own guitar transcription of Bach's *Chaconne* from the *Second Partita* in D minor for solo violin with numbers next to the notes for left-hand fingering, circles with numbers for the string to be played and some right-hand fingering directions. The guitar has the bottom string tuned down from E to D, and the excerpt below has undulating scalar invention flowing above accented bass notes for the four bars, a fifth bar without chords, and the next three and a half bars have a series of chords moving toward D major.

ANDRÉS SEGOVIA 1935
Segovia had become a renowned figure by 1935, when he performed Bach's Chaconne.

incorporating elements from flamenco. Turina's pieces include *Sevillana* (1923) and the colourful *Fandanguillo* (1925) and *Sonata*. Torroba wrote, among other works, *Sonatina in A* (1924) and *Suite Castellana* (1925), which was recorded by Segovia in 1928. Segovia became friends with Mexican composer Manuel Ponce (1882–1948) who produced a *Suite in A major* in the style of the baroque lutenist Sylvius Weiss, which Segovia recorded in 1930. Ponce drew on many strands, including Mexican folk music. The three movement *Sonatina Meridionel* (1932) has a final movement with Spanish flamenco influences, and Ponce also wrote *Concierto del Sur* (1941).

The Italian composer Mario Castelnuovo-Tedesco (1895–1968) wrote the first guitar concerto of the 20th century for Segovia, The Guitar Concerto in D (Op.99) (1939), which has a dancing energy with cadenzas after each movement.

Hermann Hauser 1

POSTWAR CAREER

Segovia continued to make recordings after the war, and his interpretation of Albeniz and Granados from the 1940s stands out. In the 1940s, he became interested in using nylon for strings. A reliable material, nylon could be used to produce strings that were well-formed and consistent with each other, giving a more even response and better intonation than gut strings. They were also less liable to break – an innovation that helped the classical guitar.

By the 1950s, Segovia was surrounded by talented pupils and generations of players who had been inspired by his recordings and performances. His avoidance of neutral interpretation and capricious idiosyncrasies with vibratos and rubatos had considerable stylistic influence. He continued to be active, giving the first performance of Joaquin Rodrigo's *Fantasia para un Gentilhombre* (1954) in 1958. A person of presence and gravitas, Segovia presided over a world in which he took a leading role in establishing the guitar as the major 20th-century instrument.

SEGOVIA'S HAUSER
Segovia played a Ramirez from 1912, and in the 1930s met the German musical instrument maker Hermann Hauser (1882–1952), who was based in Munich. Hauser later changed his method of making guitars in a Central European style and copied Segovia's Ramirez. This guitar made by Hauser in 1937 was used by Segovia until the 1960s.

MAESTRO
In a long and successful career, Segovia became the grand figure of the classical guitar; he gave concerts around the world until he was in his 80s.

COMPOSERS FOR GUITAR

The resurgence of interest in the classical guitar encouraged many composers in South America and Europe from the 1920s onward. They produced some outstanding music, which has now become part of the classical guitar repertoire.

A figure in the tradition of the great player-composers of the early 19th century, Agustin Pio Barrios (1885–1944) was born in Paraguay and developed a unique approach. At one stage early in his career, he used a steel-string guitar to perform classical pieces. Barrios is the first player of note to record, producing mechanical wax cylinders in the period from 1910–13 that feature his own compositions as well as standard works. A flamboyant and charismatic performer, he toured South America and visited Europe, and is thought to be one of the first guitarists to transcribe and perform the complete Suite No. 1 for lute by J. S. Bach. As a composer, he was inspired by Chopin and Bach, as well as by South American folk music, and his exceptional material includes *Un Sueno en la Floresta* and *Confesion*. A number of his works have survived with variants both in manuscript form and on his own recordings.

COMPOSERS FOR GUITAR

As the guitar and its possibilities started to fire the imagination, new works began to appear. The Spanish composer Manuel de Falla (1876–1946) produced one great work for the guitar, *Homenaje pour le Tombeau de Claude Debussy* (1920), which uses the rhythm

LA CATEDRAL

Inspired by Montevideo Cathedral in Uruguay, in its original version *La Catedral* (1921) consisted of the second two movements, which were recorded by Barrios in 1925. The first movement, *Preludio*, added in 1938, and subtitled *Saudade* (Yearning), conveys a sense of stillness with a shining melody over transparent arpeggiated chords with occasional close voicings and ends with harmonics. *Andante religioso*, based on hearing Bach being played on cathedral organ, has a measured rhythm and mannered chords that have a sense of processional movement with harmonies that evoke ancient traditions. The third part, *Allegro solemne*, was based on the bustle of people in the streets outside the cathedral. Its beautiful linear melodic movements interweave with shimmering cascading arpeggios with shifting harmonies. Strong thematic figures blend into each other, and the movement unfolds with inventive variations building to a perfect finale.

AGUSTIN PIO BARRIOS
A fascinating figure in classical guitar history, Barrios, named himself after a South American Indian chieftan, adding Mangore to his name from 1932. He was billed as "The Paganini of the Guitar from the Jungles of Paraguay".

VILLA-LOBOS FIVE PRELUDES

The *Five Preludes* (1940) each has its own character, and Villa Lobos uses his characteristic approaches to fingering for compositional ideas with shapes moved up and down the fingerboard, and open strings. In the example below, *Prelude No.1* in E minor opens with an emotional cello-like melody on the bass strings over open string chords, before moving to exquisite flourishes of melodic invention with strummed chords and passages of see-sawing glissandos, before

returning to the first theme. The second has an expressive turn of phrase on upper notes and is full of inventive energy with a theme in fifths over arpeggios. The third is gentle and ruminative, with delicate bell-like notes. The fourth has a beautiful simple theme against atmospheric chords and harmonics and explodes into life with arpeggiation, before returning to artificial harmonics. The fifth has elegant and stately rhythms with attractive strummed voicings.

Heitor Villa-Lobos (1887–1959).

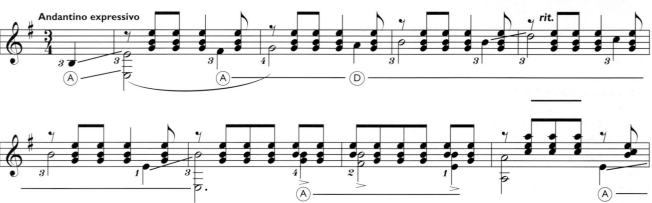

of the Cuban dance, the *habañera,* and has a stately beauty with sombre voicings and expressive lines and quotes from Debussy's piano piece *Soiree dans Granade.*

One of the most important and popular composers for guitar, the Brazilian Heitor Villa-Lobos (1887–1959) produced music with great originality and variety, showing influences as diverse as Impressionism and South American folk music. Among his music for guitar are a superb modernistic set of *Twelve Studies* (1929), which are inventive and melodic, with developing ideas that challenge the player, the *Five Preludes* (1940), and *Choros No.1,* which casts the guitar in a Brazilian-influenced ensemble.

More avant-garde composers also took an interest in the guitar. The serial composer Anton Webern (1883–1945) wrote his *Drei Lieder* (1925) for voice, clarinet and guitar, giving it a lyrical atonality. One of the few solo guitar pieces in a serial style was Frank Martin's (1890–1974) *Quatre Pièces Brèves* (1933), which uses the form of the 17th-century French dance suite.

CONCIERTO DE ARANJUEZ

The most famous piece of music for guitar with orchestra was written by the Spanish composer Joaquín Rodrigo (1901–99). *Concierto de Aranjuez* (1939) evokes the faded grandeur of the gardens of the Palace of Aranjuez and was conceived as a popular classical piece. It was premiered in Barcelona in 1940 by Regino Sainz de la Maza. The first movement starts with rhythmic strummed melodic figures that are taken up by the orchestra, and the guitar interacts with the orchestra, playing melodies and variations punctuated by strummed chords before the opening figure returns. The second-movement, *adagio,* opens with strummed chords supporting a cor anglais playing the captivating sentimental theme, which is then taken up by the guitar. The guitar plays inventive sections alone which convey atmosphere and stillness. The last movement is playful, with a dance-like 3/4 rhythm and passages of variation and interplay between guitar and orchestra.

THE MODERN ERA

From the 1950s onward the classical guitar entered an age of great popularity. A number of outstanding figures emerged, including Julian Bream, who paved the way for the development of a new modern repertoire for the instrument.

JULIAN BREAM
Emerging into the classical world of England in the 1940s, where the guitar was neglected, Bream was a unique figure in a world of amateur enthusiasts. Drive and determination led him to establish himself professionally as a self-defined visionary.

The groundwork for the modern era had been laid by the 1940s, and new virtuosos emerged, such as the French guitarist Ida Presti (1924–67). She married guitarist Alexandre Lagoya (1929–99) in 1952 and they started performing together in 1955, becoming the first great postwar duo, with Lagoya arranging a wide range of works by mainstream classical composers. Their flowing legato approach, with vibrato giving a rich tone, and their expressive interpretation, made the duo very successful. They premiered Castelnuovo-Tedesco's *Concerto for Two Guitars* (1962), and their fine musicality can be heard on their 1965 recording of a *Chaconne in G* by Handel. This reveals a range of textures, from deep vibrato to passages with staccato and muting that are played with delicacy and great dynamic control.

PRESTI-LAGOYA
Ida Presti and Alexandre Lagoya were the first well-known 20th-century guitar duo. Ida Presti played with an unusual technique, using the sides of her nails. The duo made exceptional recordings.

JULIAN BREAM

One of the great figures in the history of the guitar, Julian Bream was born in London in 1933. He has enjoyed a long and influential career as a marvellous player and recording artist who has both arranged many works for the instrument and nurtured contemporary composition.

An admirer of Django Reinhardt, Julian Bream started on steel-string guitar before hearing a recording of Segovia playing *Recuerdos de la Alhambra*. He was captivated, and devoted his main energies to classical guitar. Growing up in postwar Britain, Bream had limited resources and developed his skills by acquiring whatever music was available, practising with works such as Carcassi's *Etudes*. He was largely self taught but helped by the Philharmonic Society of Guitarists, and he studied piano harmony and composition at the Royal College of Music at a time when classical guitar was not taught by music schools.

Bream made his public debut in 1946 at Cheltenham Art Gallery, and followed this with a bigger concert in 1947, playing a wide range of material. This included arrangements by Segovia of Bach, Tarrega's arrangements of Schuman and Albeniz, and pieces by Sor, Coste and others. He started making BBC radio broadcasts in the late 1940s and played to great acclaim at his Wigmore Hall debut in 1951. He also took up the lute and played early music enthusiastically, which gave him an added perspective. Bream's album *The Art of Julian Bream* (1956) features works by Turina, Falla and Segovia, and he embarked on a prolific recording and touring schedule, visiting North America in 1958.

Bream's playing is moving, and marked by well-centred notes with a strong tone, and phrasing which has a strong musicality and depth of feeling. He felt that the guitar could convey an atmosphere and could cast a spell over the audience.

NARCISCO YEPES

Spanish guitarist Narciso Yepes (1927–97) plays with a light agility, and his recordings are precise and beautifully executed. He made the first commercial recording of Rodrigo's Concierto de Aranjuez *in 1955. In 1963, Yepes adopted a ten-string guitar made by Jose Ramirez III, which has four bass strings tuned C, Bb, Ab, and Gb. These helped him to arrange the piano music of Albeniz and Falla and to make fuller transcriptions of baroque pieces. His arrangements and recordings of Telemann and Scarlatti are an important part of his output.*

ENCOURAGING COMPOSITION

Bream felt that the guitar needed a fresh, revitalizing contemporary repertoire for it to be part of the classical world rather than becoming anachronistic. He urged composers to write for the guitar, ushering in a golden age.

BRITISH COMPOSERS

Bream mixed with a wide range of figures in the classical world in the 1950s, and actively encouraged composers to write for the guitar. He helped to demystify the instrument by explaining techniques and textural possibilities and writing articles. This was at a time when the guitar was capturing the imagination, and many composers started to produce high quality works for the instrument. Among the British composers were Reginald Smith-Brindle, who was inspired by Segovia and wrote *El Polifemo de Oro* (1956), and Lennox Berkeley, who wrote *Sonatina* (1958).

Written for Bream, Malcolm Arnold's *Guitar Concerto* (Op.67) (1959) is based around some of Bream's favourite music. The first movement features colourful strumming and incorporates folk melodiousness. The middle lento movement was written as an elegy for Django Reinhardt, and has flavours of blues and jazz, while the last movement's delicacy is derived from lute music.

In the 1950s, Bream asked Benjamin Britten to compose a work for the guitar. The new work, entitled *Nocturnal after John Dowland* (Op.70), was completed in November 1963. A brilliant work full of colour and variety, it exploits the guitar's versatility with technically difficult passages and transcends the limitations and styles of standard guitar repertoire. There are eight sections: the first, marked "Musingly", starts with single notes and offers mysterious rippling ascending arpeggios and dark mysterious chords. This moves to "Very Agitated" which is of full of nervous energy with accented chords; "Restless" offers bleak chords using fourths and seconds with a disturbing atonal melody; and "Uneasy" features flurries of short phrases which stop suddenly, and rocking hammered notes and arpeggios. "March-Like" features a double octave melody on the outer strings with rhythmic voicings using open strings, while "Dreaming" has warm open voicings and passages with artificial harmonics, and the beautiful "Gently Rocking" is rhythmic with a high weaving melodic line. This leads to the final "Passacaglia", in which a variety of upper register phrases are answered by an insistent repeating bass figure that sets up tension. Arpeggiated chords open out with intervallic invention and lead to dramatic muted pizzicato lines, plucked voicings and open and forceful lines. This gives way to a delightful ending marked "Slow and Quiet", resolving the complex feelings and moods with the graceful melody for Dowland's "Come Heavy Sleep" and gentle Elizabethan harmonies. It ends with simple

tranquil chords, and dies away with a few sustaining single notes.

The piece was recorded on Bream's landmark album *20th Century Guitar* (1967), featuring modern works played with great depth and interpretative perception.

Another major work, William Walton's *Five Bagatelles* (1972), was written for Bream and dedicated to Malcolm Arnold. Very expressive, it has touches of modernistic jazz harmony. It opens with a celebratory arpeggiated flourish on open strings, moving into an exuberant rhythmic and melodic section with constant metrical changes imparting energy and variety. Part II has a polytonal depth with major inversions over unusual bass notes. III adopts a Cuban 3/8 rhythm and a dropped 6th string to D. After a reflective part IV, the piece ends with V, which opens with a rhythmic theme before building to an exultant climax.

F&F 5

"DREAMING" FROM NOCTURNAL (OP. 70) Nocturnal *(1963) was written by Benjamin Britten for Julian Bream, who has said that it is the greatest work composed for the guitar. It consists of a series of separate episodes, with the music conveying and describing various states during the night. The sixth section shown here is "Dreaming" (Sognante). It starts with a gently strummed open-string chord, which recurs throughout, together with further voicings, which have a quiet beauty in passages alternating with magical lines with artificial harmonies. Nocturnal* was premiered at Aldeburgh in 1964.

material, challenging guitarists with inventive modern ideas. *Elogio de la Danza* (1964) has Latin rhythms, *El Decameron Negro* uses African ideas from the Yoruba region and *The Eternal Spiral* (1971) features Cuban rhythms and dramatic contrasts. At the beginning of the 1970s, Goffredo Petrassi's *Nunc* (1971) shows serialism and improvisational approaches, and Peter Maxwell Davies' *Lullaby for Ilian Rainbow* (1973) has a surreal detachment, while Toru Takemitsu's *Folios* (1973) offers meditative impressionism. Hans Werner Henze's *First Sonata on Shakespearian Characters*, *Royal Winter Music* (1976) and *Second Sonata* (1979) are difficult technical pieces in which Shakespearian figures are portrayed and dramatic situations described in music.

The more conservative repertoire expanded with the Venezuelan guitarist Alirio Diaz promoting interest in the work of his fellow countryman Antonio Lauro (1917–86), who has written attractive waltzes based on Venezuelan folk music, and *Suite Venezuelana* based on folk rhythms.

JOHN WILLIAMS

Born in Melbourne, Australia, in 1941, John Williams came from a musical family: his father Len Williams was a gifted guitarist and teacher. Guided by his father, he began playing around the age of seven. The family moved to Britain in 1952, and Williams studied with Segovia from 1953–61 at the Chigiana Academy in Siena in Italy, where he was accorded the unusual privilege of giving a full

YOUNG VIRTUOSO
John Williams astonished the music world when he emerged in the 1950s and Segovia announced that "a prince of the guitar has arrived". With faultless technical mastery and exceptional reading abilities, he performed and recorded a wide range of works. It became evident that he had the unusual capacity to master repertoire from virtually every period and style.

COMPOSITIONAL DEVELOPMENTS

During the 1950s, a number of young composers wrote experimental and challenging music for the guitar. Pierre Boulez (b.1925) included complex angular guitar lines in the sextet with voice *Le Marteau sans Maître* (1954), Luciano Berio (b.1925) used the guitar in his orchestral *Nones* (1955), and Hans Werner Henze (b.1926) created a feeling of alienation with atonal lines for a guitar in *Drei Tientos* (1958).

Cuban composer and guitarist Leo Brouwer (b.1939) started to write works based on Cuban folk music and avant garde ideas that often feature strong textural sounds and effects. Between 1959 and 1961 he produced important studies, later published as *Etudes Simples*. They are full of good musical content and are excellent developmental

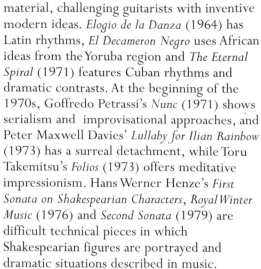

LEO BROUWER
One of the leading composers of his generation, Leo Brouwer has written music that uses both modern ideas of form and harmony, and Cuban and Latin American rhythms. During the mid-1970s, he moved from a mathematical and architectural approach to embrace melody and tonality.

recital in 1958. His first major recital at the Wigmore Hall in London in November 1958 included works by Sanz, Scarlatti, Bach and Sor; shortly after this he made his first commercial recordings. Williams started touring the world and was made professor of guitar at the Royal College of Music in 1960.

Possessed of a seemingly effortless accuracy, clarity of articulation and incisiveness, Williams' technical brilliance was to some extent moulded by Segovia's manner of interpreting works. In addition to solo

FUSION

John Williams started to experiment with classical ideas and make them more accessible to the general public: his album *Changes* (1971) features arrangements of songs by the Beatles and Joni Mitchell. One of the most adventurous pieces is the rock version of Bach's *Prelude* from the *Suite* in E major, on which he is backed by a rhythm section. Stanley Myers' "Cavatina", released as a single, also became a popular piece. In 1979, Williams formed the group Sky, a crossover fusion group working with classical, jazz and pop ideas.

recitals, he formed the Paganini Trio, which included violin and cello. Among works written for him are Stephen Dodgson's (b.1924) *Partita No.1* and *Duo Concertante* for guitar and harpsichord. Highlights in his recording output include Paganini's *Capriccio No.1* (1965) and the outstanding album, *John Williams Plays Spanish Music* (1970), with its definitive performances of "Granados" and an outstanding version of the Albeniz work "Cordoba". Williams also recorded Bach to a high standard, including the Lute Suite No. 4 in E Major. He started playing in a duo with Julian Bream and their album *Together* (1971) features pieces by Falla, Ravel, Sor, Carulli and Lawes that show how their contrasting styles are complementary and effective. During the same period, John Williams recorded Domenico Scarlatti's harpsichord works on guitar, which had been originally influenced by Spanish guitar music when they were written in the 18th century. Among 1970s works written for Williams are Andre Previn's *Guitar Concerto*.

One of Williams' most important contributions to the guitar has been the recordings of works by Paraguayan composer Agustin Barrios on his album *John Williams Plays Barrios*. These recordings brought about a widespread appreciation of Barrios' work and its incorporation within the mainstream repertoire.

During the 1980s, Williams promoted composers such as the Australian minimalist Peter Sculthorpe, premiering his *Second Guitar Concerto* in 1989, and in 1991, Williams formed the chamber group Attacca, which specialized in contemporary works.

JOHN WILLIAMS
Attempting to break down barriers between classical music and popular styles, John Williams has been open-minded in his approach to developments in music, including jazz and pop, performing at Ronnie Scott's jazz club and at rock concerts, and occasionally playing steel-string acoustic and electric guitars. He often uses a microphone to amplify his guitar in an ensemble.

SMALLMAN GUITARS
For many years, John Williams played an Ignacio Fleta guitar, but he has also used a Smallman extensively. One of the most important innovators in guitar construction, Australian maker Greg Smallman started to produce instruments with a carbon-fibre lattice-work bracing in the late 1970s. This produces extra volume and sustain and makes the guitar responsive on upper fretted notes across the strings. It also changes the tone.

DAVID RUSSELL
Scottish guitarist David Russell (b.1953) is one of the finest and most sensitive interpreters of repertoire, with a vocal lyricism and refined subtlety. He has had works dedicated to him by Carlo Domeniconi and Jorge Morel.

SHARON ISBIN
A player of eclectic taste, American guitarist Sharon Isbin (b.1956) was the first person to be appointed professor of the guitar at the Juilliard music school in New York City. She has commissioned concertos by American composers, including Lukas Foss and Aaron Jay Kernis.

THE PRINCE'S TOYS

One of the most interesting and adventurous works, which stretches the boundaries of the classical guitar, is by the Russian composer Nikita Koshkin (b.1956). The long six-movement suite, *The Prince's Toys* (1980), is a tour de force of surreal imagery, with novel sound effects, colours and textures. It contains powerful march-like rhythms and unusual harmonies, often using parallel voices, and repeating motifs. Strings are pulled hard away from the guitar to give a feeling of torsion, and occasionally snapped back percussively. After the first movement opens with melancholy harmonies, the second movement features the body of the guitar being hit percussively; staccato chords are added and there are driving continuous bass lines with rattling voicings. The third movement contains sad, plaintive voicings, scrapes along the strings and thumps on the guitar body. Strangled percussive textures are created at the beginning of the fourth movement by wrapping strings across each other, and there are surging harmonies and snare drum effects.

The fifth movement has a happier playful mood, with ascending circling figures and snapped chords. The finale contains a reflective opening, jagged lines over a pedal tone, a variety of arpeggation, short developing motifs and chords with wide voicings. An elliptical tango is created with skewed figures and string scrapes, and there are muted passages featuring a pedal tone and luminous descending passages with microtonal bends on harmonics before the piece dies away to end with a long, mysterious scraping noise that conveys a sense of three-dimensional movement.

Another adventurous work is Luciano Berio's *Sequenza XI for Guitar* (1988), which has powerful rasqueado strumming, percussive tapping, exotic arpeggiated harmonies, tremolo and shimmering legato lines.

TAKEMITSU & BROUWER

Two works have been written for Julian Bream by composers who have become important figures.

Toru Takemitsu's *All In Twilight* (1988) has a warm depth and beauty evoking a sense of mystery and the unknown. The first movement contains captivating voicings, mixed with harmonics, and there are marked shifts in tone and colour with notes near the bridge. The

CROSSCURRENTS

There has been a variety of crossover in guitar styles. The Brazilian Assad Brothers and Carlos Barbosa Lima have incorporated samba music, bringing a fresh rhythmic approach to the classical guitar. Argentinian composer Astor Piazzolla (1921–92) wrote *Tango Suite* (1984) for them after hearing an arrangement of Carlos' work. In America, minimalist composer Steve Reich's *Electric Counterpoint* (1987) uses electric guitar and was commissioned for jazz guitarist Pat Metheny. It has three movements and is made up of ten overdubbed guitar parts and two bass parts. A final live section is added by the guitar. It has continuous surging, pulsing harmonies and a theme from African horn music. Experimental composer and guitarist Glenn Branca's work, including *Symphonies 1–10* from the 1980s and 1990s, uses specially built electric instruments and systems, such as all six strings tuned to one note set at various octaves and pitches, producing awe-inspiring energy with volcanic crescendos and avalanches of sound. Born in the former Yugoslavia, guitarist and composer Dusan Bogdanovic (b.1955) draws on a range of music. His *Six Balkan Miniatures* (1991) are inventive, drawing on indigenous folk songs and rhythms with an Islamic flavour.

MANUEL BARRUECO
One of the most outstanding guitar players, Manuel Barrueco (b.1952) is an exceptional performer and a master in the interpretation of a wide range of works. He is evolving through refining mainstream works and adding new repertoire, and there is great clarity and detail in his playing. He explores pieces thoughtfully, revealing new moods and meanings and adding a deeper dimension to the repertoire. His recordings range from Bach and Mozart to Chick Corea.

KAZUHITO YAMASHITA
Japanese guitarist Yamashita (b.1961) has recorded orchestral pieces for solo guitar that include Mussorgsky's Pictures at an Exhibition *and Dvorak's* New World Symphony. *These virtuosic renditions convey some sense of orchestral fullness.*

second movement reveals a dark emotional theme with an unresolved tension, the third has dancing flurries of movement, and the fourth is entrancing with arcing lines of intervals and repeating motifs, with answering upper harmonics.

Leo Brouwer's *Sonata For Guitar* (1990) is a three-movement work that is full of contrasting episodes that collide with each other, switching suddenly from dissonance to consonance, and making short allusions to composers and different musical styles and periods.

Opening with harmonics with exotic swirling arpeggios, the first movement is full of reflective delicacy, with passages of melodic chords and juxtaposed areas of percussive dissonance, and colour effects with Spanish and Cuban flavours. The second movement contains bell-like notes with sombre melodies floating in a ruminative manner. The third movement is full of energy, with intertwining arpeggios and linear motifs, and builds with dramatic power to a sudden ending.

FLAMENCO

Unlike any other major European folk tradition, flamenco's evolution and sound have been closely linked with the guitar. It is an important part of the cultural heritage of Spain, and is a living art form which is still developing through the assimilation of ideas from other areas of music.

Paco de Lucía *An undisputed flamenco master, Paco de Lucía is a matchless interpreter of the traditional repertoire and an adventurous innovator and improviser.*

THE ORIGINS OF FLAMENCO

The origins of flamenco are complex and obscure. For many years, the music was associated with Andalucia in the south of Spain, and the first noted flamenco performers were gypsies living in the region bounded by the cities of Cádiz, Jerez and Seville.

Flamenco has three aspects: singing (*cante*), dancing (*baile*) and playing (*toque*). The flamenco tradition is the musical result of unique circumstances of geography and history. In AD 711, Moors from North Africa invaded southern Spain and established an advanced Islamic society and culture in the region they named Al-Andalus, modern Andalucia. An important part of this culture was a canon of sophisticated vocal and instrumental music. After seven centuries, the Moors were swept out of Spain by the combined might of the Christian kingdoms of northern Spain – Navarre, Aragon and Castile – leaving a large population with an Arabic identity to be gradually assimilated into Christian society. This population shared a region with gypsies, for whom music was and is a major aspect of life. Gypsy music, with its eastern influences, intermingled with the Arabic tradition, and ideas were absorbed from Jewish and early European classical and folk music, producing a unique style and repertoire now known as flamenco.

The word flamenco is variously thought to derive from the Arabic *felamengu*, meaning fugitive peasant, or the Spanish *flamencos*, used to describe the Flemish courtiers, including soldiers and musicians, who formed part of the international court of the Spanish king and Holy Roman Emperor, Charles V (1500–58), in the 16th century.

EARLY SINGERS & GUITARISTS

A flamenco singer is mentioned in Jerez c.1750, and drawings from the beginning of the 18th century show gypsies using guitars as the main instrument to accompany song and dance. The guitar had been established in Spain for a number of centuries throughout all levels of society, and written music existed that used

TORRES GUITARS
Antonio de Torres first produced modern guitars from the 1850s. This guitar from 1860 is typical of both classical and flamenco models. With its cypress body, light construction and a solid peghead, this model is similar to the traditional type of guitar used in the early period.

FLAMENCO TROUPE
Travelling flamenco groups, including singers, dancers and guitarists, were common in Spain from the 19th century onward. Taken in c.1890, this photograph shows the flamenco troupe La Zambra Gitana.

ideas occurring in flamenco, such as the rhythmic and melodic verse form called *seguidilla,* and *rasgueado* strumming with unfurled fingers. Among early guitarists to be mentioned by name are Paquirri El Guante, born c.1780 in Cádiz, who played, sang and danced, and Francisco Rodriguez "El Murciano" (1795–1848) (*see below*).

The rapidly developing Seville, with its thriving gypsy quarter in the suburb of Triana,

REFERENCES TO FLAMENCO

In his book about Spanish gypsies, *The Zincali* (1840), the English writer George Borrow (1803–81) describes "a gypsy from Melilla strumming a guitar most forcibly and producing demoniacal sounds". In 1847, Russian composer Mikhail Glinka (1804–57) heard Francisco Rodriguez "El Murciano" play in Granada. Glinka was spellbound by this indigenous music and spent many hours attempting to transcribe the music with its inventive variations. Glinka later used melodic elements of it in orchestral works such as *Night in Madrid* (1851).

became a centre for flamenco. A new type of venue appeared, the *cafe cantante*, a bar with an area for performing. Seville had a *cafe cantante* as early as 1842, and this type of environment encouraged artists to develop. Among the players who could be heard in the cafés of Seville in the 1850s was a gypsy from Cádiz, José Gonzalez Patino (1829–1902), who was an accompanist. During the 19th century, guitars were used primarily for accompaniment to the voice and as rhythmic support for dancers. Gradually, players developed short instrumental melodic interludes with variations called *falseta*s.

During this period published tutors, such as Rubio's *Metodo Elemental en Cifra* (1860), included material in a flamenco style, and the renowned classical guitarist Julian Arcas (1832–82) published pieces based on *soleares* and a *rondena*.

Patino influenced Paco El Barbero (1840–1910) from Cádiz, who was one of the first flamenco guitarists to give solo performances. He played classical pieces by Arcas and adapted and incorporated ideas for flamenco guitar. In turn, he influenced Javier Molina (1868–1956), the "sorcerer and wizard of the guitar".

EL JALEO
This painting by the American artist and society portrait-painter John Singer Sargent (1856–1925) shows dancers accompanied by guitarists in a café setting. Sargent travelled to Spain in 1879 making sketches, and El Jaleo *was finished in 1882.*

Another important early figure, Paco Lucena (1855–1930), helped to establish *picado* techniques, three-finger arpeggiation and the use of tremolo.

RAMÒN MONTOYA

The great figure who brought flamenco guitar to the world was Ramòn Montoya (1880–1949). He came from a flamenco-playing gypsy family and started at a young age. He admired Javier Molina and was influenced by Rafael Marin, who had studied with Paco Lucena and Francisco Tárrega (1852–1909) and published one of the early books on flamenco, *Metodo de Guitarra por Musica y Cifra* (1902).

RAMÒN MONTOYA
The establishment of the classical guitar on the concert stage in the 20th century led to a receptive attitude toward flamenco, enabling figures such as Ramòn Montoya to make solo recordings and tour outside Spain, bringing flamenco to other parts of the world.

His sensitivity and refinement, smooth, surging *rasgueados* and rhythmic suppleness can be heard on many early recordings from the 1920s with singer La Nina de Los Peines, on which he adds imaginative *falsetas*. His playing within the confines of the strict, rhythmically cyclical *compas* was exceptional, and at the time considered ornate and sophisticated.

Montaya's most important contribution to the genre was to break free of the role as accompanist and express himself as a solo instrumentalist, using tremendous scalar and harmonic invention, a wide range of textures, and the full scope of the fingerboard. He took the song-based melodic material and reharmonized it, developing flowing pieces with passages in open rhythm conveying a rich musicality. He can also be heard in guitar duets from the 1930s playing with a precise control, using shimmering arpeggios, burring strumming and graceful liquid lines. His passionate intensity and voluble individuality enabled him to break into the concert world, where he met with great acclaim in Paris in 1936.

MARCEL BARBERO FLAMENCO GUITAR
Flamenco guitars have a distinct sound due to light construction, cypress wood bodies and lower string action. Many of the great classical makers produced flamenco guitars, including Santos Hernandez, whose instruments were used by Ramòn Montoya. The guitar above was made by Marcelo Barbero (1904–55), who worked in Madrid.

Sophisticated arpeggiation, tremolo and scalar vocabulary were well established by the time Montoya began his career, and he soon became acquainted with the playing of the outstanding classical guitarist Miguel Llobert, who inspired him to develop an imaginative approach to the guitar.

Montoya built on traditions and added new ideas, enriching the vocabulary of flamenco, and became one of the first virtuosos of the 20th century. Early in his career he accompanied many of the major singers and dancers in the Cafe de La Marina in Madrid, performing regularly with the singer Antonio Chacon until the late 1920s and making recordings with him as early as 1922. Montoya had a thorough knowledge of the *el cante* flamenco singing repertoire.

GRANADINA

A series of solo instrumental pieces recorded in 1936 in Paris by Ramòn Montoya included "Granadina", a powerful and inventive virtuosic piece featuring an open structure, changing tempos and a series of variations. Montoya plays with a muscular incisiveness. Fast single-line phrases with rippling arpeggiation are matched by melodic bass figures with glissandi. Chords shimmer with swirling strumming and *rasgueado* flourishes. Melodies are played with a fast tremolo supported by magical, intricate, harp-like arpeggios and unusual voicings.

OTHER KEY FIGURES

Some of the earliest recordings of flamenco around the turn of the century were made by Barcelona-based Miguel Borrull (c.1880–1940), who added harmonic sophistication to chord progressions and whose work influenced Montoya. A number of leading players were not gypsies; known as *payos*, they included Manolo de Huelva (1892–1976), who was established as a young virtuoso in Seville by the age of 18. Paradoxically, in relation to Montoya he was seen as having a hard, driving rhythmic "gypsy" style as an accompanist. He enjoyed a legendary reputation as a soloist and was referred to by Segovia as "the greatest flamenco player", but he was introverted and secretive, and did not produce many recordings.

FLAMENCO PLAYING

In flamenco, the phrygian mode and harmonic minor scale are used as a framework around open strings, and function as a melodic and harmonic outline. The chants and lyrical songs that form the roots of the genre often have regional names, such as *malaguena* and *rondena*. Over time, these forms were harmonized by chords that fall within the flamenco framework to give unusual progressions and unique voicings. Rhythmically, many pieces are based on a cyclical twelve-beat *compas* form with accents in different places. For example, *solea* was traditionally counted with an emphasis on certain beats and groups of beats. This eventually became more definitive, with accents on beats 3, 6, 8, 10 and 12, or 3, 7, 8, 10 and 12. *Siguiriya* traditionally has five beats and other pieces, such as *tarantas,* are in free time. Guitarists work within these structures, adding *falsetas* and improvising.

Rasgueado strumming, in which the fingers are unfurled across the strings, is a major part of the sound of flamenco. There is often brilliantly fast arpeggiation and tremolo highlights, and melodies played with the thumb. The thumb and fingers are used for up-and-down strokes and single lines. *Golpe,* percussive tapping on the body of the guitar, is also part of the sound.

NIÑO RICARDO

Born in Seville, Niño Ricardo (1904–1972), a non-gypsy and so known as a *payo*, was one of the most important figures in the evolution of modern flamenco guitar styles. His first major public performance took place in Seville in 1917, when he accompanied figures including the singer La Maccarona. Ricardo worked with Javier Molina at the Cafe Novedades in Seville, and as a teenager played with Ramòn Montoya and was able to learn from him at close quarters. He started recording in 1927 and worked with many famous singers throughout his career.

From the mid 1950s, Ricardo made regular solo performances. His playing has a dark, earthy quality, and his unfettered spontaneity and fertile imagination make him one of the most gifted of improvisers. His rich and complex *falsetas,* characterized by interesting lines and beautiful voicings, broadened the harmonic scope of flamenco.

The many sides of Ricardo's playing range from the passionate and rhythmically abrasive to the dark and ruminative, creating spellbinding atmospheres on pieces such as *tarantas*, where he plays with an introspective dissonance using altered scales with an Arabic flavour that evokes mystery and inspires contemplation.

NIÑO RICARDO
A player with tremendous flair, Niño Ricardo's tangled and complex inventions are often conveyed in an irregular yet brilliant way. His falsetas *underpin much of the modern vocabulary of instrumental flamenco music and influenced generations of players.*

SABICAS

Born Agustín Castellón Campos in Pamplona in the north of Spain, the gypsy prodigy Sabicas (1912–90) became a virtuoso whose style would define modern flamenco. He left Spain in 1937 for Mexico, where he teamed up with the great flamenco dancer Carmen Amaya to lead a successful company that toured the world and started to make remarkable recordings. In the mid 1950s, he moved to New York, where he was able to concentrate on a solo career as a concert and recording artist. Sabicas' style is a dramatic extension of the traditional framework with a clean, polished, concise focus sharpened by brilliant all-round technical skill and panache. He displays an astonishing linear technique, faultlessly executed, and plays arpeggios across all strings, using his thumb with great flexibility. Many of his recordings, such as *Flamenco Puro* (1961) and *The Fantastic Guitars of Sabicas and Escudero*, a selection of duets with Mario Escudero (b.1928), became blueprints for succeeding generations of players.

IMPROVISATIONAL GENIUS
An inventive spirit, Sabicas stated that he could never play the same thing twice.

FLAMENCO PURO

A showcase for Sabicas' solo virtuosity, *Flamenco Puro* features characterful pieces with varied rhythms and open rubatos which lead to changes in direction. Many types of pieces and aspects of flamenco are represented. The *solea* "Bronce Gitano" features swirling arpeggios, legato and fast, incisive lines, tremolo, *golpe* tapping, staccato notes and chords and strong rhythms. An austere beauty characterizes the *tarantas* "Ecos de la Mina", with its dark harmonies and percussively struck strings. "Campina Andaluza", an *alegrias*, is full of contrasts, with its flowery delicacy, attractive arpeggiation, burring rasguedo, and tremolo. The *fandangos* "Por los Olivares" has inventive harmonized melodic passages and great tremolo playing, while captivating rhythms, superb clipped strumming and powerful lines, with expressive legato, can be heard on "Ecos Jerezanos", a *solea por bulerias*. Melodic arpeggiation and varied *rasgueados* with bewitching melodies and strong lower string figures are the foundation of the *seguidillas* "Duelo da Campanas", which shimmers with skittering tremolo underpinned by varied arpeggiation and reflective harmonies. Replete with poetic imagery, the *granadinas*, "Joyas de la Alhambra", resonates with a wonderful haunting tone and glitters with sheets of fast arpeggiation, inventive lines and unexpected shifts in direction. Dancing rhythms drive the *farruca* "Punta y Tacon", and the wonderfully evocative *bulerias* "Aires de Triana" is made haunting by a vocal expressiveness, interesting harmonies and dissonance. Ascending modulation builds the exultant *malaguena* "Brisas de la Caleta" to an exciting climax, its light, joyful rhythms, sudden cut-offs and *golpe* tapping calling dancing to mind.

FLAMENCO STYLES

There are many different forms within the flamenco genre, often derived from songs which have different levels of mood and intensity. *Cante jondo* (deep song), from which *solea* a "mother chant" springs, is full of soulful emotion and yearning. A less intense form is *cante intermedio* (middle song), from which *taranta* is derived, and the lighter *cante chico* (light song) is the basis for the *buleria*.

BULERIA (FROM JEREZ)

The *buleria* follows the 12-beat rhythmic *compas* cycle. This is played *por medio* around an A phrygian modal framework with both a C and C♯ and ends with a five-stroke *rasgueado* on an A major chord with an added A♯ (B♭). There is a *golpe* tap on the soundboard.

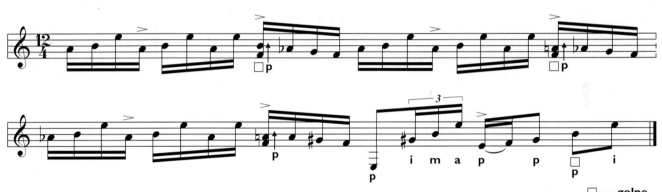

SOLEA (FROM TRIANA, SEVILLE)

This is a mother chant. Following a *compas,* it is played more slowly than a *buleria* and has a more mournful feeling. It is based on the E phrygian mode, but with both a G and G♯ (or A♭). On the third and sixth beats, the thumb plays a two-note chord while the ring finger taps a *golpe* and it ends with an ascending arpeggio.

TARANTA (FROM ALMERÍA)

The taranta is dark and ruminative with a Moorish flavour. Played around the F♯ phrygian mode with A and A♯ (B♭), it expresses rhythmic freedom while retaining an underlying moving pulse. It uses sombre chords with some dissonance, and voicings with augmented fourth and minor second intervals.

PACO DE LUCÍA

A titanic figure in the world of flamenco guitar, Paco de Lucía has an astounding technique and inventiveness within the traditions of the genre, and has continually assimilated new ideas from other styles, including Brazilian music and jazz.

IN CONCERT
Ferocious intensity and the appearance of effortless superiority are the hallmarks of Paco de Lucía's genius.

Paco de Lucía was born Francisco Sanchez Gomez in Algeciras, southern Spain, in 1947 into a family of gifted flamenco guitar players, and he started playing at the age of seven. His precocious talent led his father, Antonio de Algeciras, to encourage him and he spent countless hours practising, learning the *falsetas* of Niño Ricardo (*see page 37*), who sometimes visited the house. He later discovered the recordings of Sabicas (*see page 38*) whose speed and clean execution had a profound influence on the young de Lucía.

With his brother Pepe singing, Paco recorded an album, *Los Chiquitos de Algeciras*, in 1962. In the same year, the pair appeared at the Jerez Concurso (music festival) where they were a sensation and won top prizes. The family moved to Madrid, where Paco joined Jose Greco's dance troupe, touring the USA in 1963 and meeting Sabicas and Mario Escudero, who encouraged him to develop his own identity. Within a short time he was making records, including duets with his older brother Ramòn de Algeciras (b.1938), experimenting with Brazilian music and jazz, and broadening his vocabulary to play in more unusual settings.

Although traditional, his first solo record, *La Fabulosa Guitarra de Paco de Lucía* (1967), coruscates with characteristic fast, attacking inventiveness. On "Punta Umbria", for example, he produces a very sharp, bright sound, playing rasping lines with a taut, rhythmic drive that combines invention, speed and cutting *rasgueados*.

TRANSITION

A player with razor-sharp articulation, natural improvisational abilities and emotional power and depth, Paco de Lucía started to record pieces that modernized the sound of flamenco in the 1970s. On the album *Fuente y Caudal* (1973), the title track, a *taranta*, is wonderfully poignant and full of space, with a dark intensity featuring tremolo playing, graceful crystalline harmonies and expressive lines. The album has other traditional material, such as the exciting "Cepa Andaluza", but a track that was originally an afterthought was set to change Paco's career. The *rumba* "Entre dos Aguas" was given an added rhythm section with guitar, electric bass and percussion and became a hit in Spain, setting Paco on the road to stardom. Over the repeating harmonies of the attractive melody, he improvises in a relaxed,

thematic style using sustain with contrasting bursts of flamenco-style virtuosity. Another popular album, *Almoraima* (1976), features a title track *buleria* that blends chopping rhythms, an Arabic flavour, a delicate melody and harmonies with a latin-jazz flavour. "Rio Ancho" is a *rumba* propelled by a warm, seductive rhythm section and made dazzling by a series of melodies and countermelodies with developed themes and variations, attractive harmonies and rhythms and the fast lines of explosive invention. Paco de Lucía's music has played a major part in encouraging forms that are known as *cante ida y vuelta*, Spanish ideas that went to the Americas and returned as altered, reinvigorated styles, such as the *rhumba*.

EVOLUTION & MATURITY
In the early 1970s, Paco de Lucia made great traditional albums such as El Duende Flamenco de Paco de Lucía (1972) that demonstrate an evolving harmonic vocabulary enlivened by new voicings and chord progressions.

CONSUMMATE MASTERY

Early in his career, Paco worked extensively with singers and formed a close empathy with singer Camaron de la Isla; they recorded a series of albums, including *Soy Caminante* (1974), that highlight his sensitive approach. There are echoes of Spanish classical vocabulary in de Lucía's playing and in 1978 he recorded *Paco de Lucía Interpreta a Manuel de Falla,* on which a group freely interprets de Falla's compositional ideas.

Increasingly influenced by jazz, de Lucía was, by the end of the 1970s, playing in a trio with John McLaughlin (*see pages 114–15*) and Larry Coryell (*see page 116*), recording the live *Castro Marin* in 1979, and he went on to work with McLaughlin and Al Di Meola (*see page 116*) in the early 1980s.

The album *Solo Quiero Caminar* (1981) features a sextet consisting of three guitars, bass, percussion, a flautist/saxophonist and brother Pepe on vocals. The tight, driving title track is a *tango* starting with an attractive

guitar figure and featuring close interplay with the electric bass. Paco's guitar melds rhythmically with the band and he plays fast linear solos.

Among subsequent highlights are "La Barrosa" (1987), full of effortless delicacy with cascading phrases, bright strumming and inspired improvisation, and "Tio Sabas" (1990), a heartfelt and introspective *taranta*. The haunting beauty of this homage to Sabicas, with its beautiful swirling effects, 'ud influences and Arabic flavour, is marked by incandescent inventions that surge out of a contemplative stillness. In 1991, Paco memorized and recorded Rodrigo's *Concierto de Aranjuez,* which he plays with a flamenco feeling and a bright clarity that gives the work capricious edge. He worked with José-Manuel Canizares and José María Banderas on the album. He has continued to develop and seek out new horizons, playing a modernistic form of flamenco on *the Guitar Trio* (1996), working in a guitar trio with previous colleagues John McLaughlin and Al Di Meola.

FLAMENCO VIRTUOSO
Paco de Lucía continues to use all techniques to serve his self expression. With his left-hand flexibility, brilliant picado *picking technique for lines, fast arpeggiation, tremolo and effects including pizzicato, glissando, harmonics and legato, de Lucía is unrivalled. He is also a master of traditional styles, including all rasgueado approaches, a phenomenal alzapua technique — up-and-down strokes with the thumbnail — to play lines and chords on all strings,* apagado *damping with the left hand and golpe tapping on the top.*

FLAMENCO TODAY

From the 1960s onward, various players, including Manolo Sanlúcar, have developed both a classical and jazz-influenced vocabulary and instrumentation. Traditional players have also extended their language, and today the many styles range from the traditional to the progressive.

A number of fine players emerged in the late 1960s, including Serranito (b.1942), who has an introspective character, fine articulation and dynamic sensibilities. The guitar still takes a central role in the accompaniment of flamenco singing and dancing, and one of the great figures in this area is the gypsy player Tomatito (b.1958), whose earthy style and dramatic impetuosity is appealing, the elegant Vicente Amigo (b.1967), and Paco Peña, who has built an international career with his flamenco companies. Tradition has continued in the hands of dynasties such as the gypsy Habichuela family, and there are many guitarists working within the traditional framework of older styles feel that flamenco should be played within a limited structure in order to retain its identity and authenticity.

MANOLO SANLÚCAR

One of the major figures in the development of modern flamenco, Manolo Sanlúcar (b.1943), was taught by his father and developed his talent in the bars of Madrid. A tremendous technique and a distinctive touch and tone give his playing both a dynamic, powerful aspect and a gentle side, embodied in melodic sensitivity, harmonic sophistication and lyricism. Early in his career, he concentrated on working with singers, and in 1972 won the Jerez Catedra de Flamencologia guitar prize. One of his most significant contributions to the evolution of flamenco is his use of the guitar within classical instrumental contexts based on structured written compositions.

MANOLO SANLÚCAR
A tremendous player with an all-round skill and structured compositional and improvisational approaches, Manolo Sanlúcar has been one of the top figures in flamenco from the 1960s (above) to the present day (right).

THE ACCOMPANIST
Gypsy guitarist Tomatito (José Fernández Torres), who plays with strong colour and a powerful identity, played for many flamenco singers, forging a particularly fertile partnership with the singer Camaron de la Isla.

During the 1960s and 1970s, light strings had been added to recordings by figures including Sabicas (*see page 38*) and Paco de Lucía (*see pages 40–41*). Sanlúcar pioneered a fully integrated dialogue with orchestra when, in his early twenties, he wrote the three-movement work *Fantasia Para Guitarra y Orchestra*. This was recorded in 1977 and released with some success. He went on to experiment with jazz, and incorporated new ideas that shaped his harmonies and linear playing. Sanlúcar recorded an important guitar suite with orchestra on *Tauromagia* (1988). This features sections that evoke the series of rituals a matador goes through during a bullfight. It shows great invention and classical sophistication, achieved through subtle moods and textures.

NEW FIGURES

Gerardo Núñez (b.1961) has created fresh ideas within the tradition, using innovative tunings and modulations which can be heard on *El Gallo Azul* (1987). On his classically influenced album, *Mi Tiempo* (1990), Rafael Riqueni (b.1962) demonstrates his virtuosity and flair, particularly on the title track *bulerias*. An appealing commercial sound derived partly from flamenco-fusion *rumba* styles has been developed by The Gipsy Kings, who have built a career based on an exciting group dynamic.

The talented young guitarist Vicente Amigo plays on the recording, and unusual instruments, such as a sitar, augment the orchestra. As a homage to bullfighting, the piece relies on traditional flamenco forms, such as a slow *buleria,* an *alegria* and a *tango,* to convey festive moods and dramatic scenes.

Sanlúcar has kept a strong traditional Spanish flamenco sound in his playing and composition, and is the major innovator, alongside Paco de Lucía, in contemporary progressive flamenco.

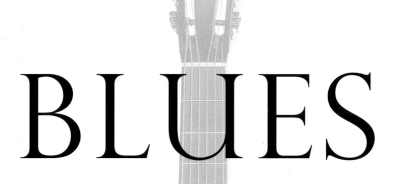

BLUES

The blues evolved primarily from a folk culture developed in the southern states of America by a black population whose ancestors had been transported from West Africa to work as slaves. It formed part of the underlying basis of popular music styles in the 20th century and continues as a traditional genre in its own right.

The young B.B. KING, who was to go on to become one of the most famous electric blues guitarists in the world and enjoy a long and illustrious career.

EARLY BLUES

The Mississippi Delta and its surrounding area was the heartland of a type of acoustic country "Delta blues" that often has a primeval sound quality. Sophisticated styles based on blues and ragtime emerged from other regions too, including Georgia, Kentucky and Texas.

The African-American people who sang and played early blues carried an ancestral heritage and were subject to a wide range of musical idioms. Music functioned directly in almost every facet of life, from work to dances and the church. Blues is a coalescence of indefinable elements. The lack of documented material means that its development has been the source of extensive conjecture. In terms of the guitar, however, the songster tradition may be the core of early styles.

Although early blues is often described generally as "country blues", the music was in fact just as closely associated with small towns and cities as with the farms and cotton plantations of rural agricultural areas. Cheap, mass-produced guitars became available throughout the United States in the late 19th century. They were taken up by singers, who used them to accompany their songs, and occasionally they were integrated into small groups. Early guitar styles probably used both standard fretted fingerstyles as well as open tunings based on a chord, with a slide object moved along the strings for basic harmonies, and notes that have an expressive, microtonal nuance. An early reference to a blues guitarist dates from 1902–03, when musician W.C. Handy passed through a southern railway station and saw a singer playing slide guitar with a knife, producing what he termed "the weirdest music he had ever heard". Sylvester Weaver (1897–1960) from Kentucky is one of the first clearly identifiable guitarists. He was recording backing for singer Sara Martin in October 1923, and the following month, in New York, he recorded two solo instrumentals with a smooth, warm sound using slide and an open E-major tuning. "Guitar Blues" is reflective, with simple phrases and chords, and "Guitar Rag" is rhythmic with a jaunty melody.

CHARLEY PATTON

Considered to be one of the seminal figures of the genre, Charley Patton (c.1887–1934) was born in Mississippi. His "Pony Blues" (1929) was the commercial success that made him well known. Patton recorded ragtime, country songs and spirituals as well as blues. His characteristic fingerstyle and open-tuning slide accompaniment often has a loose, unstructured approach with irregular bars, uneven timing and unusual accents, and his music conveys a rough, repetitive, basic earthiness with a strong, physical, rhythmic feel. His phrases, played with a lyrical subtlety, often mirror or answer his voice, and he uses slide end to end. Patton's approach incorporates additional sounds and techniques, including snapping strings against the fingerboard and drumming on the instrument. His guitar was tuned higher than normal to give a bright, penetrating sound. Among his well-known compositions are "A Spoonful Blues", showing distinctive melodic slide playing, and "Moon Going Down". By the time he died in 1934, Patton had become a legendary early figure establishing Mississippi Delta blues.

CHARLEY PATTON
Blues musicians played at small bars termed "jukes", at dances and often on street corners. One of the great blues showmen was Charley Patton whose stage tricks included playing the guitar behind his back. Showing another side to his nature, Patton recorded Gospel (see page 48) under the name Elder J.J. Hadley.

RAGTIME

A large part of the early blues repertoire consisted of ragtime, the application of classical inventiveness to the lighter side of black music. It was popularized by the compositions of Scott Joplin (1868–1917), starting in the 1890s, and was in demand through to the 1920s. This led to "ragging", the turning of popular and vaudeville songs into lively numbers using pronounced syncopation with a strong bass part.

BLIND LEMON JEFFERSON
Jefferson's inventive style of playing contrasts sharply with the Mississippi guitarists. He did not rely on slide, open tunings and basic repetitive harmonies. Jefferson also recorded under the name Deacon L.J. Bates.

STELLA GUITAR
Jefferson played a Stella guitar, developed from the type of 12-string guitars common in Latin America. The 12-string guitar is a descendant of double-coursed 12-string guitars in use in Europe until the 19th century. Stella 12-string models were ideal for performing, with a full sound and reasonable level of volume.

Son House (1902–88), an influential figure, (*see page 58*), has a rhythmic slide style that can be heard on "Walking Blues".

Other outstanding musicians of the early years included Booker T. Washington "Bukka" White (1906–77), Nehemiah Curtis "Skip" James (1902–69) and "Mississippi" John Hurt (1892–1966), but they languished in relative obscurity. Leadbelly (*see page 58*) was recorded while in Angola Penitentiary in 1933.

BLIND LEMON JEFFERSON

Texas, specifically the great city of Dallas, was one of the major regions in which early guitar-playing developed. It was here that Blind Lemon Jefferson (1897–1929) started recording in 1926. He was one of the first popular blues recording artists and his exceptional technique combines blues with ragtime virtuosity, using harmonic sequences that function as an ingenious counterpart to his vocals.

His exuberant and intricate fingerstyle is full of imaginative lines, with arpeggiation emphasizing melodies, and suggesting countermelodies woven with a dancing and infectious rhythmic propulsion. Jefferson also uses the guitar in a call and response style. "Black Snake Moan", for example, mixes single lines, strumming and independent bass in relation to upper chord voicings. "Rabbit Foot Blues" starts with a boogie and becomes a piece full of unexpected invention. Jefferson was astonishingly versatile: from the slide of "Jack O' Diamond Blues" to the percussive ragtime of "Hot Dog". He showed how the guitar could create a high level of instrumental content and supersede, rather than just accompany, vocals; "Matchbox Blues" became a popular vehicle for musical developments by later generations.

GOSPEL

From the 1920s, "Gospel" became the term for songs with an overtly religious content. Gospel guitar playing in the early period is essentially similar to blues, with fingerstyle, slide and a tendency towards occasional pieces with less rhythmic emphasis. One of the greatest individuals to express a feeling of human yearning and salvation was Blind Willie Johnson (1902–49), who began recording in 1927. His melodious, iridescent slide flows seamlessly around his intense voice and has its own peculiar singing quality, with a shaking, fast vibrato at stressed points. There is a brooding presence in "Dark Was The Night, Cold Was The Ground" with its haunting depth and spine-tingling spirituality. Floating in time with searching slide and an eerie, percussive punctuation, the guitar is no longer a familiar instrument but a vehicle for otherworldly transcendent power.

THE SOUTH-EAST

The south-east provided a flourishing blues environment. Its most important areas were Georgia, particularly the city of Atlanta, parts of Florida and the Carolinas. Some of the music from this region has been described as "Down Home Blues", and music from the area north of Atlanta is termed "Piedmont Blues". This area has its own characteristic mix and shows a closer relation to the roots of European folk, and also ragtime and country music affected blues musicians to varying degrees. The area is not unlike Texas and Dallas in its urban sophistication and mixture of cultures and there is a lighter optimism in some of the music. Atlanta produced early exponents such as Barbecue Bob Hicks and Peg Leg Howell but the major figure to emerge with strong instrumental skills was Blind Blake (c.1890–1933) who rivals Blind Lemon Jefferson in his range and complexity. "West Coast Blues"

(1926), a showcase for his playing, is one of the few early recordings to be solely instrumental. "Diddie Wa Diddie" is a virtuosic, ragtime-style twelve-bar piece and "Police Dog Blues" uses an open tuning and features harmonics. With his advanced and highly organized musicianship and almost pianistic level of controlled technique, Blake's right-hand fingerstyle with rolling bass stands out. He became one of the few players to work as a house session musician for the Paramount label between 1926 and 1932. Blind Willie McTell (1901–59) was another figure with a wonderful voice and a smooth sophistication, playing a wide range of styles on his 12-string guitar.

Many early blues musicians were blind, as music was one of the blind's few options for making a living. Both Blind Boy Fuller (Fulton Allen, 1908–41) and Riley Puckett (*see page 64*), attended Atlanta's school for the blind. Fuller mainly used a resonator guitar, putting down "I'm A Rattlesnakin' Daddy" (1935), with its puncy staccato bass and driving incisive chords, which became popular with blues and country players. Gary Davis (1896–1972) worked with Fuller in the 1930s, switching to Gospel after his ordination in 1937 (*see page 58*).

BLIND WILLIE JOHNSON
With his indelible presence almost tangible on recordings, Blind Willie Johnson's music is a primeval form of expression, imbued with religious fervour. His emotional gospel vocals are supported predominantly by varied slide with an occasional piece played fingerstyle.

BLIND BLAKE
A tremendous all-rounder with panache and flair, Blake (aka Blind Arthur) was advertised as having a "piano-sounding guitar and singing which is 'too tight' for anything".

Cordially yours
Blind Blake

ROBERT JOHNSON

In a period in which there were many blues guitarists, one of the individuals to stand out was Robert Johnson, born in Mississippi in 1911. His strength lay partly in his ability to draw on prevalent traditional elements and distil them into his own clearly articulate style. Surrounded by myth and legend, Johnson was said to have sold his soul to the devil at a crossroads (the Delta's traditional place to meet the Prince of Darkness) in return for worldly success. This myth was compounded by the fact that he died under suspicious circumstances in 1938 at the very early age of 27.

Johnson grew up in an environment full of musical crosscurrents, listening to musicians of the calibre of Charley Patton and Son House performing locally, and also drew on the sophisticated recordings of Lonnie Johnson (*see page 50*) and pianist Leroy Carr.

His improvisation is often based closely around chord positions and is characterized by an intense focus, a transparent clarity, surging infectious rhythms and an uncluttered realization of musical ideas, in which notes and harmonies are always telling. Johnson's tight boogie riffs anticipate later developments in the postwar era as he moves through parts gracefully, his guitar supporting his passionate and emotional vocals.

JOHNSON'S GIBSON
Robert Johnson is photographed with a Gibson L-1 from circa 1928 which has a pin bridge, a round sound hole and a very worn sunburst finish. The Gibson company had built its reputation on archtops but began to introduce flat-top steel-string guitars from 1926 onward.

RECORDINGS

Robert Johnson recorded 41 tracks in Texas in 1936 and 1937. These tracks comprise 29 different songs and 12 alternate takes. A great deal of his material is played using open tunings (which are thought to be E and A with a capo on the second fret, as material is often based on open F♯ and B), and Johnson draws tonal beauty and metallic percussive qualities from his guitar.

There is a telling sense of presence in his work and a clear feeling of growing out of a cultural framework. "Cross Road Blues" is based on Charley Patton's "Down The Dirt Road Blues" with Johnson playing sharp, acid slide. The slide playing on "Hellhound On My Tail" has a wavering, out-of-tune character that, along with emotional vocals, helps to project a sense of persecution and fear. The outstanding slide of "Come On In My Kitchen" shows continual expressive inventiveness. Shimmering slide runs alongside the vocals and alternates with a variety of fills composed of slide riffs that generate a sonorous melodiousness.

Johnson's rhythm is varied and he is able to move seamlessly between different techniques while keeping up a driving momentum. On "I Believe I'll Dust My Broom" he carries a steady rhythm as he moves from urgent, high-register fills to insistent boogie figures, and on "Rambling On My Mind" he puts in slide fills over a similar rhythm style. "Terraplane Blues" shows a sophisticated funkiness, "Sweet Home Chicago" rolls with the voice, and "Love In Vain" features hard, cutting vamping. "Preaching Blues" ("Up Jumped The Devil") suddenly switches from the intro into an astonishingly fast rhythm composed of chopped staccato strokes and slide.

TRANSITION & INNOVATION

The big cities, with their rapidly developing music scenes and appreciative and discerning audience, the expansion of radio and the recording industry and the influence of jazz brought a high standard of musicianship to early urban blues.

Blues was gradually expanding throughout the 1920s, moving from individual players to duos, small groups and bands. A bigger line-up allowed guitarists to experiment with both lead and rhythm roles, and combinations with other instruments brought a new, urban dynamic to the established blues styles.

LONNIE JOHNSON

LONNIE JOHNSON
One of the great figures of blues and early jazz, Lonnie Johnson worked in a number of different genres and was skilled with fingerstyle, slide and single-line playing with a pick. He used both a six- string guitar and Stella 12-string guitar in performance and for recording.

Born in New Orleans, a melting pot for all kinds of musical crosscurrents and the early centre for jazz, Alonzo "Lonnie" Johnson (c.1899–1970) stands near the beginning of blues history in terms of recording. Early in his career, he uses an open tuning and plays fingerstyle. On many pieces he is backed with piano and sings with a measured gracefulness. Jazz-influenced and suavely professional, Johnson often conveys an almost jaunty mood in comparison to other blues musicians; "Mr. Johnson's Blues" (1925), recorded in St. Louis, demonstrates his decorous fills. He is in a darker mood on the Delta-style "Blue Ghost Blues" (1927). With piano backing, he stands out on "6/88 Glide" (1927), where he succeeds in being both percussive and graceful. "To Do This You Got To Know How" (1926) is a jazzy instrumental featuring rhythmic chordal passages.

Johnson flowered as an instrumentalist early in his career and demonstrated an advanced playing style, often adding melodic lines and pairs of notes over the bass part. Later work shows him using swing rhythms and playing sophisticated diminished-chord intros and turnarounds in blues sequences. His astonishing musical growth enabled him to step easily into the jazz world, and he developed a commanding soloing technique, using a flatpick to play inventive solos that are full of decorative ornamentation.

Blues often merges with jazz and it is difficult to categorize Johnson's work in terms of genre. In 1928 he formed a duo with jazz guitarist Eddie Lang (*see page 95*) and played blues as well as swing jazz. Working within the two genres, he became a major figure in the transition toward modern blues. His reworking of earlier material in the 1930s showed how much he had developed. Johnson stepped back into traditional blues frameworks with an advanced soloing conception, using a full vocabulary of scalar invention, which brought out the guitar's capabilities within the blues genre and put Johnson ahead of players moulded by the traditional blues of the south.

URBAN CENTRES

Urban areas were flourishing all over the USA and Beale Street in Memphis, Tennessee, was an important centre. The city had its own jug-band style, exemplifying a long tradition of southern group music. Recordings made by the Beale Street Sheiks in the late1920s highlight guitar duos working closely together. The female guitarist, "Memphis Minnie" (Lizzie Douglas, 1897–1973), also worked in the city and played with a panache and ability equal to many of the Chicago innovators.

TAMPA RED

Tampa Red (Hudson Whitaker, 1904–81) moved to Chicago from Tampa, Florida, and became one of the first widely recognized guitar celebrities – he was billed as "The Guitar Wizard". After working with singer Ma Rainey, his duet recording with pianist Georgia Tom Dorsey (1899–1993), "It's Tight Like That" (1928), was a major Hokum hit. Two instrumentals from 1934, "Things 'Bout Coming My Way" and "Denver Blues", show Red's skill in fretting chords on the lower strings while gliding over the top with an individualistic and smooth slide part. In a long playing career, he became one of the major figures on the Chicago music scene.

SCRAPPER BLACKWELL

Francis "Scrapper" Blackwell (1903–62) forged interesting jazzy ideas and a muscular technique. He worked with pianist Leroy Carr until 1935. Blackwell was able to strum chord voicings with his thumb while playing a solo on the top strings with his fingers, often snapping the strings against the fingerboard to give an incisive effect, as can be heard on "Kokomo Blues". A highlight of the duo is "How Long, How Long Blues", recorded in 1928.

TAMPA RED
Using slide and fingerstyle on a resonator guitar, Tampa Red could play in a range of styles and frequently worked in the Chicago studios. A gifted multi-instrumentalist who often played kazoo solos over his guitar, he was one of the first early figures to adopt the electric guitar.

BIG BILL BROONZY
Broonzy became a godfather of the Chicago blues scene and exerted a strong influence over a long period of time, helping to nurture fresh talent. He travelled abroad and became an ambassador of the genre.

BIG BILL BROONZY

During the 1920s, Chicago was a key musical centre and a magnet for migrants from the countryside and towns and cities of the south.

An early figure who played a major part in developing a fashionable style of urban blues in Chicago was William "Big Bill" Broonzy (1893–1958) from Mississippi. After playing violin and performing from a young age, he moved over to guitar and settled in Chicago in the 1920s. He brought his own strands of country songs and ragtime from the south and started recording in 1927. Over a long playing career Broonzy recorded a large body of material and wrote many songs that have become standard repertoire. "Guitar Rag" and "Pig Meat Strut" showcase his bright, jangling tone and effervescent dancing style.

Broonzy was part of the "Hokum" craze in the early 1930s. Hokum was a light, witty style of blues with double-entendre lyrics. One of Broonzy's most important contributions was his formation of extended early instrumental line-ups, and he featured in the 1938 "Spirituals To Swing" series at the prestigious Carnegie Hall in New York, when blues began to be championed by figures such as record producer John Hammond.

National Triolian

GUITAR & PIANO
Scrapper Blackwell (left) used a resonator to be heard above Leroy Carr's piano. The resonator, with its metal body and internal cone system to project the sound, was first developed in 1926 and became widely popular with blues musicians. The economy National Duolian and Triolian models, with their loud, penetrating, percussive edge and distinctive metallic sound, appeared around 1930.

POSTWAR BLUES

After World War II, Chicago continued to be the major urban centre for blues. Guitarists moved there from the south and, as the electric guitar became widely embraced, the city gave birth to a blues style of searing intensity that drew directly on southern musical roots.

Although the first electric guitars were commercially available from 1932, it was a number of years before they became adopted by blues musicians. The key figure in the emergence of electric blues was the debonair T-Bone Walker (1910–75). Although he was the first great electric stylist, Walker was not the only figure to play electric guitar in the 1930s. Robert Jr. Lockwood and Tampa Red had also discovered the power of electricity.

T-BONE WALKER

Born in Texas, Aaron Thibeaux "T-Bone" Walker first worked in Dallas as a lead boy for Blind Lemon Jefferson, helping him to get around the city and earn a living. When he began playing himself, Walker imitated the work and style of Scrapper Blackwell and was also impressed by Lonnie Johnson. He made his first recordings in 1929, and in the 1930s played duets with Charlie Christian (see page 102), set to emerge later as the first widely influential electric guitarist in jazz. In

T-BONE WALKER
A consummate showman, T-Bone Walker developed set routines and stage antics to widen his appeal.

JUMP BLUES

In the 1940s, a vogue for a jazzy style of blues produced "Jump Blues", a swinging, uptempo boogie style. Jump blues was played by groups such as saxophonist Louis Jordan's band, the Tympany Five, formed in 1938. The group had a slick style and instrumental line-up with a brass section similar to a jazz group; the guitar was part of the rhythm section. Carl Hogan played guitar in Jordan's band.

1934, Walker moved to Los Angeles where he worked with blues and jazz groups and experimented with electric instruments. Eventually, at the beginning of the 1940s, he adopted the electric guitar professionally. In 1942 with "Mean Old World" and "I Got A Break, Baby" he moved toward creating his own special identity. His solo tone is brittle and has affinities with Charlie Christian's style. Some of Walker's jazz-chordal passages sound similar to those used by Django Reinhardt, but he also developed a particular way of using brass-style stabbed comping. His fluent use of scales and triplet-feel laid part of the foundations for sophisticated modern electric soloing.

In 1947, Walker recorded some of his finest material, including the evocative "Call It Stormy Monday", which became a major hit. Against a laid-back rhythm section, Walker plays a supple, laconic solo with chopped, rhythmic fills. His smooth voice, jazzy soloing and brass backing arrangements placed him worlds apart from his blues contemporaries. On the fast swing of "Lonesome Woman Blues" he plays riffs, and "Vacation Blues" has sounds similar to jazz soloing, with added string bending. "Too Much Trouble Blues" runs two notes at the same pitch against each other to produce a lifting, rhythmic effect, a technique that would later be adopted by rock 'n' roll players.

In his long career, Walker also recorded some exceptional instrumentals, including "T-Bone Jumps Again" (1946) and "Two Bones and A Pick" (1956), both of which demonstrate the abilities that put him in a league of his own.

During the 1940s, guitarists all over America started using electric guitars. One was Robert Jr. Lockwood, based in the south, who acquired an electric guitar at the end of the 1930s. He appeared with the singer Sonny Boy Williamson in the radio show KFAA King Biscuit Time in the 1940s, the first black radio station to play blues.

MUDDY WATERS

Born in Mississippi, Muddy Waters (McKinley Morganfield, 1915–83) started playing slide guitar in the early1930s, emulating Son House. On "I Be's Troubled" (1941), he plays slide with driving funky rhythms with chopped muting. Working in clubs in Chicago, where he had moved in 1942, Waters soon realized that he needed an electric guitar to be heard properly. After starting to record for the Chess Brothers in 1947, his first hit "I Can't Be Satisfied" was based on "I Be's Troubled".

In 1948, in a duo with Ernest "Big" Crawford on double bass, his "I Can't Be Satisfied" (1948) and its B-side "I Feel Like Goin' Home", captured a city-wide audience with its magnetically sensual vocals which combined with novel electric slide. Waters used a resonant open tuning and played with a direct melodic and rhythmic technique; his approach played a major part in establishing Delta-influenced electric blues.

He broke through to a national audience in the 1950s, writing and arranging classic standards. After recording "Rollin' Stone" (1950) solo, using a muted rhythm with short distorted riffs, he started to work with bigger line-ups. With "Long Distance Call" (1951), he plays in a trio with harmonica and bass, and mimics train and phone sounds. The measured simplicity of "Honey Bee" (1951), with Jimmy Rogers on guitar, sees slide creating buzzing effects over guitar chords. "I'm Your Hoochie Coochie Man" (1954) has a full group line-up playing powerful stop-start rhythms.

MUDDY WATERS
Waters forged a primeval urban sound utterly unlike the lighter popular urban blues that had gone before. He set the standard for groups at the beginning of the 1950s and his line-ups featured strong characters, including Little Walter on harmonica, Otis Spann on piano and Willie Dixon on bass.

BLUES ELEMENTS

Blues is based around three chords and a twelve-bar repeating structure. In the key of D, this starts with four bars of D, followed by two bars of G, two bars of D and two bars of A, and finishes with two bars of D. There are variants, and prewar blues structures can be irregular, without a sense of fixed bars and lengths. The "key" of D is not a major scale, but a loose, pentatonic structure based on the notes D, F, A, G and C, with added notes such as E, F♯, G♯ and B, and bending giving in-between notes. Guitarists often tuned their instruments to an open D, G, E or A major chord to play slide, moving up and down the strings using lines, chords and partial two-note lines in parallel thirds and fourths, as in the example below. *(See pages 234–35 for musical terminology.)*

PENTATONIC BLUES SCALE IN D WITH ADDED NOTES

SLIDE IN OPEN-D TUNING

B.B. KING

King plays with a surging exuberance and uses downstrokes to give a full sound, with string bending and his own type of finger vibrato. The feeling is sweet and soulful and he sometimes reaches tentatively into space with delicacy and controlled dynamics, the guitar dropping to a whisper.

GIBSON ES-125

The ES-125 is essentially a cheaper version of Gibson's first production electric, the ES-150. The ES-125 was modified during the 1940s and B. B. King used his with Fender amplifiers which were launched in the 1940s. The Gibson and Fender combination has been the cornerstone of blues guitar playing and recording setups for over 50 years.

ELMORE JAMES

Destined to become one of the legendary Chicago slide players, Elmore James had a particular way of taking early blues and converting it into a personal style with powerful phrases. This led to his work becoming part of the fundamental vocabulary for electric blues guitarists.

Over succeeding years, Waters became the leading figure in Chicago blues and his group recorded classics such as "I Just Want To Make Love To You" (1954) and "Got My Mojo Working" (1956). His instrumental line-ups were templates for blues groups and helped to place the guitar at the forefront of popular music.

ELECTRIC DELTA STYLES

A character who took the smouldering earthiness of the South and established himself in the north was John Lee Hooker (b.1917), who moved to Detroit in 1943. Hooker often drives just one or two scratchy, abrasive chords with rattling strings and pushes notes into primal licks with great effect. The unusual "Boogie Chillen" (1948) has a seductive primitive resonance; the whole structure is based on one chord, with a slide excursion backed by double bass. "Hobo Blues" (1949) and "Crawling Kingsnake" (1949) both conjure up the Delta. On later tracks, such as "Dimples" (1956), he snaps distinctive lower notes to end vocal phrases.

Elmore James (1918–63) stands out as a legendary electric slide player with "Dust My Broom" (1952). The unforgettable slide figure is his own extension of Johnson's "I Believe I'll Dust My Broom". James continued to develop variants on this idea, using an approach that is subtly rhythmic and wildly atmospheric.

Howlin' Wolf (Chester Burnett, b.1910) injected a rough ferocity into the blues. His recordings from Memphis in 1951–52, with Willie Johnson's added edge, were followed in 1954 by work with Hubert Sumlin in Chicago. "Smokestack Lightnin'" (1956), based on Patton's "Moon Goin' Down", is now a staple of the blues repertoire.

Gibson ES-125

B.B. KING

"B. B." King (b.1925) has become one of the most famous electric blues guitarists in the world. Early in life he admired Blind Lemon Jefferson and Lonnie Johnson, but later came under the spell of his idol, T-Bone Walker, and absorbed ideas from his cousin Bukka White. He also drew from jazz guitarists such as Charlie Christian and, in his efforts to emulate advanced soloists, created his own more direct style in relation to his voice. King eventually established himself in Memphis in 1948, playing on the radio station WDIA. He built a way of playing that does not involve the use of block chords for vocal backing or rhythms; instead, the guitar becomes a melodic counterpart to his voice, often using short expressive, hallmark phrases. Two years after his first record, "Miss Martha King" (1949), he had a hit with the slow tempo "3 O'Clock Blues" (1951), on which his distinctive fills and solo produce a colourful tone over an arrangement with sustained brass chords.

"Woke Up This Morning" (1954) is backed by a big band over which King plays a rhythmic, distorted chord intro contrasted with jazzy comping in a completely different tone.

"You Upset Me Baby" (1954) opens with swinging lines and has a melodic solo full of bending and sustain, drawing on jazz phrasing, while one of King's best-loved pieces, "Sweet Little Angel" (1956), has expressive fills and a solo built around phrases with string bending.

GENRES & REGIONS

There was an explosion of talent all over the States in the 1940s and 1950s. Sam "Lightnin'" Hopkins (1912–82) started recording in the 1940s. He went on to produce rocky, electric blues numbers with fluent soloing such as "Highway Blues" (1953) which has liquid glissando, boogie lines and chords and soloing, and the exceptional electric blues track, "Hopkins' Sky Hop" (1954). With changes in fashion and the rise of rock 'n' roll, Hopkins gradually sank into obscurity. On the West Coast, Lowell Fulson (b.1921) laid down his best-known number, "Three O'Clock Blues" (1948). The young prodigy Johnny "Guitar" Watson (1935–96) spent time in the studios in the 1950s recording many tracks, among them the amazing "Three Hours Past Midnight". Texan Clarence "Gatemouth" Brown (1924–93) mixed country elements with blues. His outstanding playing on "Okie Dokie Stomp" (1954) is full of fresh, swinging inventiveness. A simple style of muted boogie blues took Jimmy Reed (1925–76) to the top. Working with guitarist Eddie Taylor (1923–85) he had a string of hits from the 1950s. The 1950s also saw the start of Albert King's career (*see page 59*).

New Orleans had its own regional flavour: Guitar Slim (Eddie Jones, 1926–59) produced "The Things I Used To Do" (1954) and "The Story Of My Life". Slim was a great showman, often performing using a 60m (200ft) guitar lead so that he could walk outside the building still playing.

A regional genre called "Swamp Blues" emerged from the coastal areas in the south. It is associated with Louisiana and characterized by laid-back, relaxed tempos, echo and reverb, giving it a distant, sombre sound. Major players of this swamp sound included Lightnin' Slim (Otis Hicks, 1913–83) and Slim Harpo (James Moore, 1924–70), who recorded "I'm A Kingbee" (1957) and later worked with Lightnin' Slim.

OTIS RUSH

Chicago was full of talented guitarists as the scene flourished during the 1950s. After establishing himself in the city, Otis Rush (b.1934) started recording music with vibrant, innovative guitar parts that have a unique character. His recording career began in 1954, and he had a breakthrough with "I Can't Quit You, Baby" (1956). This was followed by a highly creative period that produced "All Your Love" (1958), with its beautiful, potent arpeggiated figures and bright, warm, characterful soloing, and the atmospheric "Double Trouble" (1957).

Along with Magic Sam and Buddy Guy, Rush became one of the "West Side" players associated with clubs in Chicago's western neighbourhoods.

OTIS RUSH
One of the remarkable figures emerging in 1950s Chicago, Rush has his own unique ringing tone with vibrato and echo. He plays left handed without reversing the strings, so the bass strings are at the top.

ELECTRIC GOSPEL
Gospel singer Sister Rosetta Tharpe (Rosetta Nubin, 1915–73) moved from acoustic to electric guitar in the 1950s. She played a Gibson Les Paul.

FREDDIE KING

FREDDIE KING
*An inspirational
electric blues
soloist, Freddie
King's playing is
full of invention,
with attractive
phrases and subtle
rhythmic nuances.*

Born in Texas, Freddie King (1934–76) is one of the figures who virtually created a large part of the soloing vocabulary of guitarists from the 1960s onward. Inspired by Robert Johnson, Lightnin' Hopkins, T-Bone Walker and B.B. King, he started playing at a very young age, moved to Chicago in 1954, and began recording in 1956. His all-instrumental album *Let's Hide Away And Dance Away* (1961) is refreshingly unusual.

Playing with a thumbpick and metal fingerpicks, King's sound is unmistakeably metallic without losing sonority. Rhythmically adventurous passages and elliptical phrasing unravel chorus after chorus of the sheer invention and musical content that mark him out from many blues soloists, whose improvisational imagination can tend to be limited. King moves beyond licks and expands his vocabulary by transcending pentatonic and chord-based soloing ideas toward a freer scaler expression. His bright, bubbly extemporizations are unmistakeable, and he is able to shift from punchy staccato to gentle passages with a playful, light touch.

King's compositions, written with keyboard player Sonny Thompson, are exciting and full of ideas. The *tour de force* "Hide Away" (1960) sparkles with a torrent of riffs and two-note melodic fills, as it changes time and builds and releases tension, while on "Sidetracked" (1960), he constructs his solo with a wonderful swing in his timing.

"THE STUMBLE"

Recorded in Cincinnati in April 1961, "The Stumble" was written by King and pianist Sonny Thompson. Its form is a refreshing variation on the twelve-bar blues, comprising 16 bars consisting of an initial eight bars and an answering eight bars. King plays an original expressive line, with a rhythmic structure and flowing triplets, swinging blues bends and offbeat ninth chords. The lead-in phrase ends on the first beat of the first bar. From bar nine, the band stop on the first beat, leaving King alone to play phrases and after they come back in, King plays phrases with sixths on bars 13 and 14. (*See pages 234–35 for musical terminology.*)

BUDDY GUY

Growing up in Louisiana, "Buddy" Guy (b.1936) was formatively influenced by local musicians such as Guitar Slim. Guy moved to Chicago in 1957 and made his first recordings the following year. While he acknowledged influences such as Muddy Waters and B.B. King, his style is unique and individualistic. His recordings from the beginning of the 1960s are explosive, tortured and full of an irregular phrasing across the beat that can be almost devoid of melodic invention yet full of unexpected variety. He achieves this by taking an unusual approach to stock phrases and tension release. He does not bend at obvious moments, emphasizing expressive points in his own way. With dynamics, tone and colour, his music is varied. He has a wide range of tones, ranging from a shattering physical energy to a strange, flute-like breathiness. His breakthrough came with "First Time I Met The Blues" (1960) which displays his urgent, searching

ALBERT COLLINS

A cousin of Lightnin' Hopkins, Albert Collins (b.1932) has been called the Iceman because of his song titles. He recorded "The Freeze" in 1958 and was one of the few people, apart from Freddie King, to produce idiosyncratic instrumentals. "Frosty" (1962) has a rich, reedy sound full of colour and comes across as completely individualistic: Collins' astonishing rhythmic subtlety features notes across the beat which are played with great precision. He also used his own bizarre type of open tuning which helped him to break away from convention.

Albert Collins, known as the Iceman.

vocals and fiery chip fills. Guy's sense of compressed manic intensity comes across in all kinds of arrangements and tempos. The jiving "Slop Around" (1960) features wild, high tremolo chords and a feeling of zaniness, and on "Broken-Hearted Blues" (1960) he takes a querulous emotional solo to convey instability. His tone is unmistakeable on the electrifying, iridescent intro riff for "Let Me Love You Baby" and on the voodoo chill of "I Got a Strange Feeling" (1960), with its eery intro sound and dry fills with little sustain which, along with his choked incoherence, help project fear. His touch comes across on "Stone Crazy" (1961), too, where the guitar answers vocals with great variety and he squeezes the notes on his solo with expressive feeling. With its muted arpeggio figure, the instrumental "Skippin'" (1961) is light and melodic, and "Worried Mind" (1963) displays a gentle delicacy. The smooth "Moanin'" (1963) shows him in a jazzy context, playing unexpected turns of phrase.

BUDDY GUY
Guy's work is characterized by a cutting, frenzied style, emotionalism and a trademark technique of excessively shaking notes, imparting a tight, compressed energy. He uses unusual bends, some of which are very wide, and an extensive range of left-hand vibrato effects.

FENDER STRATOCASTER
This 1950s Sunburst model is similar to the instrument used by Buddy Guy to help achieve his particular type of brittle tone.

BLUES RENAISSANCE

With enthusiastic researchers and musicians leading the way, and a growing interest from a younger generation, there was a rehabilitation of acoustic blues and a re-evaluation of existing electric blues artists. White musicians became involved and the 1960s saw a blues boom.

GIBSON J-200
The large-bodied Gibson J-200 first came out in 1937. It produces a tremendously rich tone and a reverberating depth. Gary Davis used this model of guitar in his last period.

GARY DAVIS
Among those who came to deserved prominence thanks to the renewed interest of the folk movement was the Reverend Gary Davis (1896–1972) who was encouraged by guitarist Stefan Grossman. Davis played ragtime and blues and was a technically proficient all-rounder who came out of an environment in Georgia in which he had been directly influenced by Blind Blake and had worked with Blind Boy Fuller.

The folk movement's interest in what it considered to be authentic musicians led to the rehabilitation of careers and the discovery of previously overlooked figures who were given the opportunity to record. Leadbelly (Huddie William Ledbetter, 1885–1949) had moved to New York in 1935. He was elevated to heroic status in the urban folk scene of the 1940s and 1950s and wrote numbers such as "Rock Island Line" and "The Midnight Special". His guitar work was straightforward and concise, and his ability to amalgamate country, gospel and blues in the New York coffeehouse scene helped to make him appealing to the folk movement. The work of musicologists led to a crusade to research the blues and attempt to revive the traditional music. This was effected by folk-music archivist Alan Lomax and producer John Hammond, and in 1959, the guitarist John Fahey (b.1939) and writer Sam Charters who produced an album for Lightnin' Hopkins.

An effort to research the music and seek out players in the south who had been overlooked or lost led to the rediscovery of musicians who were thought to have died, such as Sleepy John Estes (1899–1977). Slide specialist Mississippi Fred McDowell was found

by Alan Lomax in 1959 and this eventually paved the way for the recording of his first album, *Delta Blues* (1963) in his sixtieth year. Players who had been influential and recorded in the prewar era were also unearthed. Bukka White (*see page 47*) made powerful recordings from 1963 onward, using an open-G tuning to play slide with percussive and complex rhythms. Skip James (*see page 47*) was rediscovered in 1964. The writer of "Devil Got My Woman" and "I'm So Glad", he had his own type of fingerstyle with nails and used unusual tunings.

SON HOUSE
After living in obscurity and only recording in 1930 and 1941, Son House (Eddie James House Jr.) gave up playing until 1964, when he was tracked down and brought out of retirement. His album The

Legendary Son House: Father Of The Folk Blues *(1965) put him firmly back on the map. He worked consistently once more, displaying the open-tuning slide work that had inspired Robert Johnson and Muddy Waters.*

ELECTRIC BLUES

There was a marked separation between the acoustic and electric blues audience in the early 1960s. After the folk rediscovery of acoustic blues, there was a blues boom, partly due to the effect of British musicians such as the Rolling Stones and Eric Clapton who drew on a wide range of music but whose work most closely reflected 1950s and 1960s blues. This helped to bring a new interest to the blues as a whole which eventually worked its way through to established black artists who were less in vogue due to the explosion of interest in pop. Consequently their profile was enhanced which helped their recording careers.

ALBERT KING

Albert King (1923–92) was born in Mississippi and moved to Chicago, making his first recordings in the 1950s, although his recording career did not fulfil its potential until the mid-1960s. King successfully superimposes blues playing over sequences and arrangements that move away from the twelve-bar format. When he started recording for Stax in 1966, using their house musicians including the Memphis Horns, he incorporated elements of soul and other genres, creating a funkier edge to his blues numbers. He had a breakthrough with "Laundromat Blues" (1966) on which his fills have a reedy sustain and a solo builds from repetitive elements to inventive

Gibson Flying V

melodic licks. The instrumental B-side "Overall Junction" features rhythmic riffs over brass backing and a positive solo in which King develops ideas with a sequential clarity.

His seminal album *Born Under A Bad Sign* (1967), with the title track, "Crosscut Saw" and "Oh Pretty Woman", brought electric blues into a well-produced studio context with great arrangements and tempos. The solo on "Personal Manager", with its paced sustained notes against the band, surging string bending and tension release, is well constructed and holds its appeal through the use of space.

THE 1960s

Howlin' Wolf's band recorded one of the important songs of 1960s blues, "Killing Floor" (1965) with its rocky chordal style and incisive rhythms. During this period, Wolf's band featured the elliptical guitar work of Hubert Sumlin, who had moved away from rhythm to play solos at odd places or in the background throughout a song with an unpredictable course. Many leading blues players evolved and recorded their best work during the 1960s.

MIKE BLOOMFIELD
Growing up in Chicago, Bloomfield was influenced by Freddie King and played in the bars and clubs of the South Side before recording with Paul Butterfield on his album The Paul Butterfield Blues Band *(1965). The album showcased Bloomfield's exceptional talent which is fired with energy and passion.*

ALBERT KING
In the 1960s, King emerged as one of the major figures within electric blues, with a style that has had a pervasive effect on players in recent years. Primarily a linear player, King sometimes plays behind the beat, bends notes out of tune and achieves a pinched sound by squeezing notes to produce a strong tone. He is also a master of nuance and is able to create fresh-sounding ideas from a simple group of notes.

ALBERT KING'S FLYING V
A left-handed player, King uses right-hand stringing, with the lower pitched strings at the top, and his own type of open tuning.

B.B. King's *Live At The Regal* (1965) is one of his most popular albums. "Sweet Little Angel" highlights the kind of exciting fluent playing he was capable of at this time.

Magic Sam (Samuel Maghett, b.1937) made an album, *West Side Soul* (1967), that shows him to have been a player who could have broken through to a larger audience, but unfortunately he died in 1969.

Some of the greatest blues was being played by rock figures such as Jimi Hendrix (*see pages 190–95*) and Eric Clapton (*see pages 142–45*) who were blues based and recorded blues solos played against heavy rock backgrounds. A younger generation of white American players took to the blues with great fervour in the 1960s. Mike Bloomfield (*see page 59*) was one of the first. Along with Duane Allman, Johnny Winter and Roy Buchanan, he made a career in both rock and blues genres.

CONTINUITY

The 1970s was a mixed period for many long-established blues musicians. The old-guard acoustic players were passing away and the electric generation had mixed fortunes. Some, such as Johnny Guitar Watson, embraced current rock and pop trends and funk.

In 1978, Albert Collins was able to record the album *Ice Pickin'* that brought him directly into the mainstream. Emerging from the shadows, Clarence "Gatemouth" Brown enjoyed a breakthrough the following year with *Makin' Music* (1979). Less successfully, Buddy Guy (*see page 57*) was running a club in Chicago and experienced a difficult time without a record deal during the 1980s until his comeback commercial album *Damn Right, I've Got The Blues* (1991). The indestructible John Lee Hooker, on the other hand, has enjoyed a long career of continuous popularity.

GIBSON 355
Gibson symmetrical thinline guitars, which appeared from 1958, have always been a mainstay for artists such as B.B. King and Freddie King.

FREDDIE KING
One of the great soloists in blues, Freddie King (see page 56) was embraced by the pop and rock worlds and worked regularly until his death in 1976.

B.B. KING & BAND
King had a mainstream hit in the pop charts with The Thrill Is Gone *(1969) and has sustained a career at the top in the blues world by touring and releasing retrospective compilations of his work.*

TEXAS FLOOD

Recorded in Los Angeles in 1982, *Texas Flood* (1983), with Stevie Ray Vaughan playing in a trio format, showcased his approach which integrated a raunchy modern sound with blues shuffles without stepping outside the traditional framework. The album immediately made him a major force in blues. Backed by a driving, rootsy rhythm section playing strong grooves and shuffles, and accompanied by his laconic vocals, the guitar shines out with its superb tone and powerful vocal qualities. The title track highlights tremendous soloing, with long sustained notes dropping off into resolution and lurching tremolo-bar chords pulled up and down in pitch. The guitar meshes with the rhythm-section sound to produce a mesmerizing lyricism. Vaughan hangs on to sustained notes and resolves them to release tension. On the exuberant "Pride and Joy", the earthy rhythm section play great tempos, and Vaughan slides into searing figures.

STEVIE RAY VAUGHAN
With his Fender Stratocaster tuned down a semitone, heavy gauge strings, minimal effects and two amplifiers, Vaughan was able to wring a plangent, full sound from the instrument. His bristling, rhythmic fills have a contrasting, almost acoustic-sounding presence.

ELECTRIC DEVELOPMENTS

In the 1980s, electric blues started to borrow sounds from blues rock, with more modern-sounding backing and pop production.

The new star of the 1980s, Stevie Ray Vaughan (1954–90), was brought up in Texas playing blues. He grew up playing guitar with his older brother Jimmie Vaughan (b.1951), was influenced by Albert King and absorbed the blues-rock developments of the 1960s. He forged his own rich singing sound and exploited a wide vocabulary of blues licks and melodic chordal riffs in such a way as to create a fresh-sounding synthesis. Vaughan plays with great assurance and has a superb feel and musical taste, all of which can be heard on the album *Texas Flood* (1983).

Another important figure, Robert Cray (b.1953), produced strong blues recordings with a soul flavour such as *Bad Influence* (1983), and moved to a more modern accessible pop rhythm section sound on *Strong Persuader* (1986). Tracks such as "Smoking Gun" have background chords with a processed jangly pop sound and Cray plays dry, pithy breaks. "I Guess I Showed Her" has chopped chords and on "Right Next Door" he plays an expressive solo with notes that have a popping definition. Catchy, repeating riffs characterize "Nothin' But A Woman" and an attractive emotional opening break introduces "I Wonder", on which Cray plays a questioning solo.

Among other figures are Robben Ford, who draws from blues and incorporates the inventiveness of modal jazz fusion. On his album *Talk To Your Daughter* (1988), he uses a reedy, overdriven sound with long sustain and mixes blues phrasing with sonorous upper register bending and interesting lines. *Robben Ford & The Blues Line* (1992) moves back toward traditional blues and is infused with a refreshing creativity.

ROBERT CRAY
After playing with Albert Collins and releasing his first album in the 1970s, Robert Cray has found success by producing a style of blues set within a modern-sounding popular framework.

COUNTRY

COUNTRY MUSIC IS AN AMERICAN STYLE OF

POPULAR SONG AND DANCE MUSIC. ROOTED

IN EUROPEAN FOLK SONGS, IT ORIGINALLY

HAD A STRONG REGIONAL ASSOCIATION WITH

THE RURAL AREAS OF THE UNITED STATES. AS

COUNTRY HAS DEVELOPED, IT HAS GIVEN RISE

TO GENRES SUCH AS BLUEGRASS.

CHET ATKINS *The most famous country guitarist of the 20th century, Atkins developed his own versatile chord-melody technique. He has recorded a vast range of material.*

THE ORIGINS OF COUNTRY

During the early 1920s, country started to appear on commercial recordings, and by the end of the decade it was established as a popular style, helped by the first radio stations. One of the most famous was Nashville's Barn Dance Radio Show, later renamed The Grand Ole Opry.

Country musicians in the 1920s were working within a traditional framework that had been in existence for decades. Music based around country dancing, folk songs and ballads had been developing in Tennessee, Georgia, Kentucky, Virginia and adjacent states until, with figures such as Fiddlin' John Carson selling large quantities of recordings from 1923, country became recognized as a new, popular and commercial style, with a potential for widespread appeal.

In much the same way as happened with the blues, the widespread adoption of the guitar for country music was due partly to cheap mass production. British folk music had some influence on the music, but the isolation of rural "hillbilly" communities in the Appalachians led to a particular style of mountain songs and country dancing tunes. Ragtime and blues also contributed to forming early-guitar styles.

MARTIN SIZE 1
Founded in 1833, Martin developed high-quality instruments with an open, resonant sound. They were widely adopted by country musicians in the 1920s, by which time metal had replaced gut strings.

RILEY PUCKETT
Puckett was one of the first country-music guitarists to become well known. His instrumental style was influenced by Scottish and Irish dance music, as on the inventive "Miss McLeod's Reel" (1931).

EARLY GUITARISTS

A number of other important country guitarists emerged in the 1920s. Sam McGee (1894–1975), from Tennessee, was influenced by Uncle Dave Macon (1870–1952) and eventually joined Macon's group The Fruit Jar Drinkers in 1924. With the McGee Brothers, he made successful recordings from 1930. Other figures included Frank Hutchison, "The Pride Of West Virginia", and Roy Harvey (1892–1958), who played blues-influenced solos in the 1920s. Another famous group was The Sons of the Pioneers with Karl Farr, an extended family harmony group in the Carter tradition. Country music has become associated with the white population, but there were many important early black players. In Kentucky, for instance, black guitarist Arnold Shultz developed a rhythmic "choke" style that was influential.

RILEY PUCKETT

Born in Georgia, Riley Puckett (1894–1946) had a large repertoire of British folk songs, popular 19th-century songs and Broadway hits. From 1916 he played with fiddler Gid Tanner, recorded with him from 1924, and in 1926 the two formed the Skillet Lickers. Their forward-looking instrumental arrangements, put down in Atlanta, were antecedents for bluegrass. On these, Puckett plays a sophisticated style of accompaniment with floating, displaced runs and arpeggiated chord sequences.

As well as chordal strumming, Puckett added clear bass notes and melodic runs that are sometimes put in unusual places, giving an almost contrapuntal effect, often using subtle syncopation. His strong bass can be heard on "Dixie" (1927) and the instrumental "Liberty" (1928). On the uptempo "Molly Put The Kettle On" (1931), Puckett opens by playing the melody on guitar, and uses higher-register fills with occasional double-time flourishes.

JIMMIE RODGERS

Jimmie Rodgers (1897–1933) was born in Mississippi. Until he turned professional in 1925, he worked on the railroad which led to his nickname, "the singing brakeman". Like most early country performers, he was first heard on the radio before being discovered in 1927 and given the chance to record.

Among his first recordings is a folk waltz, "The Soldier's Sweetheart", which Rodgers accompanies with a country-style guitar bass note and strumming technique. At this time, the major characteristic that Rodgers brings to country music is the blues, which can be heard on "Blue Yodel #1 (T. Is For Texas)" (1927). This sees Rodgers strumming chords with a bluesy

THE CARTER FAMILY
Maybelle Carter's playing was sometimes described as "church licks" and her technique as the "Carter scratch". She was very influential and is shown here with her sister Sara, on the right, and Sara's husband A. P. Carter.

harmonic structure, with added musicians playing Hawaiian-style slide guitar and violin. On another number, "The Brakeman's Blues" (1927), Rodgers rocks rhythmically between pairs of bass notes and plays short fills. Tragically, Rodgers had only a short career, but managed to record a large body of material.

MAYBELLE CARTER

Maybelle Carter (1909–78) and the Carter Family came from Virginia and popularized hillbilly folk roots by developing an instrumental style to back their harmony singing using various instruments, including guitar and dulcimer. With Sara on rumbustious rhythm guitar, Maybelle Carter plays pronounced bass runs and melodic figures with a thick-textured tone that underpins the music and helps to give the group an appealing and instantly recognizable sound.

One of their most popular songs is "Wildwood Flower" (c.1927). Backed by Sara's infectious country rhythm, Maybelle opens by playing an attractive melody and reintroduces it with ornamentation to provide solo breaks. This approach is also used on "Keep On The Sunny Side", where Maybelle plays the melody on guitar accompanied by Sara playing rhythm. The waltz "Meet Me By The Moonlight Alone" features slide guitar on melody, often used to give a broader range of colour.

JIMMIE RODGERS
Described humourously as someone "who couldn't read a note, keep time or play the right chords", Jimmie Rodgers was nevertheless one of the first big country stars and consequently widely imitated.

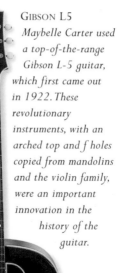

GIBSON L5
Maybelle Carter used a top-of-the-range Gibson L-5 guitar, which first came out in 1922. These revolutionary instruments, with an arched top and f holes copied from mandolins and the violin family, were an important innovation in the history of the guitar.

POSTWAR COUNTRY GUITAR

Country guitar started to evolve and become an equal partner with the instrumental mainstays of country music, the fiddle and banjo. From the 1930s, with the influence of jazz and urban blues, country styles diversified and amplification gave the guitar a more powerful voice.

THE DOBRO
Resonator guitars gave country a new sound. The wooden-body Dobro was used by Brother Oswald of the Ray Acuff Band from the late 1930s.

Country music became nationally established and spread all over the world through Hollywood movies featuring singing cowboys with guitars. One of the first popular films, *In Old Santa Fe* (1934), featured Gene Autry (1907–98), who went on to have a long and successful career. Individuals with widely differing backgrounds started to play country, and musicians from regions such as Texas brought their own distinctive cultural strands. Blues, jazz and the broadcasts of figures such as the early electric guitarist George Barnes influenced a younger generation who saw themselves as moving on from the old-time songs. The advent of electrified instruments, including steel guitar, and hits such as "It Makes No Difference Now" (1938) by The Texas Wanderers were part of changes and developments that would alter the character of country music. Amplification and new techniques gave the guitar a stronger role.

HONKY TONK & BLUES

The word "honky tonk" was originally used to describe rough and ready bars where there was music and dancing. Honky tonk became a vehicle for music with a powerful lyrical, emotional edge, dealing with the problems of everyday life; the music had a strong blues influence and was played with more volume and a strong beat. Texas singer and guitarist Ernest Tubb (1914–84) is an important figure in the development of a honky-tonk style. He took up the guitar after listening to Jimmie Rodgers and had his first radio date in 1934. An important breakthrough came with his composition "Walking The Floor Over You", a popular honky-tonk style hit recorded in 1941 with Fay Smitty Smith on electric guitar. This opens with the electric guitar introducing and embellishing the melody with a catchy feel. Tubb plays acoustic chords and Smith contributes solo breaks using the melody

WESTERN SWING

A style of overtly jazz-influenced country music became established in Texas in the 1930s. The major figure in what has come to be termed western swing was bandleader Bob Wills, who formed Bob Wills & His Texas Playboys and started recording in 1935. His music is essentially dance music with vocals in the style of swing jazz bands, arrangements with a country flavour, and instrumentation mixing brass with string instruments. Eldon Shamblin joined the Texas Playboys in 1937 and was the main guitarist associated with the group. Early recordings feature acoustic guitar playing a strong rhythmic role with a four-

in-the-bar swing style. Recorded in Dallas in 1938, "Whoa Baby" and "That's What I Like About The South" have Shamblin taking short solos that have strong affinities with the styles of both Eddie Lang and Django Reinhardt. On "Bob Wills' Special" (1940), Shamblin is joined by a second guitarist and harmonized, two-part bluesy phrases characterize the track. When the electric guitar came along, Shamblin quickly adopted the instrument, becoming one of the few high-profile electric players in country music. After 1945, the group showcased the guitar more heavily, with prominent electric solos by Jimmy Wyble (b.1922), a particularly talented jazz-influenced guitarist.

THE DELMORE BROTHERS

Guitarist and singer Alton Delmore (1908–64), and his brother Rabon Delmore (1916–52), played a key role by integrating blues boogies with country. Alton Delmore had originally been inspired by Blind Boy Fuller, and from 1946 the brothers' group often features acoustic and electric guitar playing twangy repeating boogie figures. Alton on guitar and Rabon on tenor guitar remain in the background, adding studio guitarists and creating music that anticipated the role of boogies in the popular music of the 1950s. The Delmore Brothers developed hard-driving, uptempo numbers, such as the acoustic "Hillbilly Boogie" recorded in 1946 with added guitarists Merle Travis and Louis Innis. This became a formula that was used for other tracks, such as "Freight Train Boogie" (1946). In this piece, the fast electric boogie figures played by Jethro Burns run alongside acoustic guitars to simulate a train whistle. Another number, "Boogie Woogie Baby" (1947), has tremendous energy, with electric guitar playing riffs and solos using string bends. The Delmore Brothers became famous for "Blues Stay Away From Me" (1949), which has a memorable guitar riff. The Delmores were not the only people producing country boogies at this time, however, and in 1948, Arthur Smith had an influential hit with "Guitar Boogie Shuffle".

and adding a bluesy edge with a loud raucous sound. After this recording, Tubb and his group, The Texas Troubadors, had a long run of successful records that helped to define the sound of modern country. Tubb became a major Nashville figure and, in 1943, was one of the first people to introduce the electric guitar at The Grand Ole Opry (see page 64).

(see page 64)

ELECTRIC GUITAR

In the early 1940s, the electric guitar started to become part of country music. Players could be clearly heard for the first time and the new sound started to affect approaches and styles. Merle Travis first heard studio guitarist George Barnes playing electric guitar on the radio and had a DeArmond pickup fitted to his Gibson L-10 archtop. This solidbody guitar, made for Travis by Paul Bigsby in 1948, was ahead of its time in design and construction.

BOB WILLS & HIS TEXAS PLAYBOYS
Bob Wills (1905–75) had a highly unusual ensemble in country music: a jazz-style big band line-up featuring two electric guitarists who both played rhythm and solos.

ERNEST TUBB
Inspired by Jimmie Rodgers, Tubb helped to modernize the sound of country music in the 1940s. He often played Jimmy Rodgers' guitar, which was given to him by Rodgers' widow.

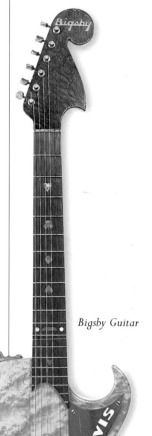

Bigsby Guitar

HANK WILLIAMS

The Alabama singer and guitarist Hank Williams (1923–53) forged a style with a forward-looking modern country backing group that had wide popular appeal and established him as one of the innovative figures in popular music. He formed his own group, The Drifting Cowboys, and started recording in Nashville in 1946. An important early track was his composition "Move It On Over", recorded in May 1947, which became one of his many hits. It features Bob McNett (b.1925) on electric guitar and Don Helms on steel guitar. On this influential track, Williams plays simple steel-string acoustic strumming. McNett creates a showy solo full of complex melodic turns of phrase with a shining tone. The sound was a precursor to the rock 'n' roll of the 1950s. Another outstanding track, "Mind Your Own Business" (1949), has a lilting melodic guitar playing solos and passages under the vocal with a jazzy style. Both McNett and guitarist Sammy Pruitt worked with the group and can be heard on songs in which electric guitar breaks, riffs and fills are woven around the vocals.

Despite a short career, Williams and his band were a major force in country music, and helped to set the scene for 1950s rock 'n' roll.

BLUEGRASS

Bluegrass is a virtuoso acoustic string-band style, often played at fast tempos. With its breakneck speed and relentless driving rhythm, it was a complete departure in style and led to an important movement in country, becoming the vehicle for a new style of guitar playing. In bluegrass, the guitar initially functioned as part of the basic rhythm and harmony. Over a period of time, it gradually absorbed the vocabulary and technique of the frontline bluegrass instruments: banjo, mandolin and violin. The architect of bluegrass was mandolin player Bill Monroe. In the 1930s he started out in a duo with his brother Charlie Monroe on guitar. In 1945 he put together a group with Lester Flatt (1914–79) on guitar and Earl Scruggs (b.1924) on banjo. They left to form their group The Foggy Mountain Boys in 1948. On most numbers, including "Foggy Mountain Breakdown" (1949), Lester Flatt plays tight rhythm chords in the background. But on "Salty Dog Blues" (1950), his offbeat guitar rhythms are distinct and he plays short runs connecting his strummed chords, which are later called Flatt runs. His instrumental skills can be heard on "Preachin' Prayin' Singin'" on which he uses slides, and plays lines and melodic chordal figures.

EARL SCRUGGS & LESTER FLATT
Flatt added distinctive fills to the taut framework of The Foggy Mountain Boys.

MERLE TRAVIS

An exceptional individualist with a unique approach to playing the guitar, Merle Travis (1917–83) grew up in Kentucky, absorbing ideas from guitarists such as Mose Rager and Ike Everly, father of the Everly Brothers. Travis adapted ragtime and bluegrass banjo techniques for the guitar, developing his own remarkable physical approach, which came to be known as "Travis picking". With an effortless grace and smoothness that astonished his contemporaries, he used his thumbpick to play independent bass lines and partial chords and his index finger to play chords, arpeggios and melodies with an astonishing variety of colour and effects. He was first heard using his idiosyncratic style on the Cincinnati radio station WLW from 1937.

Travis established himself in Los Angeles in 1944. The bouncy "Lost John", recorded in Hollywood in 1945, features fast bass lines and rolling arpeggiated fills. On his deceptively light debut album, *Folk Songs Of The Hills* (1947), he sings jocular songs, talks and tells stories. Underneath, he plays sparkling rhythmic acoustic-guitar accompaniment and takes instrumental breaks. His revolutionary approach can be heard on tracks such as the traditional song "John Henry". Travis went on to record instrumentals displaying his characteristic way of playing the blues and introducing jazzy harmonies that support sentimental melodies. He was equally at home

on electric guitar and recorded using a clipped tone and a tremolo bar to add Hawaiian steel-guitar effects, such as moving the pitch up and down slightly. His 1950s numbers vary considerably. On "Walkin' The Strings" there are surging arpeggios with a punchy staccato and slides, while "Blue Smoke" features a jaunty fast rhythm, with muted bass and melodic chords, and moves through cascading arpeggios and single lines without losing momentum. On "Saturday Night Shuffle", Travis creates a ragtime feel with an incisive rhythm. "Bugle Call Rag" becomes a wildly

elliptical development built in the form of a bugle call, with fast lines shooting off at tangents. In contrast, the delicate number "Bluebell" starts with impressionistic chords with harmonics before the rhythm enters, altering the character completely. Travis changed the approach to guitar playing, showing how it was possible to play with variety and innovative techniques. Using his thumb to stop one or two bottom strings enabled him to build mobile upper chords and, with his jazzy voicings, open strings and rolled fast arpeggios, his mesmerizing style inspired many players.

TRAVIS PICKING
Merle Travis performing in his unique style: his right hand position is slumped down near the bridge, enabling him to mute notes and parts of chords to propel rhythms and enhance the effect of syncopation. Travis was also able to strum up and down using both his thumb and index finger.

69

CHET ATKINS

One of the great guitarists of the 20th century, Chet Atkins drew from country music and jazz. His guitar arrangements and his all-round solo control with bass, chords and melody set high standards, and his catchy motifs and harmonic ideas influenced both country and pop music.

CHET ATKINS
Seen here in 1943, Atkins is holding a Martin C-2 archtop guitar, fitted with an early-style tremolo arm. He was fascinated by the playing of Merle Travis, and developed his own fingerstyle technique with thumbpick and fingers. He was also inspired by Django Reinhardt, George Barnes and later Les Paul.

Born in Tennessee in 1924, Chet Atkins started by playing ukulele and later took up violin and guitar. A prodigious talent, he turned professional in the early 1940s and developed his own technique on acoustic and electric guitar using a thumbpick and fingernails, which enabled him to play fingerstyle with great versatility.

A chopped, rolling bass is one of his most characteristic sounds, often with muting and echo-supporting flexible harmonized melody notes, chords and single lines that are supple, snappy and incisive. Atkins also plays deft, quickly rolled arpeggiated chords similar to a banjo roll and uses touches of pitch variation and vibrato on notes, with a tremolo arm. An early instrumental composition, "Guitar Blues" (1946), highlights his individual style. Played on electric guitar, it features tight rhythmic bass notes with luminous, bright, chipped chords, ringing harp-like tones, sliding chords and single-note passages.

In 1947, Atkins' prolific career took off with his close association with RCA in Nashville. He made many recordings and worked with artists who included the Carter Sisters and Hank Williams. Among his own recordings, his solo instrumental "Black Mountain Rag" (1952) uses a DGDGBD tuning and is full of invention, with swirling legato lines, powerful bass and

ATKINS' GUITARS

During the 1940s, Atkins often used a Gibson L-10 archtop. In 1950, he acquired a sunburst D'Angelico Excel that was subsequently converted to an electric guitar with the addition of two fixed pickups. He also started recording with classical guitars in the 1950s. Gretsch made a whole series of Chet Atkins guitar models, including the Chet Atkins Hollow Body 6120 which first appeared in 1954 with Dynasonic pickups, a Bigsby vibrato unit and western-style designs.

DEVELOPING SOUNDS

In 1954, Atkins started using an EchoSonic combo amp with a built-in echo unit. He experimented with various effects, including a pedal fitted with a tone control. "Boo Boo Stick Beat" (1959) has effects with a mouth organ-like sound as the chords breathe and shimmer with a distorted sound with tone and volume level fluctuations. "Django's Castle" ("Manoir De Mes Reves"), recorded in 1960, has wah wah-like tone variations and electronic tremolo

tremolo arm producing a steel-guitar type sound, with echo. The number "Oh By Jingo" (1953) also features a great deal of echo, and its gliding effortlessness with lively dancing playing exudes optimism. For this number he makes use of arpeggiation with sharp, inventive bass, twangy tones, banjo rolls and tremendous raunchy smoky-textured chordal figures.

The number "Kentucky Derby" (1953) simulates a horse race, with climbing figures and fast galloping single lines, while "Dill Pickle Rag" (1953) contains a variety of sparkling arpeggio techniques, fast chord changes,

JAZZ & BLUES

Recordings from 1964 feature Atkins' controlled melodic jazz playing. He creates a country influence, imparting a rhythmic bounce to tunes, keeping close to the melody. "Jordu" is played with a fine delicacy, "I Remember You" has smooth impressionistic chords, "Bluesette" is melodic and "Summertime" is atmospheric and spacey. "A Little Bit of Blues" features deep-toned swinging accented chords, with a raunchy edge and a vocal expressiveness.

doubled notes, staccato chords and fast descending legato lines. The instrumental "Mr. Sandman" (1955), which features his muted bass underpinning the plucked upper chord melody, was a hit.

As a guitarist, producer and arranger, Atkins played a major role in developing the smooth Nashville Sound. During the late 1950s, he started working in the studio, adding guitar parts to Elvis Presley and the Everley Brothers' recordings. He also made a major contribution to the growing rock 'n' roll and pop sound.

Atkins extended his range on his own recordings, bringing his distinctive tone and touch to "Get On With It" (1959), which has flamenco and classical flavours. His ability to mix country with popular styles can be heard on "Windy And Warm" (1962), which starts with jaunty descending chords and has a western-style theme melody. "Yakety Axe", with its bending and "chicken pickin'" staccato lines, is full of humour.

POLISHED CONTROL
Chet Atkins used a thumbpick and three fingers with nails to play sessions, record and perform his fingerstyle virtuoso pieces. Using Gretsch guitars, he produced a smooth sparkling tone with clarity and separation between the notes.

STUDIO PLAYER
A tremendously versatile musician, Chet Atkins worked on thousands of recording sessions as guitarist and producer. Using both electric and acoustic guitars, he covered all types of music.

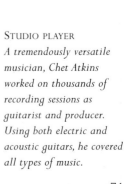

SOLOING DEVELOPMENTS

A level of sophistication in soloing in the 1950s led to a style of playing over simple chords with implied harmonies that used an approach similar to jazz. Pioneers emerged who developed the flatpicking technique to a high level of virtuosity, much influenced by jazz guitarists.

One of the first significant electric country flatpicking guitarists was Jimmy Bryant (1925–80). He was brought up in Georgia and moved to Los Angeles in 1946. Bryant had a background steeped in jazz; he was so inspired by Django Reinhardt and his soloing shows that he also assimilated the harmonic complexity of bebop. At the end of the 1940s, Bryant started working with Speedy West, a pedal steel-guitar player. They developed a close empathy, and were dubbed the "Flaming Guitars". Bryant and West often worked together as session musicians, backing singer Tennessee Ernie Ford and, between 1951 and 1956, they put down their own instrumental recordings with a backing group that included Billy Strange on rhythm guitar. Bryant and Westfunctioned as catalysts for each other and their subsequent compositions feature a daring flamboyance. The group has a country-jazz sound and the writing is full of extended lines and harmonized passages with futuristic sounds pushing colour and effect to the limit, without electronic effects, in arrangements that veer toward the experimental. "Comin' On" (1952), for example, has a bizarre mix of elements with bubbly guitar parts and calling motifs.

In 1953, Bryant recorded two uptempo fiddle tunes on guitar: "Arkansas Traveller" and "Old Joe Clark". With tremendous technique, Bryant uses inventive turns of phrase, mixing traditional fiddle material with passages of jazz improvising.

The whacky uptempo "Stratosphere Boogie" (1954) features Bryant playing a doubleneck guitar: one neck is set up as a 12-string with tunings in thirds to enable him to play harmonized ensemble lines; the other is a normal neck, allowing him to construct contrasting and jazzy solos. Another number, "Shuffleboard Rag" (1955), has a rhythm section backing with a semblance of prosaic normality, which acts as a platform to offset Bryant's intricate cameo passages that burst with imaginative ideas, mimicking vocal effects and classical motifs.

Bryant's inventiveness can also be heard in his tasteful grooving jazz soloing on "Cotton Pickin'" (1954), which ends in upper register flourishes.

JOE MAPHIS

Another sophisticated country guitarist, Joe Maphis (1921–86), was based in California and worked with his wife Rose Lee and as a session musician with singer Rick Nelson on some of his early records. Maphis' range of techniques includes highly developed flatpicking that enabled him to play fiddle tunes on guitar. His fast, linear picking can be heard on "Flying Fingers", his own composition.

JIMMY BRYANT
Bryant moves seamlessly through a variety of material, from boogies and polkas to fiddle tunes and jazz-influenced country swing. He laid the groundwork for modern country flatpicking.

THE FENDER TELECASTER
Jimmy Bryant was one of the earliest prominent guitarists to be associated with the world's first mass production solid-body Fender guitar. This was launched in 1950 with the name Broadcaster. By 1952, the name had been changed to Telecaster.

DOC WATSON

A leading architect of modern acoustic playing, Doc Watson emerged from a secluded rural community in the early 1960s. He integrated banjo and fiddle techniques with traditional folk, blues and country music, becoming one of the most important flatpicking virtuosos.

The blind guitarist and singer Doc Watson was born in North Carolina in 1923. He grew up listening to a diverse range of figures, from Jimmie Rodgers and Riley Puckett to Merle Travis and blues guitarists such as Blind Lemon Jefferson (*see page 47*). Watson played banjo and guitar, absorbing folk and bluegrass from the local musical landscape, and played fiddle tunes on guitar using a flatpick. He was discovered in the early 1960s and encouraged to join the folk revival. On his first record, *The Doc Watson Family* (1963), he plays country and folk material. His lively, dancing style, mixing single lines and strumming, can be heard on tracks such as "Every Day Dirt". Watson's appearances at the Newport Folk Festivals in 1963 and 1964 stunned guitarists, who were surprised to hear someone from the backwoods with such technical virtuosity. He revolutionized acoustic flatpicking and helped to set the stage for modern bluegrass guitar.

During the 1960s, Watson produced many exceptional recordings with his son Merle Watson and various important figures, such as Bill Monroe and, later on, Chet Atkins. He has set the standard for acoustic country playing since the 1960s, recording a large body of traditional work with musical depth, and has bridged disparate strands in country, developing them on the guitar without losing their authenticity.

Martin D-28
Doc Watson sometimes refers to his guitar as "the old flog box". Early on he often used a Gibson J-35, until about 1964, when he adopted a dreadnought-shaped Martin D-28, and later other makes. The Martin D-28 came out in 1931 and has been one of the most popular and widely-used instruments in country and other genres.

Early life
As with many other figures, Doc Watson's background is full of surprises. His mother sang English folk songs to him when he was a child and, ironically for someone who has become one of the godfathers of acoustic playing, in the 1950s, he played early rock 'n' roll using an electric guitar.

DOC WATSON (1964)

Doc Watson emerges fully on the album *Doc Watson* — a fascinating mixture of folk, country and bluegrass. The record had a tremendous impact at the time and the guitar playing was widely admired. Watson approaches the blues with depth and sophistication. "Sitting On Top Of The World" has a graceful rolling bass and inventive decorative arpeggiation, and manages to convey a haunting beauty with a resonant tone. Another number, "Deep River Blues", opens with a chord melody played with a relaxed command and Watson adds a measured accompaniment with occasional fast fills.

On the country instrumental "Black Mountain Rag", he turns the traditional fiddle tune into an infectious piece, showcasing his expressive flatpicking. Another instrumental, "Doc's Guitar", is inspired by Merle Travis. On this fast, intricate instrumental, Watson makes his guitar sound like a duo with interweaving parts and fingerstyle played with a bright urgency. Watson shifts into folk on the moving "Omie Wise", where he plays picked chords with a gentle undulating gracefulness before stating the tune as a short chord-melody break. In "St. James Hospital", Watson plays with great sensitivity and dynamic control; he moves through the harmonies, conveying movement with swelling dynamics and scurrying arpeggios.

MODERN COUNTRY

While pop music dominated record charts during the 1960s, country music continued to develop. Its rich heritage of songs and instrumentals produced figures who combined musical skill with popular appeal, while virtuoso instrumentalists developed new crossover ideas.

JERRY REED
Jerry Reed (b.1937) typifies many country musicians, showing a wide range of abilities, from songwriting to singing and playing. His rock 'n' roll and pop approach and sinuous melodic nylon-string soloing stand out in country. He emerged in the 1950s, and after recording tracks such as "Hully Gully Guitar"(1962), went on to have a hit with "Guitar Man"(1967) before recording duets in 1970 with Chet Atkins.

CLARENCE WHITE
In a career that reflects the fast-evolving crosscurrents of the times, Clarence White moved from acoustic bluegrass to country rock. In a few short years, he stamped his personality on both acoustic and electric guitar.

With the smooth high-quality production of the "Nashville Sound", the ground-breaking innovative guitar styles coming out of Los Angeles, and a diverse range of influences from jazz to rock 'n' roll and bluegrass, country music moved into the modern period. A key event was the development of a "Bakersfield Sound" in California which is primarily associated with Buck Owens and Merle Haggard.

Singer and guitarist Buck Owens (b.1929), with his group the Buckaroos, which included guitarist Don Rich (1941–74), helped to forge the Bakersfield Sound. Their first big hit was "Act Naturally" (1963), on which the guitar has a thick-textured metallic cable twang sound with string bending. One of the group's most interesting tracks is "Memphis" (1965), Owen's version of a Chuck Berry song (*see pages 176–78*). This opens with bluesy chordal figures and has a well-executed raunchy sound, which anticipates country rock.

The talented Roy Nichols worked with singer and guitarist Merle Haggard from the mid 1960s. His licks and riffs have been widely admired on many of Haggard's songs. James Burton also did sessions with Haggard, adding touches such as the "chicken pickin'" technique (*see opposite*).

THE BUCKAROOS
Building a sound around Fender guitars and amplifiers, the Buckaroos established a bright, glassy texture with a full treble that can be heard on numbers such as "Buckaroo" (1965), where the guitar plays jangling arpeggios.

B. BENDER
At the end of the 1960s, Clarence White helped to develop the Parsons White B. Bender with Gene Parsons. It revolutionized the possibilities for mimicking pedal-steel effects. Activated by the strap button, it raises the pitch of the B string by a tone to a C♯. Later, more sophisticated, devices raise two strings, and also raise notes by a third.

CLARENCE WHITE

One of the most exceptional prodigies to emerge in the 1960s was Clarence White (1944–73). He started in bluegrass with The Kentucky Colonels, recording with them from 1963 and producing one of the greatest instrumental bluegrass albums, *Appalachian Swing* (1964). White's virtuoso acoustic bluegrass picking and harmonic interplay with the other instruments are highlighted on an album that has a seamless flowing quality. His intermingling of swinging lines and fills with slides and chordal elements is heard on "Nine Pound Hammer". "Listen To The Mocking Bird" and "Billy In The Lowground" feature his characterful melodic phrasing and individual approach to stretching time into a relaxed and personal style of syncopation. White has an ability to transcend the mechanical-sounding edge in guitar picking, and this can be heard on the deceptively loping yet subtle solo on "I Am A Pilgrim", the elastic phrasing on "Sally Goodin" and on "John Henry", where his guitar sound forms a pleasing contrast to the mandolin. Among other skills are White's arpeggiated crosspicking variations across three adjacent strings to achieve a banjo-roll effect.

White adopted a different approach when he started using a Fender Telecaster electric guitar with a B. Bender device. His distinctive steel-guitar style additions made a new contribution to his vocabulary, and can be heard on many of his recordings.

White worked with The Byrds from 1968, and played on a number of their albums, including *Dr. Byrds and Mr. Hyde* (1969) and *Untitled* (1970), which feature his sharply executed yet subtle melodic country fills using slides and multinote bends. He also played on sessions for the Everly Brothers and Joe Cocker. Highlights toward the end of his career are with Muleskinner and recordings by the reformed Kentucky Colonels. White's progressive style, his rhythmic originality and his subtle lines form a link between an older style approach to bluegrass and a supple improvisational medium. He has been enormously influential.

GRAM PARSONS

An exceptional songwriter and an innovator who helped to define the beginnings of country rock with his first album *Safe At Home* (1967), Gram Parsons (1946–73) formed the International Submarine Band. He worked for a short period with

The Byrds in 1967–68, when he released some of his finest work. As a guitarist, Parsons uses the instrument to play chords and adds further guitarists, including James Burton, to his recordings. Burton contributes a variety of attractive touches to *GP* (1973) and works closely with Al Perkins' pedal steel. "We'll Sweep Out The Aisles In The Morning" has a beautifully executed melodic slide break on Dobro, and on "Kiss The Children", a short section with double stopping and bending is played with smooth technical mastery. The rocky "Big Mouth Blues" has driving upper register solos with a brittle tone and echo. The number "Grievous Angel" (1974) features acoustic and electric guitar parts from Parsons and Burton with added work from Bernie Leadon.

SONGWRITER
A lyrical songwriter, Parsons' music bridges country and rock with warm harmonies and country-style fills.

JAMES BURTON

Country-guitar parts are often made up of well-crafted elements using licks and melodic phrasing. In a long and illustrious career, James Burton (b.1939) has been one of the best session and backing guitarists, laying down a vast number of superb guitar tracks.

JAMES BURTON
With his paisley Telecaster, James Burton emerged as a recognizable figure late in his career after backing Elvis Presley and Emmylou Harris. Using thumb and fingerpicks, he achieves an incisive right-hand control and is able to emulate steel-guitar sounds with multiple string bends using light gauge strings.

Burton has a technical versatility that enables him to use devices such as "chicken pickin'", in which the guitar plays triplets with the first two

NEW GRASS

Bluegrass became an umbrella term for an evolving area of acoustic country music that could range from the traditional to open-minded music that is close to jazz and classical music with harmonic shifts and conceptual approaches to form. Groups such as The Kentucky Colonels in the 1960s set a high standard and pointed the way for a new sophistication in bluegrass. During the 1970s, a number of talented guitarists worked in the bluegrass area, one of the most skilled being Norman Blake (b.1938), who produced albums ranging from the down home *Back Home in Sulphur Springs* (1972) to the outstanding *Whiskey Before Breakfast* (1976). One of the most remarkable new guitarists to emerge is Tony Rice (b.1951), a modern-thinking flatpicker who merged country with jazz and progressive folk elements. Rice started working with traditional bluegrass groups before launching a solo career in the mid 1970s. With a full reedy tone and supple rhythmic

flexibility, Rice helped to forge a new style of single-note playing; on *Tony Rice* (1977), mandolinist David Grisman's instrumental "Rattlesnake" is a quantum leap in terms of arrangement compared with traditional country notions, with time changes and impressionistic harmonies. Rice plays melodic excursions that weave in and out of the arrangement in a style that defies generic boundaries. "Plastic Banana" opens with the guitar playing an extended folk-inspired line that develops in alternating sections with the other instruments. On the uptempo bluegrass number "Farewell Blues", Rice holds his own with a stream of inventive lines and solos. The development of this area has been an important addition to country, reflecting an artistic side of acoustic country music with depth and vision. One of Rice's techniques is to pick notes and lines and mix them with open-string notes that ring at upper and lower registers. This gives lines extra floating notes and a sense of rolling continuity. In 1980, he formed the Tony Rice Unit.

TONY RICE
An innovator who developed a smooth style of picking and use of controlled harmonies, Tony Rice has been at the forefront of progressive song arrangements, as can be heard on Cold On The Shoulder *(1984).*

WILLIE NELSON
Singer/songwriter Willie Nelson's important albums include Shotgun Willie Phases and Stages *(1974) and* Red Headed Stranger *(1975). Nelson, who has a leaning toward jazzy melodic inventiveness, produces recognizably individual earthy sounds on his nylon-string guitar. With Waylon Jennings, he was part of the "outlaw" country movement.*

notes muted to mimic clucking. He is one of the greatest country session players, yet despite producing albums such as *Corn Pickin' & Slide Slidin'* (1969) and *Guitar Sounds of James Burton* (1971), Burton remained largely unrecognized as a leading guitarist until he started to work with high-profile artists in live concerts. In the late 1960s, he joined Elvis Presley, working with him until Presley's death in 1977. He added classy country-style breaks on records such as *In Person at the International Hotel Las Vegas* (1970). After Gram Parson's death, members of his group continued to work with Emmylou Harris. Burton too had a key role in Harris's Hot Band, and played on a number of her albums. His concise solos can be heard on "Queen of the Silver Dollar" on the album *Pieces of Sky*, recorded in 1976.

ALBERT LEE

Coming from a tradition of playing in a voluble style with a dense complexity, Albert Lee (b.1943) fits into a way of approaching country that stems back to figures such as Jimmy Bryant. One of his obvious characteristics is that he improvises as well as working within set licks and motifs. Lee started working in the US, joining Emmylou Harris' Hot Band in 1976, and taking over the role filled by James Burton. His playing at this time is featured on "Luxury Liner" (1977) and "Quarter Moon In A Ten Cent Town" (1978).

Lee produced a debut solo album *Hiding* (1979), on which he plays "Country Boy". First written with "Head Hands And Feet" in the early 1970s, "Country Boy" has also become a *tour de force* signature track, showcasing Lee's technical dexterity. Using a sharp snappy tone he plays countermelodies, fast skittering melodic motifs, and contrasting sections with double stopping using muting and echo.

Lee worked as a top sideman with Eric Clapton, the Everly Brothers and many others, but he also produced an instrumental album, *Speechless* (1987), which demonstrates his ability to run complex long lines made up of attractive variations on stock country licks, tricky turns and his own improvised ideas. His own composition, "T-Bird to Vegas" shows him using a stinging tone and snappy percussiveness on the head, with its hammer slides and ringing notes followed by a tightly articulated propulsive solo break. Another side of his playing can be heard in the tremulous melody for "Seventeenth Summer", which features a graceful solo with bluesy bending over arpeggiated acoustic guitar, and on "Romany Rye", with its wistful melody with tasteful simple phrases using a dry, bright sound. On traditional material, he brings his metallic twangy string sound to the fiddle tune "Arkansas Traveller" and the folky "Salt Creek".

COUNTRY TODAY

In the 1980s, country veered toward pop influences with glossy overproduction and the use of synths. During this time, a number of guitarists who were beginning to establish themselves gained a strong grounding in the more artistic side of country, drawing on the best traditional music and bluegrass. Country music has always had a high standard of instrumental skill, and in the 1980s figures such as guitarist and mandolinist Ricky Skaggs (b.1954) helped the mainstream to rediscover its rich musical heritage and steer away from the lighter side of pop. The rock-crossover instrumental group, The Hellecasters, with Jerry Donahue, John Jorgensen and Will Ray

ROCK GUITAR IN COUNTRY

In the 1990s there was a move toward modern pop and rock guitar sounds in country. The shift in style came in from the end of the 1980s with figures such as Clint Black. On "One Emotion" (1994), guitarist Dan Huff brings modern guitar styles to the music and today there is a shift in style and a tendency for country to reinvent itself as rock on albums. This is evident on albums where session guitarists such as Dan Huff and Brent Mason play in a completely different non-traditional country style. A new generation has assimilated the developments of the modern pop and rock era, using blues rock and heavy-metal type fast lines with effects.

has recorded some of the most impressive guitar music, combining traditional country style with rock. On the album, *The Return of the Hellecasters* (1993), they play a fusion of country with rock jazz, combined with other influences that use intricate guitar parts. The album's showcase is "Orange Blossom Special" with its cutting stacatto, rock effects and steel-guitar type lines.

VINCE GILL
A major figure in country today, the gifted guitarist Vince Gill (b.1957) began as a session musician and broke through to became a singing star with "When I Call Your Name" (1993) and "Don't Let Our Love Start Slippin' Away" (1994), on which he plays heartfelt solos.

ALBERT LEE
One of the only major figures born outside North America to have had an impact on country is English guitarist Albert Lee. He spent his early career in the UK and, although highly rated among guitarists, was largely unrecognized until he established himself on the US scene in the 1970s.

STEVE WARINER
Although seen today as a vocalist, Steve Wariner (b.1954) was one of the new generation of country guitarists who emerged in the 1980s with his debut album No More Mr. Nice Guy *(1982).*

FOLK

FOLK MUSIC HAS MANY DIFFERENT STRANDS, WITH ORIGINS GOING BACK TO UNACCOMPANIED SINGING AND INSTRUMENTAL DANCE STYLES BASED ON THE VIOLIN, BAGPIPE AND OTHER INSTRUMENTS. MANY FOLK GUITARISTS ARE ESSENTIALLY SINGERS AND SONGWRITERS, BUT THEY HAVE ASSIMILATED A WIDE RANGE OF INSTRUMENTAL STYLES AND TECHNIQUES. TODAY, THE GUITAR IS A VEHICLE FOR MANY TYPES OF FOLK MUSIC.

RICHARD THOMPSON *embodies the folk developments of the past 40 years. A talented instrumentalist, he works in many key areas of folk music in Britain and North America.*

FOLK MUSIC IN NORTH AMERICA

In North America, folk music is bound up with blues and country music. Early figures have a guitar accompaniment style that is hard to distinguish from some country and blues, but folk stands apart through its adoption of traditional folk material, politics and changing fashions.

WOODY GUTHRIE
An outsider and political radical, Woody Guthrie was the most important early figure in urban American folk. He used the guitar to play simple accompaniment to his songs, which were often social commentaries.

ELIZABETH COTTEN
When she was a child, Elizabeth Cotten wrote "Freight Train", one of the most famous American songs. She finally released her first album in 1958, at the age of 63.

The overlap between folk and country music is highlighted by figures such as the Carter Family (*see page 65*) who, from 1927, recorded guitar-accompanied folk songs, creating a dual role for themselves as part of folk heritage and the country-music world.

One of the first pre-eminent folk singers who played guitar was Woody Guthrie (1912–67). Born in Oklahoma, he moved to Texas, where an uncle taught him to play. Guthrie's guitar style comes from early country music and supported his songwriting, in which the melody is sometimes based on traditional songs, while the lyrics deal with the Depression and the plight of the poor and socially disadvantaged. Guthrie started recording in the

1940s, basing himself in New York and playing residencies at clubs, including the Village Vanguard. A Greenwich Village scene grew up around figures such as Leadbelly (*see page 58*), who had moved to New York in 1935, and among Guthrie's hits, "Tzena" had as its B-side "Goodnight Irene", written by Leadbelly. One of Guthrie's most powerful songs was "This Land Is Your Land" in which the guitar part is made up of basic strummed chords with separate bass notes played in a plain homely style. Guthrie's songs helped to mould the folk group The Weavers, formed in 1948, and following Guthrie, a number of guitar-playing folksingers emerged, including Burl Ives and the extraordinary Elizabeth Cotten.

ELIZABETH COTTEN

An important early guitarist with a sophisticated and versatile fingerpicking style, Elizabeth Cotten (1895–1987) was born and raised in North Carolina. Influenced by local banjo styles, she only played guitar in church for many years, until encouraged to perform and record by Mike Seeger. He made recordings of her at home in Washington that were released, in 1958, as *Folksongs And Instrumentals With Guitar*, a moving testament to America's heritage of music-making. The instrumental "Wilson Rag" features Cotten playing her own distinctively toned, syncopated country-ragtime style. Her composition "Freight Train" embodies the spirit of an earlier period, with a chugging bass, rolling arpeggios and a clear expressive melody. Other numbers include the brass band-inspired "Graduation March", church hymns such as

INSTRUMENTAL DEVELOPMENTS

John Fahey, born in Maryland in 1939, was the first folk guitarist to stand out as a solo instrumentalist. For his time he is considered to be startlingly original. His primary source appears to be the blues, but his crossover experimentalism has a feral intensity that cuts across prevalent trends. After his first album, *Blind Joe Death Vol. 1* (1959), he recorded, edited and re-recorded his early material, resulting in, among other pieces, the ten-minute "Transcendental Waterfall" (1964), notable for its use of atonal chords. One of his greatest albums, *Transfiguration Of Blind Joe Death* (1965), demonstrates his improved technique. The slide-based "I Am The Resurrection" and "The Death Of Clayton Peacock", with its microtonal variations, draw in the listener, while mesmerizing landscapes of sound move along with a flow of imaginative ideas on tracks such as "Orinda-Moraga" and "On The Sunny Side Of The Ocean". Other musicians who emerged with a strong instrumental style include Dave Van Ronk and Sandy Bull, with his eclectic mixture of material on "Fantasias For Guitar And Banjo" (1963). Doc Watson, too (*see page 73*), recorded a large repertoire of folk material.

"Sweet Bye And Bye", "When I Get Home" and the fiddle tune "Run…Run", played on lower strings against a background of open strings. On "Vastopol" Cotten uses an open tuning and plays the melody with bluesy bends and passages of arpeggiation supported by a steady bass. The unusual bluesy folk song "Spanish Flang Dang", also on this album, is an old open-tuning parlour piece that harks back to a lost era.

BLIND JOE DEATH VOL. I

John Fahey produced his first album, *Blind Joe Death Vol. 1*, himself, pressing 100 copies. The playing on the album is rough and shambolic, but, with his compelling sound, Fahey brings an emotional intensity to the instrumentals. His version of W.C. Handy's "St. Louis Blues" is quirky and characterful with textural colours, its choppy stacatto bass and chords and notes with bends and slides conveying his individuality. "Uncloudy Day" has percussive harmonics and murky bass notes, moving into a bluesy modal 3/4 rhythm. Among the most interesting tracks is Fahey's arrangement of the traditional "John Henry", which has an insistent repeating bass figure and, with its dissonant elements, verges on the avante-garde. He takes this approach further in "Sun Gonna Shine In My Back Door Someday Blues", an atmospheric piece with clashing notes.

JOAN BAEZ
On her first album, Joan Baez *(1960), the singer uses the guitar to create a variety of backgrounds. "Silver Dagger" has bright up-tempo guitar with sliding bass notes and hurrying chords, while "East Virginia" features gentle arpeggios. A throaty drang characterizes her sombre low-register accompaniment to "House Of The Rising Sun".*

JOHN FAHEY
An artistic visionary who drew emotional soundscapes using unconventional forms and harmony, John Fahey gave his guitar a primitive power. He used a blues-based folk fingerstyle technique to put together an idiosyncratic mix of unlikely elements, some of which anticipated New Age sounds.

MARTIN 0-45
Baez used a variety of Martin guitars. This 1929 model has ornate decoration, with abalone edge binding and soundhole ring, snowflake and other designs on the fingerboard and a torch inlay on the headstock.

BOB DYLAN

One of the great figures of 20th-century popular music, Bob Dylan (b.1941) used the guitar to support his songs and their inspired lyrics. Although he was influenced by Woody Guthrie, his first album, Bob Dylan (1962), shows tremendous originality and features guitar playing that is full of energy and drive. Dylan went on to write classic songs such as "Blowin' In The Wind" (1963) and had a tremendous influence on the course of folk and pop music. In a defining moment that anticipated changes in folk music, he made a controversial appearance at the Newport Folk Festival in 1965 backed by an electric band. This alienated folk purists who saw it as a betrayal of tradition.

FOLK MUSIC IN THE UK

In Britain, it was during the 1950s that the guitar began to appear in folk music, inspired by blues and the American folk movement. Guitarists emerged who developed both traditional material, based on a rich folk heritage, and a diverse range of styles from jazz to ethnic music.

Britain was a crossroads of cultural diversity with its own peculiar mix of American influences and indigenous music. One of the early folk groups, led by Ian Campbell, started out playing skiffle in the 1950s and eventually incorporated ceilidh dance music, with the guitar playing simple chords and rhythms.

DAVY GRAHAM

Davy Graham (b.1940) was the first strong instrumentalist. An adventurous pioneer, with a powerful fingerstyle technique, he called on a blues-based foundation to explore jazz and non-European music. In the early 1960s, Graham wrote "Angi" (1962) which, with its classical-sounding theme, descending bass line and jazzy flavour, became one of the most popular folk instrumental pieces.

On his first album, *The Guitar Player...Plus* (1963), Graham's music is a mixture of melodic blues guitar and compositional jazz approaches. Graham played an important role in the developing British folk movement, his discovery of DADGAD tuning, and arrangement of "She Moves Through The Fair" being widely influential. His album *Folk Roots, New Routes* (1964), with singer Shirley Collins (b.1935), was one signpost for British folk. During a personal voyage of discovery, his guitar became a conduit for all types of music. On the instrumental "Maajun" (1964), for instance, he adapted Arabic music to his style of playing, becoming a figurehead for those who see folk as a catchall that draws on music worldwide. His open-minded eclecticism epitomizes the split with revivalists that can occur in the folk scene.

MARTIN CARTHY

A very different line of development came from the work of Martin Carthy (b.1941), a major English folk revivalist who sang traditional songs with guitar. He drew on collections amassed by folk archivist Cecil Sharp and many others, and absorbed material from all over the country.

MARTIN CARTHY
A champion of the English folk song who reinvested traditional material with fresh impetus, Martin Carthy developed an unobtrusive style of accompaniment, using the guitar to support his voice and parts played by other instruments.

DAVY GRAHAM
Graham plays the guitar with strength and conviction, projecting clear melodies and improvisation, accompanied by chords with a good rhythmic feel.

Carthy plays accompaniment to the song line, using earthy harmonies and tunings with low drone notes that run along under the music. Early in his career, he found his own way of working with traditional melodies, using a DADEAE open tuning.

On his first album, *Martin Carthy* (1965), his attractive, understated accompaniment lets the melody and words stand out on songs such as "The Wind That Shakes The Barley". One of the most memorable guitar parts in folk, "Scarborough Fair" has captivating original guitar voicings that help to carry the vocal line and create a haunting timelessness. On "Sovay", with Dave Swarbrick on violin, Carthy plays interesting bass movements and rhythms, which act as a counterpart to the vocal. With this and *Second Album* (1966), Carthy started to establish an authentic-sounding English folk-guitar style.

BERT JANSCH

An artistic individual with a highly personal style, Bert Jansch (b.1943) has an intuitive musicality that led him to develop his own technique and approach to the guitar. On his exceptional debut album, *Bert Jansch* (1965), his guitar playing is characterized by a unique sound, depth and feeling of mystery, and the guitar parts that he created through writing and singing his own material have a marked originality. With its rolling drone note and expressive arpeggios, "Oh How Your Love Is Strong" produces a gentle intimacy, and "I Have No Time" has a magical, haunting depth. Jansch's guitar is expressive in its muted understatement on the powerfully moving "Needle Of Death", with its dark subdued tone.

Jansch's remarkable guitar technique and physicality can be heard on the short instrumental "Finches", which unfurls organically with cross rhythms and a feeling of movement and release. The instrumental "Veronica", with its hypnotic rocking bass figure, includes falling, scattering upper parts. Whether using standard or open tunings, Jansch often achieves a harmonic and rhythmic idiosyncrasy that is indefinable; his touch and essence are also retained when playing his exquisite arrangement of Jimmy Giuffre's impressionistic jazz composition "Smokey River".

The album *Jack Orion* (1966) includes "Black Waterside", one of Jansch's most famous pieces, with its mesmeric descending figure and snapped percussive touches. Using a low drone note, its changing accents defy bar-line structure.

JOHN RENBOURN

A classical guitar student, John Renbourn (b.1944) established a close rapport with Jansch, working with him on a number of recordings, including "Lucky Thirteen" (1966), a duet that established their own style of instrumental interplay. Renbourn's playing moved in various directions, including a meditative early-music flavour which can be heard on "Lady Nothynge's Toye Puff" (1966) from his second solo album *Another Monday* (1966). He had developed this area further by the time he recorded *Sir John Alot Of Merrie England's Musick Thynge And Ye Grene Knight* (1968). William Byrd's "The Earl Of Salisbury", and his own composition "Lady Goes To

PENTANGLE
Pentangle, with Bert Jansch, John Renbourn, Jacqui McShee, Terry Cox and Danny Thompson, produced folk with a strong leaning toward jazz. One of their best-known pieces, "Light Flight" (1969), has a distinctive acoustic intro and guitar rhythms with time changes and attractive fills.

FAIRPORT CONVENTION
With a shifting line-up composed of individualists, Fairport Convention forged a folk-rock sound.

Church" demonstrate Renbourn's ability to play in an evocative early-music style on steel-string guitar with a remarkable variety of tone and a supple technical liquidity.

In 1967, Pentangle formed, with Renbourn and Bert Jansch, putting out their first album *The Pentangle* in 1968. Tracks such as "Bells And Waltz" demonstrate Renbourn and Jansch continuing their instrumental style, backed by the rhythm section.

FOLK-ROCK

Developments in mainstream rock and pop arrived on the British folk scene in the mid to late 1960s, through the music of Fairport Convention. Formed in 1967 with guitarists Richard Thompson (b.1949) and Simon Nicol (b.1950), Fairport Convention started out playing American folk-influenced pop, blues and rock 'n' roll. The group also explored traditional folk music and rearranged it, extending form, harmony and rhythm. These elements gradually synthesized, and Fairport developed their own type of folk-rock. With Thompson playing lead and Nicol rhythm, both guitarists used mainly electric instruments, which was then unusual in the British folk scene. Their first albums feature guitar styles that have an American West Coast sound. *Unhalfbricking* (1969) reveals country influences and original touches on "Who Knows Where The Time Goes" and "Genesis Hall". Importantly, some tracks such as the extended "A Sailor's Life" show Fairport incorporating traditional British material.

LIEGE & LIEF

For the album *Liege And Lief* (1969), Fairport Convention used arrangements that stamped their own identity on traditional material to create a British folk-rock sound. The guitar often has a rocky edge and plays around with rythmic patterns in an original way. Guitar solos and fills are often based on expanding folk phrases and melodic themes; this can be heard on "Matty Groves", which features an instrumental section with unison riffs and a driving rhythm, and on "Tam Lin", characterized by a signature sustaining riff and distorted rhythm chords on emphasized accents.

"Medley", with four traditional jigs and reels, sees guitar doubling the lines with Dave Swarbrick's violin. A brooding atmosphere is created on "Renardine": here, a wash of electric and acoustic guitars using space and reverb provides imaginative support for Sandy Denny's vocals. "The Deserter" offers a contrast between relaxed acoustic and menacing electric backing, and "Crazy Man Michael" includes attractive chords and a short solo with effects.

NORTH AMERICAN SONGWRITERS

With the 1960s pop-music explosion, folk-inspired songwriters emerged in North America who crossed over into the commercial mainstream. They accompanied themselves on steel-string guitar and developed innovative arrangements, using many different guitar styles.

Paul Simon (b.1941) and Art Garfunkel (b.1941) started playing together in the 1950s, as Tom And Jerry, and formed their Simon And Garfunkel duo in 1964. Using classical approaches and folk fingerpicking styles, they produced bright acoustic backings, their two guitars working closely together with strumming, arpeggiation and melodic lines, an approach that can be heard on "Wednesday Morning 3am" (1964). Their number "Kathy's Song" (1965) includes intricate fingerstyle, and "The Sound Of Silence" (1965) opens with simple acoustic ideas layered with harder-edged jangly electric chords and bluesy bending over a rhythm section pushing the tempo. The number "Homeword Bound" (1965), with its passages of intimate acoustic strumming alternating with driving sections, shows the duo using acoustic guitars with a rhythm section very effectively.

JONI MITCHELL

Canadian songwriter Joni Mitchell (b.1943) has produced material with floating open-ended acoustic guitar. Interesting backings function without following the conventions of directional harmonic sequences and resolutions. Her album *Blue* (1971) includes the funky "All I Want" and "A Case Of You", both with interweaving upper and lower parts. Mitchell employs many original open tunings, often with very low notes, to create impressionistic jazz and classical voicings and harmonies, using parallel block movements and wide-interval voicings against open pedal-tone strings. On the album *Hejira* (1976), she plays electric guitar with effects and explores rhythms with a jazz-fusion line-up. The title track has atmospheric low tuning figures draped across the background. She strums with a loose texture on "Black Crow", "Amelia" features flowing electric guitar parts, and there are arpeggiated electric chords on the jazz-based "Blues Motel Room."

SIMON AND GARFUNKEL
Paul Simon and Art Garfunkel's duo, Simon And Garfunkel, was one of the most successful partnerships to cross over from folk into pop. After visiting England, Simon adapted Martin Carthy's version of "Scarborough Fair" (1965), with its beautiful arpeggiated voicings, to create "Scarborough Fair-Canticle" (1966).

JONI MITCHELL
Continually evolving, Joni Mitchell has developed new ideas and original voicings to create fresh harmonies. The influence of dulcimer playing gives her music a percussive quality.

JAMES TAYLOR
Influenced by blues, pop and country, James Taylor (b.1948) has written songs with attractive guitar harmonies, such as "Oh Susannah" (1970).

DEVELOPMENTS IN FOLK

As times changed, socially and musically, from the 1960s to the 1970s, folk music continued to develop. New musicians emerged, while established players refined their ideas and explored new areas. In Britain, there was a great interest in playing the traditional repertoire.

One of the innovators of the guitar, Leo Kottke (b.1945), developed a highly personal blend of folk with ragtime and blues, creating dense sheets of sound. His ground-breaking album, *Leo Kottke & His 6 & 12 String Guitar* (1969), has a rumbustious energy which can be heard on "The Driving Of The Year Nail", in which his 12-string guitar displays rattling strings and low-tuned notes. His bouncing fingerstyle has bluesy runs, slides and harmonics and a fast tempo and attack, while retaining a loose feeling. The melody on "Ojo" turns round rhythmically and has a country flavour, using reflective arpeggios, low-tuned strings and pairs of resonating notes at the same pitch. Using a 6-string guitar, the number "Vaseline Machine Gun" starts with an atmospheric slide quoting "The Last Post" with whirring notes, before breaking into surging arpeggios. Figures pushing and sliding against pivotal notes are followed by slide with a metallic wire sound. On the following album, *Mudlark* (1971), Kottke is supported by a rhythm section that sounds almost superfluous alongside his full sound. His arrangements are full of character; they include "Cripple Creek", in which his tangled arpeggios and rhythmic sounds combine folk, country and ambient music, and his arrangement of Bach's *Bourée*, which he plays on steel-string guitar with a hard-edged rigidity. Kottke's electric playing is more concise on "Bean Time" (1972), which has

jazzy strumming, and he develops chordal ideas with bouncing musical rhythms, creating a high-register electric bass-like sound.

JOHN MARTYN

Scottish songwriter John Martyn (b.1948) uses hauntingly beautiful dark modal voicings with a powerful acoustic guitar tone. On his album *Bless The Weather* (1971), the title track and "Go Easy" show deep resonant harmonies, while "Back Down The River" reveals close voicings over a low pedal tone. Martyn uses a percussive attack on "Walk To The Water" and "Just Now", which has a tough sound with strumming near the bridge. On "Head And Heart" he plays linear fills, snapping the strings against the fingerboard.

LEO KOTTKE
Inspired by Stravinsky, Leo Kottke later developed his own approach to American musical styles with the 12-string guitar. He creates his unusual crossover style with intense energy, and has an insistent rhythmic momentum with rippling arpeggios. Using a thumbpick with fingerpicks, Kottke plays open tunings and low bass notes.

MARTIN D12-28
Kottke's first album features a Gibson B-45 12-string. He moved onto a Martin D12-28, before switching to handbuilt guitars with cutaways.

JOHN MARTYN
Martyn blends acoustic guitar with double bass and other instruments to create drifting soundscapes with hypnotic figures. With a muscular physicality, he plays instrumental fills and additions with a spiky minimalism and thick texture, hitting the guitar to make percussive, accented notes and sounds.

ESTABLISHED FIGURES

Richard Thompson (b.1949) has one of the most distinctive electric-guitar voices in folk, and on the album *I Want To See The Bright Lights Tonight* (1974), with his wife Linda, he continued to hone and develop his sound. He creates a strong sustain and finger vibrato, and his inventive ideas are underlined by strummed chords with a trebly, breaking sound. "When I Get To The Border" has a variety of sinuous linear fills, and "Calvary Cross" opens with his typically distinctive threading metallic lines.

Martin Carthy develops stark, imaginative, almost primitive-sounding guitar parts for a wide range of traditional material. On "The Cottage In The Wood", (1974) he beats out a rhythmic version of the melody with an indeterminate-

MARTIN 000-18
Martin Carthy puts a contact mike inside his Martin 000-18 guitar to retain a natural sound.

MARTIN CARTHY
A champion of traditional British material, Martin Carthy had, by the 1970s, evolved his open tuning to an unusual yet adaptable low-register CGCDGA. Using string-damping, right-hand rhythmic control and use of a thumbpick and fingerstyle, he continued to refine his song-accompaniment style.

sounding bass and basic harmonies that have a static quality, enabling the tune to retain its evocative power on the album *Right Of Passage (1989)*. "Eggs In Her Basket" has him playing a rough yet magical guitar part with idiosyncratic timing, melodic voicings and a low pedal tone. "The Banks Of The Nile" has a scratchy sound with reverb and out-of-kilter guitar loosely following the voice and conveying a melismatic sadness.

Carthy uses various well-chosen colours for different material – a light tone on "Bill Norrie", with its distinctive fills and melodic strummed figures, and strong morris-dance rhythms, with tough cutting stacatto, on the instrumental "Swaggering Boney".

NIC JONES
A gifted guitarist who developed a highly effective approach to traditional material, Nic Jones built his playing around rhythmic propulsion and sustain, using a trebly sound to give projection and clarity.

NIC JONES

Working within a traditional English framework, Nic Jones (b.1947) developed a guitar style that has a cutting rhythmic clarity and resonant low drones. On "Canadee-i-o", from his album *Penguin Eggs* (1980), he produces bright snappy percussiveness and a lilting feel. He builds his guitar parts around an open-string tuning on the plaintive "Humpback Whale", which has a pulsating energy with a grainy strummed texture, strings buzzing against the frets to create a sitar-like sound. Jones' trebly sound and dry and sweet tones can be heard on "Courting Is A Pleasure", in which upper parts ride over low strings.

MARTIN SIMPSON
Emerging in the 1970s, Simpson (b.1953) is featured on June Tabor's album of traditional songs A Cut Above (1980). He is one of the finest modern folk guitarists.

CELTIC FOLK MUSIC

During the 1970s, the guitar started to assume a more prominent role in traditional Scottish and Irish music, moving from a rhythm role to playing single lines. Violin and pipe music, and mainstream bands and crossover folk groups, brought in progressive ideas from pop and rock.

Historically the guitar had a minor role in Celtic music; only recently has it been adopted seriously. Scottish guitarist Dick Gaughan (b.1948), for instance, emerged in the late 1960s, playing Scottish and Irish instrumental music. His album, *Coppers & Brass* (1977), was a landmark in the development of a linear technique and style for the guitar.

ARTY McGLYNN

Irish guitarist Arty McGlynn marks a move forward in Irish music. On his album, *McGlynn's Fancy* (1980), the number "Carolan's Draught" features double-tracked chords with a single line weaving through them. He creates a feathery-light phrasing on the reels "The Floating Crowbar" and "The Star Of Munster", and his picking dances through the pieces as he hits accents incisively. The jigs "Peter's Byrne's Fancy" and "Creeping Docked" have a resonant

IRISH BANDS

The guitar has often played a peripheral role among major Irish groups. Planxty, for instance, with guitarist and singer Christy Moore (b.1945) and guitarist and bouzouki player Donal Lunny, use it for chordal harmonic layering, as can be heard on the album, *Planxty* (1973). Irish folk-rock was developed by Horslips, who formed in the early 1970s. Guitarist John Fean joined in 1977 and plays on the album *The Man Who Built America* (1979), which features rock and blues as well as traditional material. One of the most influential groups, Moving Hearts, emerged in 1981 with Christy Moore and Donal Lunny. They fused uilleann pipes with jazz-rock, contributing to the foundation of modern folk fusion. With Declan Sinnott joining on guitar, their high-powered sound is featured on the album *The Storm* (1985).

depth with finely-played ornaments. "The Blackbird", a slow air, starts with the unaccompanied single-line melody played with a sweet tone. McGlynn then adds sedate and tasteful chordal accompaniment. Vibrating the pick, he plays "Jenny's Welcome To Charlie" and "The Connacht Heifers", hitting a pivotal drone note before he is supported by a low drone from a keyboard.

ARRANGING MUSIC

In recent years musicians have shown a tremendous interest in playing "Celtic" music, with jigs, reels, hornpipes and other forms being widely performed. These forms are not meant to be harmonized; instead guitarists use drones and open tunings such as DADGAD and CGDGAD. The lower string is damped to play rhythms, mimicking the bodhran drum. A number of guitar players have been developing material and differing styles, including Dave Evans, who uses attractive open tunings. One of the finest albums in this "Celtic" genre, *The Swans At Coole* (1989), has Steve Tilston bringing a classical flavour to Celtic music.

DICK GAUGHAN
Recording a stream of albums through the 1970s, Dick Gaughan evolved as a guitarist and helped to establish the instrument in the Scottish and Irish repertoire. He has a thick-textured acoustic tone and muscular approach, drawing from pipe styles with doubled-up and repeating notes.

ARTY McGLYNN
With his bright clear sound and excellent pick technique, Arty McGlynn plays single-line melodies and phrases with a light rhythmic flexibility and control. He uses translucent chords without resorting to thumping bass strings.

CROSSOVER & FUSION

The 1980s saw the continued fusion of folk music with rock and pop. Simultaneously, a new group of guitarists emerged in Europe and America, playing with distinctive styles that draw on a wide range of music, creating crossover music and outstanding instrumental pieces.

PIERRE BENSUSAN
With unfolding melodic and semi-improvised variations, Pierre Bensusan's fingerstyle playing unfolds organically with uplifting modulations and flexible rhythms. His innovative thinking retains echoes of old musical traditions.

Individualists have emerged outside mainstream folk styles, playing music that is almost impossible to categorize in terms of genre, and which ranges from crossover styles to ambient music.

PIERRE BENSUSAN

The French singer, guitarist and composer Pierre Bensusan (b.1957) produces music with a rich depth and warmth, and his approach has been a major influence on New Age and ambient guitar playing. Bensusan's mastery of the open DADGAD tuning is tremendous, and he creates an expansive harmonic beauty, incorporating Gallic, Celtic, Arabic and Latin-jazz ideas. He plucks with controlled attack, producing chiming chords that are combined with flowing arpeggios. His playing is full of decorative ornaments, and he uses slides, muting, tapping and string snapping. Natural and artificial harmonics are employed for melody and chords, and he bends the guitar body and neck slightly to create ethereal pitch movements.

MICHAEL HEDGES

The American guitarist Michael Hedges (1956–97) uses the acoustic guitar to build multi-layered music with progressive folk and jazz influences. He uses multi-tracking to produce drifting soundscapes in which melodic and harmonic ideas mutate in a fashion that has affinities with the work of minimalist classical composers. "Aerial Boundaries" (1984), for instance, features guitar with an orchestral sound suspended in reverb, delay and echo.

BENSUSAN RECORDINGS

On the album *Solilai* (1981), "Nice Feeling" is bright and optimistic, with early-music harmonies. These can also be heard on "Au Jardin D'Amour", with its romantic courtly beauty, and on "Soliai", which breaks into an Irish jig. The captivating "Suite Flamande Aux Pommes" draws on Celtic music, and Bensusan sings with the guitar lines and over the chords with a series of melodies. Strong rhythms propel the number, which sees Didier Malherbe playing soprano saxophone, and it fades with atmospheric harmonics. The numbers "Bamboule" and "Santa Monica" feature Latin rhythms and jazzy scat-singing, with long improvised melodic lines, twirling hammered ornaments and percussive notes. "Milton" features beautiful, rocking, transparent harmonies, while "Doatea" has a Gallic soulfulness. On the album *Spices* (1987), Bensusan started to incorporate flamenco and Arabic 'ud music into his playing and developed jazz-fusion backings. "Agadiramadan" uses cyclical lines in 7/8 and 'ud-like sounds played with a driving percussiveness, and has an improvised solo. "Presquile" suggests Arabic flavours with open arpeggiated chords and lines, while Irish music is heard on "La Femme Cambree".

MICHAEL HEDGES
Creating compositions with guitar, Michael Hedges produces a huge sound, as if recorded in a cathedral. His first album, Breakfast In The Field, *came out in 1981 but his career was cut short tragically when he died in 1997.*

RICHARD THOMPSON

During a long and creative career, Richard Thompson has constantly developed as a player, embracing elements from all types of music and successfully accommodating pop and rock sounds while retaining his identity as a writer and modern folk musician. By the time he recorded the last album, *Shoot Out The Lights* (1982), with his wife Linda Thompson, he had developed a sharp rocky edginess with processed sound effects and distortion. The title track has powerful dark crunching chords and a raw angular solo with a tearing tone with echo, and a highly expressive passage. His nervous energy can be heard on "Walking On A Wire", which features fractious solo breaks and fills that have an iridescent cutting sound with twisted phrasing. Hard-edged rhythms characterize "Don't Renege On Our Love", with its insistent muted foundation and shimmering guitar chords.

Thompson is equally powerful on electric and acoustic guitar, whether backing his singing or playing solos and instrumentals. A highlight is "52 Vincent Black Lightning" (1992), a song with a fast instrumental section on steel-string acoustic with interweaving parts based on a CGDGBE open tuning.

Hedges builds sumptuous harp-like intertwining harmonies, moving from delicate touches to cavernous barrages of resonant sound. He also incorporates cascading harmonics and hits the guitar for a crashing percussive attack.

ADRIAN LEGG

An astonishing guitarist, Adrian Legg (b.1948) emerged in the early 1980s with a propulsive funky style, playing a quirky individualistic synthesis with sound processing that creates new guitar colours. He uses open tunings and his technique incorporates chordal arpeggio and linear playing with single and double-string bends. His album *Technopicker* (1983) illustrates his style. The opening number, "Pass The Valium", reveals liquid legato lines with a smooth sound and biting incisiveness. The chordal rhythm draws unusually on blues and country music. The amazing "Een Kleyne Komedye" is a futuristic folk-style technical tour de force, with country-guitar techniques and sounds.

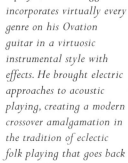

JAZZ

One of the great American art forms, jazz has evolved by integrating elements from all types of music. Many jazz guitarists have developed their style primarily by emulating the innovations of the jazz greats on brass instruments and keyboards, and by absorbing classical and world music to produce some of the most sophisticated music for guitar.

WES MONTGOMERY *One of the great jazz guitarists, Wes Montgomery solos inventively and with feeling on all types of material, bringing to it his own sound and touch.*

EARLY JAZZ

The first jazz music developed in New Orleans in the late 19th century and was derived from many different strands, including blues, ragtime and vaudeville. It was essentially an urban dance music, and the first jazz guitarists played only a peripheral role as part of a rhythm section.

Early jazz guitarists did not leave any recordings behind and much of what is known about their music has to be deduced from hearsay or later recordings. Guitarist Jeff "Brock" Mumford (1870–1937) appeared in one of the most famous New Orleans bands, that was led by cornetist Buddy Bolden in the 1890s. The band is said to have played a Dixieland style and the guitar would have supported the brass and reed instruments. During that period, the banjo eclipsed the guitar because of its percussive penetration. However, a younger generation of New Orleans banjo players emerged who later

also adopted guitar for their rhythm playing. Johnny St.Cyr (1890–1966), for instance, played with Kid Ory and, from 1904, joined Armand Piron. He started on banjo, then moved to 6-string guitar-banjo and guitar. He can be heard, with Jelly Roll Morton and Louis Armstrong, on "Jelly Roll Blues" (1926) and "Grandpa's Spells" (1926), playing guitar with a chord and bass-note rhythm style using linking low-register fills. Bud Scott (1890–1949) had a similar style and, from 1904, played with the John Robichaux band and Freddy Keppard. He remembered a time when it was a novelty to play four straight downbeats. On "Apex Blues"

BROCK MUMFORD
One of the first recognizable jazz guitarists, Brock Mumford played with the legendary Buddy Bolden's group in New Orleans, on numbers such as "Maple Leaf Rag".

LONNIE JOHNSON & EDDIE LANG

The most important early jazz-guitar duo was formed in 1928 by Lonnie Johnson and Eddie Lang. Much of their material was created around a blues framework but also had a dense sound and powerful swing. Johnson plays melodies and inventive solos with an improvisational fluency virtually unheard of at the time, while Lang provides complex and equally virtuosic accompaniments, as can be heard on numbers such as "Two Tone Stomp" (1928) and "Hot Fingers" (1929). Slow melodic blues phrases characterize the soloing on "Blue Guitars" (1929), while "Deep Minor Rhythm" (1929) reveals twirling phrases with string bending, cutting dry staccato notes and improvising based on the variation and development of phrases, with short fast passages. "A Handful Of Riffs" (1929) features uptempo soloing, with great rhythm, and Johnson's typical delicacy with developed motifs, fast hammered runs and unusual rhythmic emphasis.

LONNIE JOHNSON
Arguably the first improvising soloist in jazz guitar, Johnson recorded a great solo with Duke Ellington on "The Mooche" (1928), and an unaccompanied "Playing With The Strings" (1928) jumps with energy with its single lines and tight, driving rhythm.

EDDIE LANG
An influential figure, Eddie Lang also recorded a range of material with Joe Venuti. It included "The Wild Dog" (1928), with a quartet including sax and piano, enabling Lang to play a solo with a poised bluesy melodiousness, and "March Of The Hoodlums" (1929).

(1928) and "King Joe" (1928), he uses chords for soloing, snaps single strings to cut through, and plays bass phrases.

Eddie Lang (1902–33) developed a superb pick technique and a style that draws on jazz and classical music, creating impressionistic blues moods. He recorded duets with violinist Joe Venuti, including "Stringing The Blues" (1926) and "Black And Blue Bottom" (1926), accompanying Venuti with an alternating chord and bass movement, and subtle choking in the left hand for rhythmic impetus. He also developed inversions and passing chords, with short connecting fills for sequences.

Lang composed and arranged, recording a number of beautifully balanced guitar and piano duets. On "Eddie's Twister" (1927), his compositions have a modern harmonic sophistication, with smooth melodic lines integrating blues, ragtime and classical ideas. Fast lines and melodic bass links with strumming feature on the waltz "April Kisses" (1927), and Lang demonstrates his virtuosity by transposing and playing Rachmaninoff's "Prelude in C# minor" (1927), which he plays with a pick and a fingerstyle section.

"Melody Man's Dream" demonstrates single-line guitar with a strong tone and vibrato on notes over the piano. The guitar on "Rainbow Dreams" is powerful, matching the piano with lines and broken chords. Lang also worked with Lonnie Johnson (1889–1920), and, in 1929, with the great blues singer Bessie Smith.

KRESS & MCDONOUGH
Carl Kress and Dick McDonough's duo, with its interwoven roles, took guitar arrangements to a new level, creating highly polished set pieces with a small amount of improvisation. They drew from jazz, ragtime and classical ideas: strong classical influences can be heard on "Danzon" (1934). In comparison, "Stage Fright" (1934) has jazzy swing with finely articulated guitars, both playing chords and single lines with countermelodies and linear passages, as well as short, improvised sections.

RHYTHM PLAYING

As jazz developed in the 1930s, many big-band guitarists, such as Fred Guy (1897–1971), who worked with the Duke Ellington Orchestra, were simply rhythmic adjuncts who blended into the background. Bernard Addison (b.1905), who joined Fletcher Henderson's band in 1933, was a more sophisticated player, and on "Yeah Man" (1933) and "Queer Notions" (1933) uses interesting chords and lines. Destined to become the most famous rhythm player, Freddie Green (1911–87) joined Count Basie in 1937 and became synonymous with a solid style of jazz rhythm guitar, playing four downbeats in the bar.

PREWAR SOLOISTS

Teddy Bunn (1909–78) demonstrates an early style, with slow, deliberate lines that have melodic jazz and bluesy phrases using string bending. With singer Spencer Williams, his short, grainy staccato notes and simple jazzy phrasing can be heard on "It's Sweet Like So" (1930) and "Pattin' Dat Cat" (1930). He developed a more flowing style and, as a featured soloist with The Five Spirits of Rhythm, plays a short single-note introduction and takes a complete chorus with a swinging solo using bubbly upper-register phrasing on "I Got Rhythm" (1933). "Four Or Five Times" (1937) has a lilting solo full of character. His colourful inventive solos, with surprising twists and a twangy buzzing string sound, are evident on "If You See Me Comin'" and "Gettin' Together", both recorded in 1938, with a quintet.

Another talented figure with great rhythm and a chordal style, Al Casey (b.1914), worked with pianist Fats Waller. His swinging soloing, arpeggiation, block chords and harmonics can be heard on "Buck Jumpin'" (1941).

IN SEARCH OF VOLUME

The guitar became increasingly popular but it was drowned out in group settings, and the need to find acoustic and electric solutions led to the development of new instruments. The electric guitar revolutionized the guitar's jazz role, enabling it to interact equally with other instruments.

A musician who was to take a major role in jazz-guitar amplification, Eddie Durham (1906–87) played a resonator guitar in Bennie Moten's band from 1929, and recorded with one in Jimmie Lunceford's band on "Hittin' The Bottle" (1935). After taking up the electric guitar, he made historic recordings in New York in March 1938 with The Kansas City Five that feature loud electric solos in which his volume level easily matches Buck Clayton's trumpet. "Laughing At Life" features background electric chords played with staccato, and blues and Hawaiian-style slides. Two bright linear solo breaks have a bouncy rhythmic style with liquid runs and touches of partial chords. "Good Mornin' Blues" starts with single lines, moving into a skillful and attractive chord solo with partial voicings, and "I Know That You Know" has an infectious, nimble solo.

"Love Me Or Leave Me" opens with broken chords and the tune is played as a chord melody before Durham plays a solo using a wide register with single notes, then adds broken chords and a chord solo. Subsequently, with tenorist Lester Young added to make The Kansas City Six, Durham's more flowing solo style can be heard on "Way Down Yonder In New Orleans", which shows the influence of Django Reinhardt. "Countless Blues" opens with the type of riffs that later made the guitar pre-eminent in other genres.

OSCAR ALEMAN

One of the most brilliant and overlooked guitarists, Argentinian Oscar Aleman (1909–80) was based mainly in Paris in the 1930s and used a Style 1 National tricone. His unaccompanied pieces recorded in 1938, "Nobody's Sweetheart" and "Whispering", are exceptional. Virtuosic passages display his remarkable technique and fertile imagination.

EARLY ELECTRICS

Lloyd Loar, a visionary designer and engineer at Gibson, experimented with electric guitars in the 1920s at a time when it was felt they were not commercially viable. After Rickenbacker produced their electric lap steel in 1931, the company launched the world's first production electric guitars, the Electro Spanish models, in 1932. These had a single horseshoe magnet pick-up, no rotary controls and a flat top with upper bout f-holes. The company expanded and developed the range, producing instruments such as The Ken Roberts model in 1935, which was named after a studio guitarist. Gibson finally adapted their archtop L-50 model and launched their own ES-150 electric model in 1936.

EDDIE DURHAM
Playing electric guitar from 1937, Durham was at the forefront of a revolution that established the guitar as a major ensemble instrument for melodies, soloing and chords. This opened up possibilities in jazz for the guitar to develop stylistically.

RICKENBACKER ELECTRIC
In the 1930s, Rickenbacker produced various electric guitars, sometimes with bodies made by other manufacturers. This 1930s model has a standard acoustic archtop configuration, a single horseshoe pick-up, and rotary tone and volume controls.

DJANGO REINHARDT

The guitar genius of the 20th century, Django Reinhardt was a brilliant jazz improviser with a flamboyant style that is unparalleled. His flair and virtuosity were witnessed with disbelief, and his visionary solos, technical control and sound greatly raised the standard of guitar playing.

A manouche gypsy born near Liverchies in Belgium, Django Reinhardt (Jean-Baptiste Reinhardt, 1910–53) came from a family of performers. Constantly on the move, the family settled for a period in the "zone", a shanty town on the outskirts of Paris, where Reinhardt could wander into the city and absorb music in the bars and clubs. He started playing banjo and violin when he was 12, moving over to guitar in his teens. In 1928, an accident turned his caravan into an inferno and he was badly injured; with the ring and little finger on his left hand immobilized, he was forced to rebuild his guitar technique. After a year, and with prodigious willpower, he emerged with a

dexterity that enabled him to co-ordinate both his left-hand fingers and his right-hand pick so he could glide up and down strings, hitting notes accurately.

Reinhardt learned tunes from jazz records imported from the United States. He started working in a swing setting, with a style that incorporates elements of gypsy and classical music. In 1934, he began a fruitful partnership with violinist Stephane Grappelli (1905–97), and by the end of the year they were playing their first engagements and recording with a

EARLY DAYS
Le Quintette Du Hot Club De France toured Europe successfully during the 1930s and, through its recordings, was the first European jazz group to make a big impact in the United States. Reinhardt's ringing notes and angular lines and Grappelli's lyrical sustain complemented and offset each other superbly.

DECEMBER 1934 RECORDINGS

Early recordings reveal the sound of the Quintet. "Tiger Rag" is arranged with fast unison violin and guitar lines, and Reinhardt's solo features plaintive string-bending opening out to razor-sharp lines, with fast, attractive staccato phrases and a ringing note with a vibrated pick. On "Dinah", Reinhardt weaves around and embroiders the melody without playing it directly. His imaginative soloing contains both delicate melodic lines and surging passages with chromatic motifs, fast scalar phrases and cutting octaves. He supports Grappelli with a powerful chugging rhythm. "I Saw Stars" sees Reinhardt's graceful lines build in intensity until he reaches cascading scales and arpeggios and throws in pairs of strings in a witty tuning-procedure phrase.

line-up known as Le Quintette Du Hot Club De France, a string quintet, with a variable line-up that included his brother Joseph on rhythm guitar.

During 1935, the group developed a wide range of material, such as "St. Louis Blues", in which Reinhardt plays a lovely impressionistic intro with lines and chords and takes an enchanting solo. One of his early compositions, "Djangology", features opening arpeggios, strummed chords and a lively melody built around simple short phrases packed with decorative fills; he plays a solo full of slow-turning trills and octaves with ascending arpeggios and hits certain emphasized notes.

A highlight of that year's recordings is "Swanee River". With its propulsive rhythm playing, it surges with exuberance and includes a snappy solo full of brilliant turns. "Sunshine Of Your Smile" reveals his style of using pronounced backing bass notes with chords. In "I've Had My Moments", Reinhardt breaks into a fizzing solo with fast, strummed

DJANGO'S GUITARS

Reinhardt's main instrument was a Selmer Maccaferri which, with its flat cutaway and two octave fingerboard extension, helped him to play in the high register. These guitars contained an internal sound chamber that was developed to enhance volume and sustain. Django often used later models with a small oval soundhole and 14-fret neck that came in during 1936–37. He played acoustically, with a microphone for added volume. At the end of the 1940s, he fitted a Stimer pick-up to his Maccaferri, using a small combo amplifier to achieve an electric sound.

discordant elements, and in "Limehouse Blues", he is incredibly inventive, using catchy discords, and fast bursts of buzzing strummed chords to add lift.

By 1937 Reinhardt's playing had developed a deeper dimension and mood. The adventurous "You're Driving Me Crazy" reveals powerful rhythm playing and a solo with atonal motifs and melodic double-stopping.

His individuality can be heard on "In A Sentimental Mood", where his solo is perversely abrasive and flippant. Two early unaccompanied solo pieces provide a fascinating insight into Reinhardt's playing. "Improvisation" starts with open strings and has beautiful classical-style harmonies, whole-tone chords and elegant lines. Astoundingly fast scalar flourishes act as linking runs to romantic guitaristic harmonies with an instinctive balance and form. In contrast, "Parfum" displays a looser, more romantic flavour and sounds ad libbed.

The group also took classical pieces as vehicles for improvisation. Liszt's piano work "Liebestraum No. 3", for instance, is turned into a showcase for Reinhardt's ideas. During the 1930s, Reinhardt also recorded with Coleman Hawkins' All Star

IN THE STUDIO
Django Reinhardt and the Quintet recording in Decca Studios in London on 2 August 1939. A simple microphone set-up, skillfully placed, records the instruments so that there is an acoustic balance. Live takes were limited, etched with a needle onto a recording surface and duplicated onto 78rpm shellac discs.

SELMER MACCAFERRI
These revolutionary instruments with their D-shaped soundhole were first developed by classical guitarist and maker Mario Maccaferri in 1931. They were launched commercially as a Selmer range from 1932. Django used the steel-string Orchestra model, later known as the Jazz model.

Jam Band, adding a tasteful solo to "Honeysuckle Rose" (1937).

World War II split the group, with Grappelli staying in London. Back in Paris, in December 1940, Reinhardt recorded his composition "Nuages". This was played in a sextet including second guitar, two clarinets and a rhythm section. It opens with a dramatic clarinet part and has a lush romantic melody and a solo with artificial harmonics and sumptuous phrases. His composition "Djangology" (1942), with an orchestra of strings and brass, the latter opens with a captivating introduction of lines and chords, before moving into a theme and improvisation that blends well and sails over the background.

In 1946, Reinhardt visited the United States and toured with Duke Ellington. When he returned to France, he resumed playing with Grappelli. He began to create an electric sound with a fitted pick-up, playing a plainer style with less flowery ornamentation and a mature assurance, and relying less on octave passages in solos. Reinhardt's playing at this time evolves with lines that start to show he was assimilating some of the harmonic advances of contemporary American jazz. In 1946, tremendous solos highlight his compositions "Nuages", "Melodie Au Crepuscule" and "Belleville". "Del Salle", recorded in 1947, builds to an explosive change of gear, with astonishing fast turns from semiquavers to triplets. His harmonic invention is also outstanding on "Anniversary Song".

Recordings from 1949–53 show Reinhardt in stunning form on numbers such as "The World Is Waiting For The Sunrise", "Stormy Weather" and "It Might As Well Be Spring". His electric tone has a sharp edge on "Place De Broukere" and the virtuosic "Boogie Woogie".

CHARLIE CHRISTIAN

> The first well-known electric guitarist with a highly developed soloing style, Charlie Christian became a star in Benny Goodman's band. With his infectious riffs and sophisticated phrasing, Christian brought the guitar onto an equal basis with the other instruments in a group.

CHARLIE CHRISTIAN
The first influential electric-guitar soloist, Charlie Christian emulated the style and role of the saxophone as a solo instrument. His soloing, with its coherent linear vocabulary, influenced virtually all subsequent American jazz guitarists.

Charlie Christian (1916–42) grew up in Oklahoma City and started playing when he was 12. In the mid 1930s he copied Django Reinhardt's solos and absorbed the vocabulary of players such as tenor saxophonist Lester Young, whose distinctive phrasing and harmonic sophistication was to form a link between swing and bebop. Christian saw Eddie Durham using an electric guitar in 1937, and by 1938 he too was playing one with

the Al Trent Sextet. Christian had a remarkable aptitude for the new instrument, taking advantage of its sustain and carrying power to develop a commanding linear technique with a smooth flowing style.

He gained a tremendous reputation and in August 1939 joined bandleader and clarinettist Benny Goodman. With Goodman, Christian's swinging solos give a feeling of easy mobility. His complex turns of phrase, sitting over the chords in a swing context, have affinities with

"SOLO FLIGHT"

Recorded in New York in March 1941 with the Benny Goodman Orchestra, "Solo Flight" is a showcase for Charlie Christian. After a short intro from the band, the guitar enters, followed by the rhythm section, with Christian articulating ideas clearly over punchy staccato reed and brass

chords, figures and sustained notes. On a long solo, he uses rhythmic control and swings with an uplifting gracefulness. There are statements and answering ideas using both simple lines and arpeggios and altered chords over the modulating harmonies. As he builds the solo, he adopts a rougher attack as he responds to the brass expressively, ending with edgy unison bent notes.

BENNY GOODMAN
ORCHESTRA
*Charlie Christian featured
in various of Benny
Goodman's extended line-
ups. Here he can be seen
in 1940 playing a
natural-finish Gibson
ES-250 in the Benny
Goodman Orchestra, his
Gibson amplifier tucked
behind him.*

bebop approaches, with diminished arpeggios and chromatic links. He often plays long lines with a control that gives an even sound to the notes, and uses subtle accenting and emphasized offbeats with occasional slides and bends. His riff-based ideas, which sometimes lean toward a bluesy flavour, were often used for unison compositional heads for the band.

Christian moved to New York and began his legendary recordings with Goodman in October and November 1939. These include "Flying Home", in which his clear and incisive solo, arcing lines and rhythmic subtlety are immediately evident as he switches from simple combinations of notes to longer phrases, and "Stardust", on which he plays a varied solo with melodic chords before introducing melody-based lines and using bluesy phrases and octaves. His solo on "Rose Room" starts with graceful relaxed lines, then swings hard and digs into the beat with faster phrasing. "Seven Come Eleven" has catchy riffs and an exuberant solo with long lines and bluesy bending. "Honeysuckle Rose"'s solo is light and airy, working around pivotal notes.

In 1940, he recorded "Gone With What Wind" and "Air Mail Special". The latter, with its jiving upbeat figures, followed by a solo

with a bright clear bell-like sound and snappy lines repeating notes and motifs placed across the harmony, is reminiscent of Django Reinhardt.

Some of Christian's last recordings were made while he was jamming in the cutting-edge hothouse environment of the Harlem clubs Minton's and Monroe's Uptown House in May 1941. On these, he stretches out alongside the pioneers of bebop with wonderful invention on pieces such as "Swing To Bop". Christian died in March 1942 and his recordings became a template for many jazz guitarists in the 1940s and 1950s.

GIBSON ES-150
*Charlie Christian used a
sunburst Gibson ES-150
that was first launched
commercially in 1936. It
was based on the company's
L-50 acoustic archtop,
with the addition of a
single bar pick-up and a
tone and volume control.*

POSTWAR DEVELOPMENTS

In the 1940s, the electric guitar became established in jazz, enabling guitarists to play a more equal role. New harmonically sophisticated innovations in bebop changed soloing styles and, with the advent of impressionistic classical influences, harmonic colours expanded.

Jazz guitar evolved during the 1940s and 1950s in a vibrant creative milieu with a host of instrumentalists forging styles from bebop to classically influenced jazz. Among leading guitarists of the early 1940s were the inventive Oscar Moore (1912–81), with the Nat King Cole Trio, and the sparkling Tiny Grimes (1916–89), with the Art Tatum Trio. A revolution was under way in bebop, led by virtuoso players such as Charlie Parker, Dizzy Gillespie and Bud Powell. Guitarists were challenged by a new sophisticated linear vocabulary over an expanded harmonic framework. Various players started to work in this area including Bill De Arango (b.1921), who played with Charlie Parker in 1943 and Dizzy Gillespie in 1945, and Arvin Garrison (1922–60), who recorded with Charlie Parker in 1946 on "Yardbird Suite" and "Night In Tunisia".

In 1946, another development taking place was led by the innovative pianist Lennie Tristano, whose trio recordings with Billy Bauer (b.1915) on guitar are experimental and veer toward the avante garde. Bauer plays unusual lines and atonal elements across Tristano's advanced harmonies on tracks such as "Out On A Limb" and "Atonement". He refined his ideas and on Tristano's important album *Crosscurrents* (1949) reveals a smooth cerebral approach, playing angular lines with a dark intensity.

TAL FARLOW

One of the first players to adapt scalar and arpeggio bebop vocabulary and evolve a fluent improvising technique was Tal Farlow (1921–98). He moved to New York and worked in the city, absorbing the sounds being played in the clubs around 52nd Street. In late 1949 he joined vibes player Red Norvo, playing in a trio with Charles Mingus on double-bass. The trio often played fast tempos and Farlow rose to the challenge, recording astounding solos on "Move" (1950) and "Zing! Went The Strings Of My Heart" (1950); with their fast unison lines, they are a showcase for his uptempo facility. Farlow's solos consist of streams of long phrases, made up of complex bebop phrasing, played over a wide register with a singular style of accenting and occasional bending on a note for added expression. He also developed techniques that included playing rhythm by beating time percussively on the top of the instrument.

In 1952 he left Red Norvo and started making his own albums as leader and developing his chordal ideas. On his

MARY OSBORNE
A talented hard-swinging soloist, Mary Osborne (b.1921) took up electric guitar after hearing Charlie Christian and worked with pianist Mary Lou Williams. In the 1940s she led the Mary Osborne Trio, and played with many other musicians, including Coleman Hawkins.

FARLOW'S TECHNIQUE
Tal Farlow developed his own positional system on the fingerboard using long stretches.

great album *The Artistry Of Tal Farlow* (1955), "Little Girl Blue" has a thick-textured chord melody with lower strings detuned. Farlow plays passages with the group and solo, ending with artificial harmonics. "Autumn In New York" uses chords with a large span in the voicings and features a heartfelt melodic solo. There is a scintillating fast solo on "Cherokee" in which Farlow's playing excels, creating virtuosic bebop lines through the harmonic changes.

In his subsequent recordings, Farlow again uses very low detuned bass strings on his solo guitar chord-melody arrangement of "Autumn Leaves" (1955), which has classical influences and fast fills in the melody with thirds. Farlow was a master of various techniques: on "Isn't It Romantic" (1956), he improvises lines with skillful artificial harmonics. He went on to expand his techniques, using tapped notes on upper and lower frets to stretch chords, and developing rich harmonic chord substitutions on standards.

BARNEY KESSEL

Emerging in the 1940s, Barney Kessel (b.1923) has a style that was initially influenced by Charlie Christian. He worked with Artie Shaw in 1945, and recorded with Charlie Parker in 1947. From 1952–53 he worked with the Oscar Peterson Trio, playing a strong comping role. His solos and swinging bebop phrasing can be heard on tracks such as "Fascinating Rhythm" and "Night And Day".

On his albums where he is leader, Kessel produced arrangements using a variety of approaches with chords and harmony, textures and tone colours. His soloing shows interesting tasteful lines. *Easy Like Vol.1* (1956), a hallmark of Kessel's playing, displays his adventurous and creative chord-melody openings to songs such as "Tenderly" in which he goes on to play a solo over the rhythm section with lines, chords and strummed rhythms. "What Is There To Say" also has interesting voicings and clean melodic lines. On *Kessel Plays Standards*

THE SWINGING GUITAR OF TAL FARLOW

This 1956 album features a driving trio, with pianist Eddie Costa and bassist Vinnie Burke playing with a joyful, swinging optimism. Farlow and Costa play unison heads and swap fours *(see pages 234–35)*, working closely, rhythmically and harmonically. Farlow's playing is at its most exhilarating on uptempo numbers, including the exciting "You Stepped Out Of A Dream" in which he is rhythmically incisive and plays long flowing lines, and his composition "Meteor", which has a bubbly solo. He also plays with melodic depth in his interpretation of "They Can't Take That Away From Me", while his chord melody playing is smooth and controlled on "Like Someone In Love".

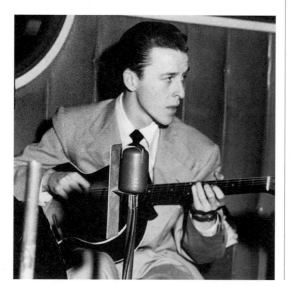

BARNEY KESSEL
A high-profile postwar figure, Barney Kessel's style is drawn from swing and his own approach to bebop. Rather than running the changes on solos with fast-flowing ideas, he uses swing lines, space and a bluesy feel.

GIBSON ES-350
Barney Kessel and Tal Farlow used the Gibson ES-350. Launched in 1946, it was Gibson's first electric archtop with a cutaway.

JIMMY RANEY
One of the few players to assimilate bebop sophistication was Jimmy Raney (1927–95). His flowing speed, smooth tone and astonishingly fluent linear ideas can be heard in a quintet with Stan Getz on Parker 51 *(1951). His long imaginative lines through the harmonies based on "Cherokee" are remarkable.*

CHUCK WAYNE
With the popular George Shearing Quintet from 1949–52, Chuck Wayne's middle-register lines merge with Shearing's piano, and he adds short bop solos.

Vol. 2 (1956), "Love Is Here To Stay" reveals a use of chords with a reflective depth and fast harmonized passages for melody. The numbers "How Long Has This Been Going On" and "I Didn't Know What Time It Was" feature Kessel supporting the oboe with rich adventurous harmonies incorporating close voicings. Barney Kessel expanded the guitar's ensemble role and developed his own concepts.

JOHNNY SMITH

An exceptionally gifted individualist with his own approach to technique, soloing and harmony, Johnny Smith (b.1922) worked with Benny Goodman in the early 1950s and established himself as a session musician at NBC in New York. His original soloing style is not primarily derived from bebop and it contains unusual motifs and angular ideas that blend smoothly into his solos. Smith has almost faultless execution and a compositional conception in his approach to jazz. He incorporates classical phrasing and plays lines with a precise control, breaking into double-speed phrases with a graceful effortlessness in solos that are played with sensitive dynamics. Smith developed a technique for playing chords which gives a legato effect: he holds down pivotal notes which keep ringing to give a flowing sustain to his beautiful close-voicing impressionist harmonies. His glistening string tone and colour on gently strummed chords is breathtaking.

In 1952 Smith recorded his arrangement of "Moonlight In Vermont" in a quintet with tenor saxophonist Stan Getz; it became an

LES PAUL

A pioneer of the solid-body electric guitar, Les Paul (b.1916) has had a long and adventurous career with recordings that range from jazz to lighter popular styles. Influenced by Django Reinhardt, Paul has a witty and expressive swing style, as can be heard on "Blues" with Nat King Cole from *Jazz At The Philharmonic*. After World War II, Paul led a fine jazzy trio and started experimenting with multi-tracking and recording material at different speeds on electromagnetic tape. His wizardry in the studio enabled him to add guitar parts in different registers using speeded-up and slowed-down tapes, which can be heard on the astonishing "Little Rock Getaway". He also used echo and sparkling sonic touches with tone. This complements his extroversion and technical style with glissandos and vibrato. "Lover", recorded in 1947 with eight electric guitar parts and multi-speed effects, was ahead of its time. Paul built his own studio and worked with

many figures as a producer, arranger and guitarist. He teamed up with singer Mary Ford and their commercial treatments of songs led to a succession of hits including "How High The Moon" (1951), built from 12 layers of sound.

IN THE STUDIO
Les Paul made use of evolving sound technology, developing multi-tracked guitar parts on tape and using effects to give added colour to songs. He also worked with tape speeds and echo.

LES PAUL MODEL
Gibson involved Les Paul and used his name for their first electric solid body, launched in 1952. The new guitar had similar appointments to the ES-295 archtop guitar. With its solid body and P-90 pick-ups, it has sustain and a clear, ringing sound.

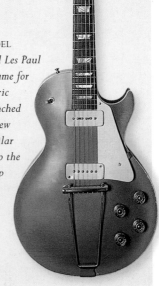

D'Angelico Excel

unexpected hit. He plays the tune as a chord melody with a harp-like sound and dreamlike close voicings that blend into each other with ringing sustain and clarity. On his solo he surges right up through the register of the instrument and plays delicate and unusual lines and chords with harmonics. Among other recordings from 1952 that use stunning chordal harmonies and solos are the romantic "Stars Fell On Alabama", "A Ghost Of A Chance" and a moving version of "Tenderly". The lush "My funny Valentine" has two-part guitar lines and chords.

Smith creates adventurous harmony lines with the sax on "Tabu", which has a fast, cleanly articulated short bebop solo, and "Where Or When?" and fast harmony lines with sax on "Jaguar".

He also takes "Vilia" from a Lehar's operetta and turns it into a swinging jazz chord melody and solo. During the following year, "Cherokee" (1953) with saxophonist Zoot Sims is arranged with frequent passages of fast unison lines and "Yesterdays" (1953) has lush harmonies and a solo with unusual ascending partial chord motifs.

Tracks from Smith's great album *Moods* (1953) are astonishing — melodically advanced and musically fresh. The stunning "What's New?" (1953) contains slow, gently strummed languorous voicings, attractive harmonized rising lines and a marvellous solo in which phrases swing right up through the full compass of the guitar to singing high notes. "I'll Remember April" has a wonderfully conceived melodic solo and on "Lover Man", Smith plays a beautiful emotional solo bursting with musicality, unusual motifs and explosive phrases that portray a deeper dimension. His near perfect conception and execution sounds almost composed. "Lullaby Of Birdland" has double-tracked guitar in a contrapuntal classical style with both chords and notes merging together. The album has one of Smith's most well-known compositions "Walk Don't Run" with its line based on graceful minor classical architecture.

HERB ELLIS

Playing straightforward bop style with strands from the blues, Herb Ellis (b.1921) worked with pianist Oscar Peterson from 1953–58. His clean lines with singing tones and

JOHNNY SMITH
In New York during the 1950s, Johnny Smith worked extensively in studios. He was an excellent sight-reader with a passion for classical music which he played with a pick, adapting classical ideas for his meticulous arrangements of popular standards.

D'ANGELICO EXCEL
This type of hand-made archtop guitar by New York maker John D'Angelico with a floating De Armond fitted pick-up has an even response, sweet tone and tremendous sustain, making it ideal for Smith's style.

HERB ELLIS
Ellis replaced Barney Kessel in the Oscar Peterson Trio, with Ray Brown on bass. His comping style, with its light airy sound and smooth uncluttered soloing, fitted in well and provided an ideal third voice between the powerful Peterson and Brown.

KENNY BURRELL
Using a style derived from swing, blues, bebop and classical guitar, Kenny Burrell emerged in the hard bop period of the 1950s playing with a clean swinging soloing style and a harder-edged tone. His albums cover a diverse range of material and his style is a link between different eras.

straightforward ideas for soloing can be heard on the group's outstanding live album *At Zardi's* (1956). The solo on "I Was Doing Alright" is one of the many fine moments on the album. Ellis' interwoven countermelodies with Peterson can be heard on "Herbie's Tune" and "Noreen's Nocturn" as guitar and piano play seamless passages of soloing and work off melodic motifs. Ellis produced his own fine albums, including *Nothing But The Blues* (1958). From 1959–63, Ellis worked with singer Ella Fitzgerald.

KENNY BURRELL

One of the figures who took the guitar toward a more modern hard bop style with considered lines and a bluesy atmosphere was Kenny Burrell (b.1931). He drew from Charlie Christian (*see pages 102–03*) and his cool, controlled improvising has a clear string tone. After working with trumpeter and band-leader Dizzy Gillespie in 1951, Burrell's early album *Blue Moods* (1957)

has lean well-paced lines on "Don't Cry Baby", while he stretches out with an inventive solo using swinging bop lines, motifs and bluesy phrases on "Drum Boogie".

The following year on *Kenny Burrell And John Coltrane* (1958), Burrell plays with a swinging, muscular dry tone and conceptual clarity, opening out with adventurous intervallic ideas on "Freight Train". The duet "Why Was I Born?" sees Burrell supporting Coltrane with crisp, ringing harmonies.

On organist Jimmy Smith's funky *Back At The Chicken Shack* (1960), the title track has Burrell playing bassy, thick-textured comping chords, and a spare bluesy solo using space. The number "Messie Bessie" shows him playing an extended bop solo featuring fast inventive passages.

Burrell's popular album *Midnight Blue* (1963) sees him taking a turn toward a simpler rootsy feel as his soloing incorporates a more overt blues flavour on tracks such as the beginning of "Mule", at the start of which he plays phrases and chords in a vocal style. Burrell takes off on the title track, which is a modal blues, while "Soul Lament" contains simple calling notes and contrasting darker chords. The number "Saturday Night Blues" witnesses Burrell playing simple stabbed chords and chips and playing a laid-back rhythmic solo.

THE CLASSICAL GUITAR

Until the 1950s, the classical guitar was rarely used in jazz because of its lack of volume and the traditional use of steel-string instruments. However, in 1947, Brazilian guitarist Laurindo Almeide (b.1917) started using a classical guitar with the Stan Kenton Orchestra, working in the studios and recording "Lament" (1947). By the mid 1950s Bill Harris (b.1925) was using nylon string effectively for jazz melodies, chords and bass lines on recordings such as "Cherokee" (1956). He was followed by Charlie Byrd (1925–99), who studied with classical guitarist Andres Segovia in 1954. Byrd played electric guitar, but decided to concentrate on classical guitar. His debut album, *First Flight* (1957), contains lyrical versions of "My Funny Valentine" and "Spring Is Here". In the late 1950s he

mixed repertoire in concerts and put out albums with classical pieces, before touring South America in 1961 and discovering Brazilian music. In early 1962 he recorded "Desafinado" with Stan Getz – a turning point in the profile of the instrument (*see page 219*). Other major jazz musicians also started to use classical guitar. On *Guitar Forms* (1965), with atmospheric arrangements by Gil Evans, Kenny Burrell plays a range of styles, starting with the traditional blues of "Downstairs To Lotus Land" which he plays with a Spanish classical and flamenco flavour through to the bossa "Moon And Sand", and his picked soloing style can be heard working well on nylon strings. On the sensitive, classically-inspired "Last Night When We Were Young", he imparts acoustic textures, vibrating the pick, arpeggiating and strumming chords.

CHARLIE BYRD
The guitars Charlie Byrd played were produced by great European makers Herman Hauser and Ignacio Fleta.

JIM HALL

A major jazz guitar figure, Jim Hall (b.1930) has a history of exceptional recordings in a variety of settings. Initially inspired by tenor saxophonist Lester Young, his deceptively spare and economical playing is full of subtle rhythmic nuances, and clever use of space, with interwoven melodic lines and tasteful chords. After working with Chico Hamilton in 1956, his role on *The Jimmy Giuffre Three* (1957) in an advanced chamber-jazz setting is innovative as he uses classical and folk elements and a rubato approach. There is thoughtful interplay in the ensemble exchanges, and Hall plays with understated swinging intensity and introspective mood using close voicings and

digging into the beat. "Two Kinds Of Blues" and "Crawdad Suite" are episodic with Hall playing colourful and unusual voicings, with a solo interlude. "The Train And The River" features countermelody lines with trills and a strange repeating nursery-rhyme motif.

Hall's first album as leader, *Jazz Guitar* (1957), is a contrasting trio with piano and bass playing traditional standards such as "Stompin' At The Savoy". On the Sonny Rollins album *The Bridge* (1962), Hall's guitar replaces piano with great effect. On "Without A Song", he embellishes Rollins' strong melody line and adds a link to a punchy solo using single notes and chords with a deep bassy jazz-guitar sound. "John S." has tight comping with close voicings to give an edge. The uptempo title track sees sax and guitar playing a short figure and a scatter of descending notes; Hall's solo is a mixture of intervals, developments of motifs and fast skittering lines. He contributes a sympathetic accompaniment on "God Bless The Child" and thoughtful solo breaks that use space and the instrument's wide register with slides and the occasional subtle string bend, and beautiful harmonies at the end.

HALL & EVANS' DUETS

On *Undercurrent* (1962) Hall works with pianist Bill Evans in a combination that can be difficult harmonically, but Hall complements Evans' rich impressionistic harmony and displaced phrasing. They turn "My Funny Valentine" into a jumping, syncopated rhythmic dialogue with Hall taking a florid solo over Evans' comping; Hall then supports Evans with an acoustic strumming tone and simulates double bass. On "Romain" the interrelationship of registers is captivating, and on the delicate "Skating In Central Park" Hall plays bell-like upper notes and sensitive comping and climbing lines. On *Intermodulation* (1966), the piano and guitar float together. He contributes gentle chords, bass notes and an emotional solo on "My Man's Gone Now".

GIBSON ES-175
The ES-175 first came out in 1949. Jim Hall acquired his single P-90 pick-up model from Howard Roberts in 1956, and used it on The Jimmy Giuffre Three *album (1956) and his own debut album. He felt it sounded "less tubby" than his L-5, and the 175 suited his sound, which was less fat and rich, more lean and precise.*

JIM HALL
Playing with compositional sensitivity and sincere emotional expressiveness, Hall has a thoughtful approach. He transcends standard jazz-guitar styles and his arrangements of material are intelligent and unusual.

109

WES MONTGOMERY

The embodiment of the jazz guitar tradition at its best, Wes Montgomery draws from bop and plays with an intuitive genius. On all types of material his great feel, emotion and sublime invention have made him one of the greatest figures in jazz guitar.

A fabulous jazz player with a natural musical ability, John L. (Wes) Montgomery (1925–68) was born in Indianapolis, surrounded by a musical family with brothers Monk playing bass and Buddy on vibes and piano. Wes was inspired by Charlie Christian; when he was developing his technique in the 1940s, he memorized Christian's solos and absorbed ideas from Django Reinhardt, including the use of octaves.

Montgomery plays with his thumb, giving him a full sound for single lines and chords, and his remarkable tone is deep and almost acoustic. His percussive phrasing is surprisingly complex, with arpeggios full of slides and hammered grace notes with a touch of bluesy vocabulary giving a speech-inflected expressiveness. His long lines sometimes use whole-tone scales and altered scale patterns.

Montgomery worked with Lionel Hampton in the late 1940s before returning to Indianapolis where he took a day job and worked around the clubs. Recordings in a group from the end of 1957 include "Sound Carrier" which displays his finely controlled rhythmic comping and bubbly soloing style. On "Lois Ann" he uses a harp-like sound for the chord-melody playing; his clear tone and rhythmic octaves and chord playing can be heard on his composition "Fingerpickin'".

His first album as leader was *The Wes Montgomery Trio* (1959). This has a magical version of Thelonius Monk's "Round Midnight"

GIBSON L-5CES
During the 1960s, Wes Montgomery played a special sunburst-finish Gibson L-5CES archtop guitar with a round cutaway and a single humbucking pick-up. This was often played through a Fender combo amplifier, giving projection and a strong full-bodied tone.

WES MONTGOMERY
Montgomery had a wide appeal and was revered in the 1960s. His rhythmic swing and strong physicality often make him sound as if he is propelling the musicians around him.

STANDARDS & ORIGINALS

The album *The Incredible Jazz Guitar Of Wes Montgomery* (1960) is split between standards and Montgomery's own compositions, including "West Coast Blues". "Airegin" burns with articulate bop ideas, while Montgomery's chord melody on "In Your Own Sweet Way" has a harp-like sound. There is a rounded bassy tone to "Gone With The Wind" and finely articulated lines with rhythms and accents including slow triplets. Octaves hang in the air on a sentimental piece "Polka Dots And Moonbeams". His "Four On Six" has a rhythmic head and relaxed groove, including ascending arpeggio-based flourishes.

Wes Montgomery hits sonorous melody notes over the prevailing harmony.

"WEST COAST BLUES"

One of Wes Montgomery's best-known and most appealing compositions, "West Coast Blues" was recorded in New York in January 1960. It is unusual with a 3/4 time signature and a 24-bar length, and sections with chord changes modulating through tonal centres. With Tommy Flanagan on piano, Percy Heath on bass and Albert Heath on drums, the graceful attractive melody is deceptively complex, with triplets, expressive upper tones with grace notes and sinuous harmonic links. Wes Montgomery takes a well-paced extended solo that swings and is full of melodic invention, with his hallmark octaves and short passages of fast strumming. As with many of his solos, it has a sense of direction with a beginning and end conveying meaning, architecture and form.

with understated background organ layering and drums with brushes. Montgomery's improvising is profound and moving as he plays and embellishes the melody with a relaxed mastery. Fresh ideas burst forth in this slow-tempo piece and at the end Montgomery conjures sublime flourishes. His debt to the blues can be heard on his composition "Missile Blues" with its calling riffs and elegant octave solo passages.

Montgomery produced other outstanding albums including *So Much Guitar* (1961). The hard-driving "Cotton Tail" contains erupting phrases, "I Wish I Knew" is lyrical and rhetorical, and "I'm Just A Lucky So And So" bouncy and optimistic. On "While We're Young", Montgomery creates deep-toned voicings and is soulful on "One For My Baby".

The live *Full House* (1962) demonstrates an assertive Montgomery in a steaming quintet session with Johnny Griffin on tenor sax. The title track offers cascading lines, there are exuberant solos on "Blue 'n Boogie", and "S.O.S." features a fast unison guitar and sax head and repeated figures, and an exciting climax where the band swap fours.

At the end of 1964 Montgomery began putting down lighter music using big band and string backing arrangements. Albums include *Movin' Wes Parts 1 and 2* (1965), *Bumpin'* (1965) and *Smokin' At The Half Note* (1965), which provides a showcase for a purer jazz setting.

NEW FIGURES

There were seismic changes in jazz in the 1960s: an expansion in improvisational vocabulary, a broadening freedom with compositional approaches and an interest in different genres. Guitarists drew from modal jazz, popular genres and blues, and absorbed new developments.

GEORGE BENSON
One of the few guitarists in jazz who also sings, George Benson came to jazz as a remarkable young player with a style that drew on popular music. His smooth technique conveys a sense of effortlessness, even on fast, complex lines, and he plays with a bubbly invention and a mood that often borders on the excitable. In both fusion and straight-ahead jazz settings, he uses a rhythmic eights feel and includes riffs and modal vamps.

At the beginning of the decade, Grant Green (1931–78) played in a light, positive style with a bright tone, using short bop phrases and a bluesy slant with occasional sustained notes and bends. On *Born To Be Blue* (1962), the title track shows blues phrasing, while "If I Should Lose You" has a delicate touch and clean bop lines and arpeggios with sustain on certain notes.

A major new figure, George Benson (b.1943) started in rock 'n' roll but soon turned to jazz. Within a short time he was working as a sideman with organist Jack McDuff, and his debut album *New Boss Guitar* (1964) with McDuff and saxophonist Red Hollway features unison heads as well as riffs, with blues and soul influences, as well as a linear style with bop and pentatonic elements, snappy staccato, and fast exclamatory phrases. "Shadow Dancers" has a funky edge with Benson playing rhythmic chipped chords on the head, and slides and partial chords in his solo, while he shows a bluesy, bop extroversion

on "I Don't Know", and plays unison riffs with bubbly guitar fills and solos on "Rock-A-Bye". *It's Uptown* (1965) contains both jazz and a lighter fusion with popular styles of music. The exceptional "Willow Weep For Me" features improvising of great originality with ideas flowing over the edges, as Benson moves from the slow theme to explosive passages with chattering, speech-inflected contours.

Pat Martino (b.1944) brought out his debut album *El Hombre* in 1967, which features bop-style playing and bluesy phrasing. His long transparent lines can be heard on the title track and "A Blues For Mickey-O".

Following this album, Martino took a more cerebral approach, expanding his vocabulary with new harmonies and building in motifs and intervallic ideas. He absorbed ideas from John Coltrane and Indian music and mixed bop with modal ideas on albums such as *East* (1968).

LARRY CORYELL

In 1966 Larry Coryell (b.1943), with his group Free Spirits, was playing in a style based on blues and rock as well as jazz. He joined vibes player Gary Burton's influential quartet for the album *Duster* (1967), on which he plays modern-sounding, technically constructed lines, blues motifs and introspective classical harmonies, his refreshing approach complementing the progressive compositions. The album *Lofty Fake Anagram* (1967) offered an opening for improvisation, notably the solo on "June the 15, 1967" which is made up of blues-guitar and intervallic playing and chords. "Fleurette Africaine" has bluesy additions. He uses inventive strumming for the duet "Lines", which has a touch of country, and plays a searching angular solo on "The Beach". "General Mojo Cuts Up" is a foray into free jazz, Coryell playing dissonant harmonies and an eastern-flavoured solo.

FREE IMPROVISATION

The early 1960s saw the emergence of free jazz and a reappraisal of collective improvisation. Stimulated by modern avant-garde classical composers, new music appeared that broke away from the constraints of regular time-keeping and improvisation based on chord progressions.

Remarkable figures working in this field include Sonny Sharrock (b.1940) who joined the Pharaoh Sanders group in 1965, appearing briefly on *Tauhid* (1966) and taking off on *Izipho Zam* (1969), on which he plays screaming ascending lines and wild atonal excursions, tremulous vibratos, volcanic sonic noises and see-sawing slide within a cacophonous stream-of-consciousness music. Fred Frith (b.1949) worked at the frontiers of experimentation with prepared guitars in the 1970s, adapting the instrument with added objects, loosening strings and creating unfamiliar sounds on *Guitar Solos* (1973).

DEREK BAILEY

In Britain, the revolutionary Derek Bailey (b.1930) sought a new, more contemporary language. He can be heard in a recorded rehearsal from 1965, with drummer Tony Oxley and bass player Gavin Bryars, playing

John Coltrane's head "Miles Mode", which they use as a springboard for open-time based modal interplay, and for new harmonic, melodic and spatial explorations. This work culminated in the decision to create music through free improvisation without preconceived material.

After this he made a quantum leap, with a complete departure from American jazz. Fascinated by unusual sounds and timbres, electronic music and the serial methods of Schoenberg and Webern, Bailey started by-passing standard harmonies and modal jazz, and developed a new, dissonant style. With the Spontaneous Music Ensemble on *Karyobin* (1968), his attack, colours, glass-toned clusters, use of unexpected noises, and unfamiliar angular lines are astounding. Characteristic of his style are sophisticated voicings made up of stopped notes, open strings and compound intervals, with harmonics and notes behind the bridge and fast changes between atonal clusters. He also uses a volume pedal to remove the attack from sounds, producing long, gliding notes and grainy atonal soundscapes, and in 1970 he added stereo amplification.

On his solo recording, *Solo Guitar* (1971), Bailey plays four different free improvisations, in which he uses staccato notes and chords, taut percussive sounds, harsh dissonances, string bends giving microtonal pitch variations, and effects with strings pulled out of position and off the fingerboard, often with volume fluctuations and gliding volume techniques, feedback and harmonic distortion. Three compositions range from sound-processed continuous rhythms to a shambolic sight-reading interpretation, and there is a piece on which he plays two guitars at once.

DEREK BAILEY
A radical individualist, Derek Bailey pioneered free improvisation on the guitar. Passionate about the instrument and its unlimited possibilities, he retains standard tuning and plays normally with a pick for single lines and the majority of voicings. He works with reasoned concepts, retaining technical control, yet also explores intuitively.

SONNY SHARROCK
At odds with American trends, Sharrock's gospel feeling and futuristic expressiveness challenged audiences. On Black Woman *(1969), he stretches slow melodies and scatters wild runs across meditative backgrounds.*

JOHN McLAUGHLIN

At a point at which the sound and style of the jazz guitar were changing radically, John McLaughlin emerged as a pivotal figure who brought all the elements together. He incorporated rock, 1960s modal jazz and the harmony and structures of Indian and 20th-century classical music.

John McLaughlin (b. 1942) was brought up with classical music and was initially inspired by the blues before discovering jazz. On his first album, *Extrapolation* (1969), he plays his adventurous compositions with a distorted edge in a quartet with frequent unison guitar and saxophone lines, such as on the elliptical head for "Spectrum"; his solo, too, has an angular quality with flurries of lines and chords. He uses interesting rhythmic strumming on "Binky's Beam", while beauty and depth characterize the harmonies of the arpeggiated "This Is For Us To Share", and "Peace Piece" which combines folk and Indian music.

In 1969, McLaughlin was invited to play on the Miles Davis album *In A Silent Way*. On the title track, he contributes plangent chords and melody notes and is given the space for tentative exploratory lines on the extended open compositions. He also joined Lifetime with Tony Williams and Larry Young, playing a high-energy fusion. On the album *Emergency* (1969) he takes off as a soloist in an explosive setting of the title track, and on "Spectrum" his inventive articulation and original phrasing, derived from bebop and contemporary jazz thinking, has forceful declamatory accenting with a mixture of motifs, pentatonic elements and bending.

Further Davis albums followed, including *Bitches Brew* (1969), where he adds lines to the polytonal collage, *Live Evil* (1971), with a burning solo on "What I Say", and *A Tribute To Jack Johnson* (1970), on which he plays in a bluesy chordal groove. Other highlights include Miroslav Vitous' *Mountain In The Clouds* (1969), where he adds dissonant chordal edge and plays a furious elliptical solo on "Freedom Jazz Dance", and the contrasting *Joe Farrell Quartet* (1970); here he takes an emotional solo on "Follow Your Heart". With its rock settings and riffs, McLaughlin's first US solo album *Devotion* (1970) points to the future.

OVATION CUSTOM LEGEND

These unusual guitars were first developed in the late 1960s and feature a rounded bowl back made of lyrachord, a type of plastic. John McLaughlin often used an Ovation at the beginning of the 1970s.

JOHN McLAUGHLIN

At the end of the 1960s McLaughlin managed to realize his conception for improvisation, developing an intense, focused style based on modes and altered scales, and using rhythmic ideas from Indian music.

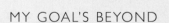

MY GOAL'S BEYOND

On the outstanding acoustic album *My Goal's Beyond* (1970), "Peace One" and "Peace Two", with their vina-like sound, create a strong Indian flavour with an ensemble. There are double-tracked standards and originals, such as the sentimental "Hearts And Flowers", the emotional "Follow Your Heart" and the surging "Goodbye Pork Pie Hat". The driving, rhythmic "Something Spiritual" and "Song For My Mother" display inventive modal improvising. "Blue In Green" reveals a magical tone, with low tuning and a thoughtful solo.

THE MAHAVISHNU ORCHESTRA

In 1971, John McLaughlin formed his own group, The Mahavishnu Orchestra. Their debut album, *The Inner Mounting Flame* (1971), was a groundbreaking template for jazz rock. The group is driven by ferocious drumming with an uncompromising "heavy eights" feel, often using compound time signatures such as 10/8, anchored by minimal bass and washes of sustaining synth harmonies. The guitar, violin and keyboards play fast, extended unison parts and solos with a yearning, spiritual feeling, over unusual harmonies with elements from jazz, classical, blues, rock and Indian music. McLaughlin's soloing is built around modes, pentatonic scales and bluesy bends, which often sound similar to synth pitch-wheel movements, and he uses a compressed, sustaining distorted sound, as on the intense "Meeting Of The Spirits", where it rides over a repeating violin figure, and the soft lyrical "Dawn". "Noonward Race" opens and ends with a funky guitar and

drum duet – McLaughlin playing tearing lines with the fills around the kit – and builds up to a solo with cascading motifs and lines. An arpeggiated progression with unusual root movements forms the opening to "Dance Of Maya", which goes into a compound time boogie and then a solo over vamped chords. "Awakening" and "Vital Transformation" feature surging riffs with the drums, but a peaceful side can be heard on "Lotus On Irish Streams" which sees acoustic guitar, violin and piano creating a classical impressionist vision.

MAHAVISHNU ORCHESTRA
With Jerry Goodman on violin, Billy Cobham on drums, Rick Laird on bass and Jan Hammer on keyboards, John Mclaughlin's Mahavishnu Orchestra (above) first appeared in 1971. Their approach revolutionized jazz fusion.

GIBSON EDS-1275
John McLaughlin performed with a double-neck guitar with 6-string and 12-string necks. His fluent soloing with fast lines and keening bends brought him to rock audiences and has had a considerable influence across many musical genres.

SHAKTI
McLaughlin put together the Indian crossover group Shakti in 1976; it included L. Shankar on violin and Zakir Hussain on tablas. There are razor-sharp unison lines, ragas and rhythmic exchanges. He used a custom-built guitar with drone strings and scalloped fingerboard.

THE EARLY SEVENTIES

At the beginning of the 1970s, jazz form and harmony had been shaped by various influences, such as modal jazz and classical music. New figures had arrived who had a fresh approach to guitar techniques, and their soloing and electric effects broadened the voice of the instrument.

LARRY CORYELL
A figure whose output reflects the shifting crosscurrents of the times, Larry Coryell played an important part in the development of jazz-rock in the 1970s. In the duo "Stiffneck" (1968) with drummer Elvin Jones, long lines of motivic phrases using feedback typify his style.

Players from different backgrounds started to work in areas with a crossover flavour, producing an eclectic variety of tracks that mixed swing and modal jazz with rock, blues and fusion. On his album *Spaces* (1970), with guest John McLaughlin, Larry Coryell (b.1943) plays an electric solo on the driving title track and swaps fours on the acoustic swing-based "Rene's Theme", using a synthetic modal soloing style with cutting phrases.

One of the most creative and cerebral of improvisers, Pat Martino (b.1944) mixes standards with fusion, and plays with an insistent metronomic compression over the beat, building a hypnotic intensity. On *Desperado* (1970), he plays electric 12-string guitar with a distorted edge: "Blackjack" is an open-ended jazz-rock piece in which manic pentatonic and blues licks are mixed with intervallic ideas and long, graceful bebop lines. On "Oleo", based on rhythm changes, Martino plays precisely constructed modern bebop lines, where he swaps fours. His long controlled lines can be heard on "Impressions": here he uses a stream of bluesy minor bebop ideas, intervallic motifs and repeating cyclical phrases played with great control, and there are no fast flurries and little use of sustain.

AL DI MEOLA

Al Di Meola joined one of the most powerful jazz-rock fusion bands, Return To Forever, with Chick Corea for the album *Where Have I Known You Before?* (1974), which features his cutting, overdriven rock sound and a style of soloing based on scales, motifs and exercises. He uses a cleaner sound for funky rhythms, and octaves for backings. Di Meola went on to bring out solo albums, including *Elegant Gypsy* (1977) where he plays fast solos such as "Race With The Devil On A Spanish Highway". He also developed his writing, using flamenco and Latin flavours.

Di Meola developed his own type of slick Latin jazz-rock with a seamless fusion soloing style.

ALLAN HOLDSWORTH

One of the most important and original innovators on the guitar, Allan Holdsworth (b.1948) virtually created a new way of playing single lines: using long streams of smooth legato, his left hand plays most of the notes through controlled hammer-ons and pull-offs. Shifting cyclical phrases, composed of unusual lines with long stretches on each string, ascend and descend and curl back on themselves, creating a sense of unending creativity. He also uses close-voiced chords and interesting tonal shifts on sequences with unexpected bass notes and movements.

The album *Velvet Darkness* (1976) has a heavy jazz-rock sound with sustained melodic heads stating the tune, and Holdsworth uses a processed distorted sound, pulling notes out of

RALPH TOWNER

A unique figure, Ralph Towner (b.1940) brought modern classical composition and classical-guitar techniques to a chamber-jazz setting, using nylon-string classical and 12-string guitars. From 1970 he worked with the crossover group Oregon, developing a mixture of classical, Brazilian and Indian flavours. On *Ralph Towner With Glen Moore – Trios / Solos* (1973), "Brujo" features 12-string guitar with shimmering and percussive staccato chords, inventive voicings and arpeggios, single lines and harmonics. The solo piece "Winter Light" on nylon string has a classical flavour in its angular phrases and deep resonant chords with added harmonics, while "Noctuary" contains shattering percussive, atonal chords with harmonics and sustaining reverb, moving to free-form passages with fast strumming. The dynamics and rumbustious fingerpicking of "Suite 3x12" demonstrate a fusion of many genres including bluegrass and bluesy folk idioms.

Tower's album with Gary Burton, *Matchbook* (1975), features dreamy, sustained passages where guitar and vibes merge, as in "Drifting Petals" and "Song For A Friend", while the intro to the title track demonstrates a muted repeating pattern like African percussion.

Solstice (1975) places Towner's guitar in a quartet that includes saxophonist Jan Garbarek. Towner creates a haunting atmosphere with shimmering arpeggios, and a solo on "Oceanus And Nimbus" reveals airy voicings with harmonics supporting single lines, before breaking into a broad range of surging arpeggios. "Train Of Thought" provides a variety of textures with Japanese koto-like sounds, tapping and rattling harmonic colours over murky bass figures and dissonant passages. *Solo Concert* (1980) features an arrangement of "Nardis", that is played on a nylon-string guitar, creating a classical flavour.

ALLAN HOLDSWORTH
Using original fingering positions and technique, Holdsworth creates a floating, harmonic style in which he plays fast inventive lines. He also uses impressionistic harmonies drawn from modern jazz and classical music.

pitch with the tremolo arm. The title track has a lyrical head, and powerful swirling lines, interspersed with slower melodic phrases, Holdsworth shaking sustained upper notes with the tremolo arm. There is an imaginative, complex solo on "Gattox".

On the Allan Holdsworth / Gordon Beck album *The Things You See* (1980) Holdsworth uses mainly acoustic guitar, notably on "Golden Lakes" with its melodic head and exuberant, flowing solos. "Diminished Responsibility" has fast unison heads and free open passages with modern classical harmonies, and Holdsworth plays an unaccompanied linear passage full of exploratory atonal lines that resolve into melodiousness; a later passage of piano and guitar interplay shows astonishing virtuosity.

JOHN ABERCROMBIE
On Gateway *(1975), John Abercrombie (b.1944) plays elliptical lines with a mixture of rigid motifs and legato lines, which can be heard on "Back-Woods Song" where he adds touches of blues and country, using a volume control and tremolo bar for detuned passages. "Sorcery 1" has an ethereal, searing rock sound combined with sonic effects.*

RALPH TOWNER
The acoustic player Ralph Towner has a classical right-hand technique, with highly-developed damping and rhythmic accent control and varied arpeggiation. He frequently makes use of harmonics, low strings, and close-voiced chords, including open strings.

THE MODERN PERIOD

The last quarter of the 20th century saw major jazz guitarists working with new sounds derived from rock, and developing music around original compositions with a leaning toward impressionism and free jazz. Innovations in approach have widened the guitar's role and potential.

PAT METHENY
Using floating legato phrasing with reverb over impressionistic harmonies, Pat Metheny gives his music a "backwoods" flavour with touches of country-style music.

Pat Metheny (b.1954) on his debut album *Bright Size Life* (1976) conjures up vast soundscapes with his compositions for a trio. He has a relaxed approach, with attractive, ringing chord voicings, and plays smooth solos with languorous stretched notes and phrasing. The title track has an extended solo with a liquid tone, in which Metheny uses slides and hammer-ons on notes and chords, with touches of country music. "Sirabhorn" has a feeling of stillness with attractive bell-like plucked voicings and a graceful overdubbed melodic solo. He plays a bubbly head on "Missouri Uncompromised", and one of his strongest solos, which contains rippling flurries of legato notes moving to passages with double stopping and chordal improvising. The gentle "Midwestern Nights Dream", based on a melodic figure with fifths and close, resonant voicings on an echoing 12-string guitar, embodies his distinctive compositional style.

With his quartet The Pat Metheny Group, formed in 1978, he incorporates jazz-rock, fusion and Latin influences. Guitar and guitar-synthesizer are put together for mellifluous backgrounds on *Offramp* (1982), creating an orchestral sound for tracks such as "The Bat Part II". On the contrasting title track, Metheny takes a fast, powerful violin-toned synth-guitar solo with inspired improvising. One of his most accomplished albums *80/81* (1980) puts Metheny in an acoustic jazz setting, where the inventive

thinking on his solos often draws strongly on Ornette Coleman's work. The title track has skittering rhythms and free-jazz-style boppy lines, while there is a searching lyricism to "The Bat" and atonal phrasing on "Turnaround"; "Pretty Scattered" has a sinuous head that allows Metheny to explore spiralling lines that slide into singing upper notes over straight-ahead, open-ended jazz rhythms. Metheny took his experimentalism further on *Song X* (1985) with Ornette Coleman, where he develops an angular free-jazz style with frenetic complexity.

GIBSON ES-175
Pat Metheny is usually associated with his modified natural-finish Gibson ES-175, but has also used guitar-synthesizer both live and in the studio.

LARRY CARLTON
Starting out as a studio player, Larry Carlton (b.1948) launched his solo career with the debut album Larry Carlton *(1978). He plays in a melodic fusion style, with a rich, reedy tone. His well-centred strong tone and soaring melodiousness made him widely popular.*

JOHN SCOFIELD

Emerging in the late 1970s, John Scofield (b.1951) draws from jazz and fusion and absorbs the motivic improvising of the Brecker Brothers using a grainy, rock sound. He improvises with bluesy lines, altered scales and dislocated phrasing, making minor alterations to some of the motifs to create a sense of the unexpected. Hard, driving riffs with thick-textured distortion and country-style two- and three-note chords with hammered notes reflect another side of his style, and his solos often include two-note melodic improvisation on intervals such as sixths. *Shinola* (1982) shows Scofield in a live jazz-trio setting, and showcases his writing abilities. On "Why'd You Do It?", Scofield uses a broken, distorted sound for jazz chord voicings, which gives his playing a gritty edge, but on "Yawn" he creates a dark, introspective stillness and sad wistfulness with glimmering harmonies. "Dr. Jackie" features fluent legato phrasing, using arcing lines with a bop architecture and phrasing that curves back on itself. In the duet with bass, "Jean The Bean", the guitar voicings and solos fit together organically. The title track is based on rock riffs and chords, but given a more modern edge, and Scofield plays with a blues-rock sound and vocabulary, augmented with his own jazz lines. As well as playing with Miles Davis, Scofield also led his own fusion group, which can be heard on the live album *Pick Hits* (1987).

MIKE STERN

Mike Stern (b.1954) played with Miles Davis from 1981, creating a hybrid style of bebop and blues with a modern rock sound. His solo on the title track of *Star People* (1983) is a bubbly blues, but on "Come Get It" it is full of dark intensity and passages of modernistic bebop. On Stern's jazz-rock fusion album, *Upside Downside* (1986), his sound is processed with effects, while the mainstream *Standards* (1992) features creative playing with a cool, liquid tone.

JOHN SCOFIELD
Working with Miles Davis from 1982–85, Scofield played alongside Mike Stern and brought a contrasting approach. This can be heard on Star People *(1983) – the loping, bluesy lines behind the beat give a relaxed feel to "It Gets Better", and he digs in with a cutting drive on "Speak".*

JAZZ & FLAMENCO

In 1979 John McLaughlin started playing in an acoustic guitar trio with flamenco virtuoso Paco De Lucía and jazz and fusion player Larry Coryell, and later with Al Di Meola. Jazz, flamenco, classical and Brazilian music mould their rhythm and harmonies as each player brings his own background improvising style to arrangements that include blindingly-fast unison lines, strummed rhythms and dazzling arpeggios. On *Passion, Grace And Fire* (1983), the crossover-style "Aspan" opens with *rasgueado* strumming and has fast unison lines, arpeggiation and stop-start rhythms, with contrasting solos from Di Meola, McLaughlin, and De Lucía. "Orient Blue" has harp-like arpeggiated arrangements using

interwoven notes with close voicings, inventive soloing from McLaughlin, flowing melodiousness from Di Meola and fabulous lines from De Lucía. "Chiquito" is flamenco-like.

With De Lucía on nylon-string with nails, McLaughlin on nylon-string with a pick and Di Meola on steel-string with a pick, the trio constantly interchange ideas and techniques from jazz, Latin and flamenco music.

STANLEY JORDAN
Appearing with a revolutionary two-handed technique, Stanley Jordan plays with a pianistic style, tapping solos and extra chord notes with his right hand. His arrangement of "Eleanor Rigby" (1984), with its extended harmonies, and his soloing with bass lines and moving harmony on "Jumpin Jack" (1985) astonished guitarists.

FRANK GAMBALE
Australian guitarist Frank Gambale developed a style of sweep picking and broadened the vocabulary of guitar soloing with his seamless, arpeggiated phrasing. This can be heard in his work with Chick Corea, and on his own signature album Brave New Guitar *(1986).*

Here he plays seamless lines and motivic improvisations over a solid groove, especially on tracks such as "Protocol".

In the late 1980s, Scofield moved toward a more traditional jazz-quartet sound, teaming up with saxophone player Joe Lovano and further developing his compositional ideas. On *Time On My Hands* (1990), he rides with the bass and drums, filling the sound and varying the duration of his comping with chips and volume-control layers. His muddy, broken harmonic ambiguity keeps the music open-sounding, and "Farmacology" provides a vehicle for his creatively fluent soloing. Ringing lines and chords are used for the atmospheric "Nocturnal Mission" and "Time And Tide".

SCOTT HENDERSON

An expressive fusion player, Scott Henderson (b.1955) with Tribal Tech has reinvigorated the area combining blues, rock, metal, and jazz. On their album *Nomad* (1988), and subsequent recordings, his playing combines intelligent and creative fusion phrasing with refreshing linear ideas. With this type of soloing, Henderson has created his own modern synthesis and identity. His flowing musicality and melodic ideas with a visceral edge set him apart from many others in the genre.

ATAVACHRON

Allan Holdsworth, on *Atavachron* (1986), uses both guitar and SynthAxe for layering and soloing. "Non Brewed Condiment" has a fabulously explosive linear head and a solo that successfully explores intervallic ideas and sustained notes. There is a joyful exuberance as he tears through phrases full of inventive energy, and the chord progressions are spiced with unusual voicings and ringing harmonies. The title track has a futuristic, sci-fi flavour with flowing, melodic harmonies, and uses a solo violin-like sound with high-spirited turns of phrase.

BILL FRISELL

An iconoclast and one of the leading contemporary innovators, Bill Frisell (b.1951) creates futuristic textures on guitar with extensive and carefully thought-out electronic and synthesized processing, together with unusual arrangements and instrumental line-ups. On his album *In Line* (1983), "The Beach" contains a number of sustained parts, each with its own sound and texture, and he uses pitch movements to create a colourful soundscape. The contrasting "Throughout" features acoustic broken-chord figures with ethereal, layered electric melodies and harmonized lines that float and die away. Frisell's unique lyrical soloing voice is processed to give a range of cello- and violin-like sounds in different registers. A remarkable timbral resonance chracterizes "Tone" on the album *Rambler* (1985), in which Frisell takes a solo full of swerving, crying notes and puts down low-register yawning, throaty noises.

Frisell's music is humourous and poignant on *Lookout For Hope* (1988). The title track contains remarkable

SYNTHAXE
Developed in Britain in 1984, the SynthAxe is played via an innovative fretboard touch system.

It acts as a MIDI controller, enabling players to produce a full range of synthesized and sampled sounds.

sustained textures and broken chords, and notes swell and run across the sound-field, disappearing into the distance and punctuated with searing upper-register calls. He creates a peculiar, futuristic country-style guitar sound and waltz sections for "Little Brother Bobby" by using volume control and a swelling pedal steel-guitar style. "Hangdog" reflects elements of Frank Zappa (*see pages 196–97, 205*) and minimalist composers, with interesting textural arrangements of repeating motifs and sonic effects. Lush, exotic background chords produce a landscape of sheets of sound in "Remedios The Beauty", over which there are strange melodic lines on acoustic guitar and a surprising rock-guitar entry. Harmonized lines and layered electric and acoustic guitars unfurl with a complex resonance, and Frisell takes a melodic solo with a deep sound, the strings vibrating against the frets. The poignant "Melody For Jack" has simple motifs with modern classical harmonies, and "Hackensack" uses a steel-guitar sound for a sonorous solo with partial chords. Shining chords unfold on "Little Bigger", with individual notes hanging in the air to form layers. Expressive individual characters are conjured up for "The Animal Race", and the haunting "Alien Prints" merges ethereal voicings, arcing lines and crying upper notes with distortion and a pungent, trailing after-sound.

Changes are apparent on Frisell's *Have A Little Faith* (1993), the guitar on "Scenes From Across America" being given a disciplined role for arrangements of music ranging from Aaron Copland and Charles Ives to Muddy Waters and Bob Dylan.

BILL FRISELL
Playing a futuristic Klein guitar and electronics, Bill Frisell improvises using a modern extended tonal vocabulary with elements of fusion and country styles. His parts are always thoughtful and considered, and his lines and chords carefully processed through sophisticated sound effects to give new textures and echoes of other instruments.

TRADITION & MODERNITY

There is today a considerable divide between the many different types of jazz, in spite of crossover and fusion, and there continues to be a number of different playing styles that co-exist but are largely separate from each other. Traditional players working within a framework of standards and conservative material include the talented Americans Russell Malone and Howard Alden, while in Britain, Martin Taylor's playing is largely inspired by Joe Pass. In France there has been a long-standing school of guitarists working within the Django Reinhardt style, which has produced players such as Birelli Lagrene. In contrast, Derek Bailey — one of guitar's few true innovators — explores new territory and records freely improvised music that has been increasingly embraced by the mainstream. His *Guitar, Drums 'N' Bass* (1996) with D.J. Ninj is a wild mixture of programmed drums and percussion with shrieking, distorted atonal guitar sitting over the background with remarkable cohesion.

MARTIN TAYLOR
One of the success stories of recent years, Martin Taylor has worked extensively as a solo chord-melody player. He improvises within a swinging metrical framework, using the traditional vocabulary built over the years by the great mainstream players.

ROCK & POP

THE UK & EUROPE

SONGWRITING AND INSTRUMENTAL MUSIC IN EUROPE IS ROOTED IN THE TRADITIONS OF FOLK AND CLASSICAL MUSIC. POP AND ROCK GUITAR MUSIC, ALTHOUGH DERIVED FROM AMERICAN POPULAR STYLES, HAS ABSORBED MANY TRADITIONAL INFLUENCES AND EMERGED WITH A DISTINCTIVE IDENTITY.

THE BEATLES' *highly creative and imaginative use of the guitar stands out in popular music. The instrument's immense popularity worldwide is due partly to their influence.*

ROCK 'N' ROLL & POP

The new generation of guitarists that appeared in the 1950s looked to American rock 'n' roll and pop for their inspiration. In a vibrant and quickly expanding British music scene, other styles, including blues, jazz and country, also made an influential impact on the new instrumentalists.

During the late 1950s, the guitar became established as a popular and widely played instrument throughout Britain. American artists such as Scotty Moore, Chuck Berry, Eddy Cochran and Carl Perkins (*see pages 176–82*) were capturing the imagination with music that reached a large and receptive audience through records, radio, television and concerts.

Inspired by their American idols, many young musicians took up the guitar. One of the most popular line-ups featuring the guitar at this time was the skiffle group – an ensemble performing in a variety of styles, frequently playing traditional jazz alongside blues and rock 'n' roll. Skiffle instruments were often crude, but very effective. Many players made their own guitars and played with a basic rhythm section made up of a washboard and a one-string bass. In 1956, the chart success of skiffle-pioneer Lonnie Donegan's version of Leadbelly's "Rock Island Line" turned grass-roots interest into a skiffle boom.

As well as giving musicians a chance to perform their own material, skiffle enabled British guitarists to develop and hone their skills playing covers of American songs. Many players who found fame in the 1960s emerged from a skiffle background, including members of The Shadows and The Beatles.

INSTRUMENTAL HITS

Popular instrumentals, with guitar as the main element, became fashionable in Britain with the release of Duane Eddy's 1958 single "Rebel Rouser". Bert Weedon (b.1920) was one of Britain's first, and now most legendary, guitarists to work in this area. Weedon's version of Arthur Smith's "Guitar Boogie Shuffle", a hit single in 1959, sees him playing twelve-bar blues riffs and using a jazz-influenced soloing style. Following on from this unprecedented chart success, composer Jerry Lordan wrote the instrumental "Apache" for Weedon, and it was released as a single in 1960.

Two years later, one of the most original and "futuristic" instrumentals of the period was released. Produced by Joe Meek, The Tornados' "Telstar" (1962) is an advanced and highly sophisticated number that features Alan Caddy (b.1940) on guitar. A number-one hit single in Britain in 1962, it also became a landmark first number-one hit in America by a British group.

HANK MARVIN

In 1958, Hank B. Marvin (Brian Rankin, b.1941) and Bruce Welch (b.1941) began working as part of the backing group for Cliff Richard. Marvin played the solo on Richard's third hit, "Livin', Lovin' Doll" (1959). Many other records followed, with Cliff backed by Marvin on lead guitar, Welch on rhythm guitar, Jet Harris on bass and Tony Meehan on drums.

The Shadows, as the group came to be known, became a successful act in their own right with their recording of "Apache" (1960), a definitive and beautifully executed arrangement that eclipsed Bert Weedon's version. In this atmospheric instrumental, sounding like a theme from a Western movie, Marvin shows himself to be a master of dynamics and controlled, tasteful melodiousness and he convincingly conjures the image of a galloping horse with guitar and echo effect.

HOFNER CLUB 60
The "Club" series of German-made Hofner guitars was popular in Britain during the 1950s, when import restrictions made it hard to get American instruments.

BERT WEEDON
A pioneering figure with a long performing and recording career, Bert Weedon has produced many fine instrumentals. His guitar tuition book Play In A Day, *first published in 1957, has been used by generations of players.*

EARLY FIGURES

Many talented players emerged in Britain during the 1950s, including the outstanding Big Jim Sullivan (b.1942), who played with Marty Wilde and the Wildcats and became a top session guitarist. Many figures are now overlooked, such as Joe Moretti who performed one of the period's most memorable guitar parts on Johnny Kidd and the Pirates' "Shakin' All Over", a number-one hit single in Britain in June 1960.

With Marvin taking the lead work, Bruce Welch provides accurate and equally tasteful accompaniment. Other Jerry Lordan themes followed, including "Wonderful Land" (1962), with its sublime and other-worldly sound, and "Atlantis" (1963). In their early period, The Shadows recorded many diverse and varied instrumentals, such as the 1961 hits "FBI", "Kon-Tiki" and "Frightened City". Typically, these and other tracks were thoroughly rehearsed and recorded, at Abbey Road Studios in London, in just a few takes.

Hank Marvin's versatility is evident on the group's first album, *The Shadows* (1961). Here, he retains his distinctive touch and sonority, and occasionally plays with a gritty, slightly distorted edge. His precision and control can be heard on "Shadoogie", a track on which he plays boogie riffs and uses double-time picking – a technique that gives the number lift. In contrast, he creates a relaxed Hawaiian sound on "Blue Star" with skillful use of the tremolo arm with echo over Welch's steel-string rhythm. A jazz-style solo is featured on the palindromic "Nivram", a number with a walking bass line and harmony lines on the melody; harmony lines are also used on "Theme From A Filleted Place". In "Gonzales", a track typical of The Shadows' ability to evoke images of the Wild West, Marvin answers a melodic phrase with a change of tone over a fast acoustic rhythm. Contrast is used in "Sleepwalk". Here, a 3/4-time acoustic rhythm supports a muted, high-register introduction that moves into an extended thematic section.

Since releasing their first single in 1960, The Shadows have maintained their position as Britain's premier instrumental group.

THE SHADOWS' GUITAR SOUND

The Shadows' early, seminal recordings feature Hank Marvin playing a Fender Stratocaster, launched in America in 1954, through a Vox AC15 combo amplifier, first produced in the late 1950s. The combination of the Stratocaster, a Binson or Meazzi echo unit and Vox combo amplification enabled Marvin to create his sonorous tone.

Fender Stratocaster

Meazzi echo unit

HANK MARVIN
The popularity and chart success of Cliff Richard and The Shadows' records exposed Hank Marvin to a wide and appreciative audience. His distinctive style and unique sound has been much imitated and is highly influential on guitarists the world over.

EARLY BEATLES

When The Beatles emerged in 1962, they were set to change musical history and ensure that the guitar dominated popular music. They produced a large body of music and stand as talented and innovative songwriters who were also highly creative in the recording studio.

EARLY BEATLES
The Beatles worked extensively on the club circuit in Britain and at the Star Club in Hamburg, Germany. During these years they played a wide range of covers, including material recorded by Elvis Presley, Chuck Berry and Buddy Holly.

TV APPEARANCES
The Beatles made dozens of radio recordings and TV appearances. They appeared a number of times on popular music shows in the UK, such as Ready, Steady, Go *and* Thank Your Lucky Stars, *in which they mimed along to their records and strummed guitars that were not plugged in.*

The four members of the group all came from the Liverpool music scene of the 1950s. John Lennon (1940–80) and Paul McCartney (b.1942) both played the guitar and started out together in 1957, playing in a skiffle group called The Quarry Men. The following year they were joined by George Harrison (b.1943) on guitar, Paul McCartney switching to electric bass. Their instrumental line-up was the same as The Shadows', with lead, rhythm, and bass guitars and a drummer. The group used a number of drummers before they finally settled on Ringo Starr (Richard Starkey, b.1940) in 1962.

After signing a record deal with EMI, the group started to evolve, encouraged by musical direction from producer George Martin who helped them with recording and arrangements. At this time Lennon and McCartney wrote most of their music using two acoustic guitars. Their open-minded acceptance of a wide, eclectic range of influences led the group towards greater sophistication. This can be heard in their guitar work and in instrumental harmony that often contains imaginative chord sequences and an ambiguous tonality.

RECORDINGS 1962–65

The Beatles' first single, "Love Me Do", recorded in June 1962 at Abbey Road Studios, London, is hardly auspicious in terms of guitar. Harrison and Lennon play simple chords strummed on acoustic guitars. There are no melodic fills or solos, and the track has a bare, sparse feeling. It is unrepresentative of the group's instrumental capabilities. The second single, "Please Please Me" (1963), has a driving electric rhythm and harmony that complements the vocal melody line – a hallmark of The Beatles' sound.

During 1963, the group developed the role and sound of the guitars with solos, fills and varied rhythms, using combinations of electric and acoustic instruments. The solos on "I Saw Her Standing There" and "Twist And Shout" are the first Harrison recorded using the electric guitar. The energy and excitement that the group was able to convey comes across on tracks such as "She Loves You" and "I Want To Hold Your Hand". On "All My Loving", Lennon plays a fast-triplet strumming pattern against Harrison's rhythm part that generates a great feeling of energetic exuberance.

In 1964 The Beatles continued to search for tonal colour and soak up influences that expanded and developed their music. At a time when Brazilian composer Antonio Carlos Jobim's music was popular (*see page 219*), The Beatles used steel-string and nylon-string guitar with Latin rhythms. Harrison plays nylon string in the song "And I Love Her", with a solo based on the melody. With electric sounds, "I Feel Fine" begins with feedback, then features a catchy riff with a bright, metallic tone. The haunting "She's A Woman" has a blues-influenced solo, unusual for a Beatles song in this era.

ALBUM DEVELOPMENTS

When the group recorded the album *Help!* in 1965, McCartney emerged as a guitarist as well as a bass player. On "Yesterday" (*see page 131*), he uses fingerstyle on steel-string guitar, playing an attractive chord sequence with moving bass and melody parts. He also plays the repeating opening riff and takes solo breaks on "Ticket To Ride". Harrison continues to play with country-style fills and solos, but contributes more unusual colour with the use of a Leslie speaker cabinet to create an unusual texture on "It's Only Love" and a volume pedal for swell effects on "I Need You".

With the album *Rubber Soul,* recorded during 1965, the group continued to expand into new areas. McCartney plays an innovative

NORTHERN SOUNDS

In the wake of The Beatles came an explosion of new groups from all over the north of England. The Liverpool Merseybeat scene produced groups including Gerry And The Pacemakers whose atmospheric hit, "Ferry Across The Mersey" (1964), has a light guitar figure; in Manchester, The Hollies, with guitarists Graham Nash (*see page 199*) and Tony Hicks, had a string of hits with catchy melodic pop-guitar parts, starting with "(Ain't That) Just Like Me" (1963). The Newcastle group The Animals had a major hit in June 1964 with the traditional song "The House Of The Rising Sun" featuring guitarist Hilton Valentine. His understated, arpeggiated chord progression with Alan Price's organ became one of the most popular and widely played chord sequences for guitarists.

slide solo on "Drive My Car". On "Nowhere Man", Harrison adds bright, shimmering chord fills and a chord melody solo, ending on a high harmonic. "If I Needed Someone" has chiming arpeggiated chords on an electric 12-string, and on "Wait" there are volume-pedal chord swells. The acoustic tracks are just as interesting. On "Norwegian Wood", guitar and sitar melody play in unison. "Girl" sees Harrison and Lennon playing with a mandolin-like sound and a solo in a Greek folk style. The single "Day Tripper", recorded during this highly creative period, opens with one of The Beatles' best-known repeating riffs played by two guitars that are doubling the bass.

GEORGE HARRISON
The sound of Harrison's Rickenbacker can be heard on "Eight Days A Week" and at the beginning of "A Hard Day's Night".

RICKENBACKER 360-12
This instrument was built in December 1963 and given to George Harrison in February 1964 when The Beatles were on their first American tour. The lower four strings have an extra higher-octave string and the top two strings are doubled.

129

THE BEATLES' GUITARS

Harrison and Lennon used electric guitars for their concerts and kept the Gibson J160E electric acoustic and other acoustic guitars for studio use. Lennon used his black Rickenbacker 325 models for all his live work; Harrison used a number of different Gretsch guitars, including the black 1950s Duo Jet that was his main instrument until 1963, when he switched to Country Gentleman and Tennessean models.

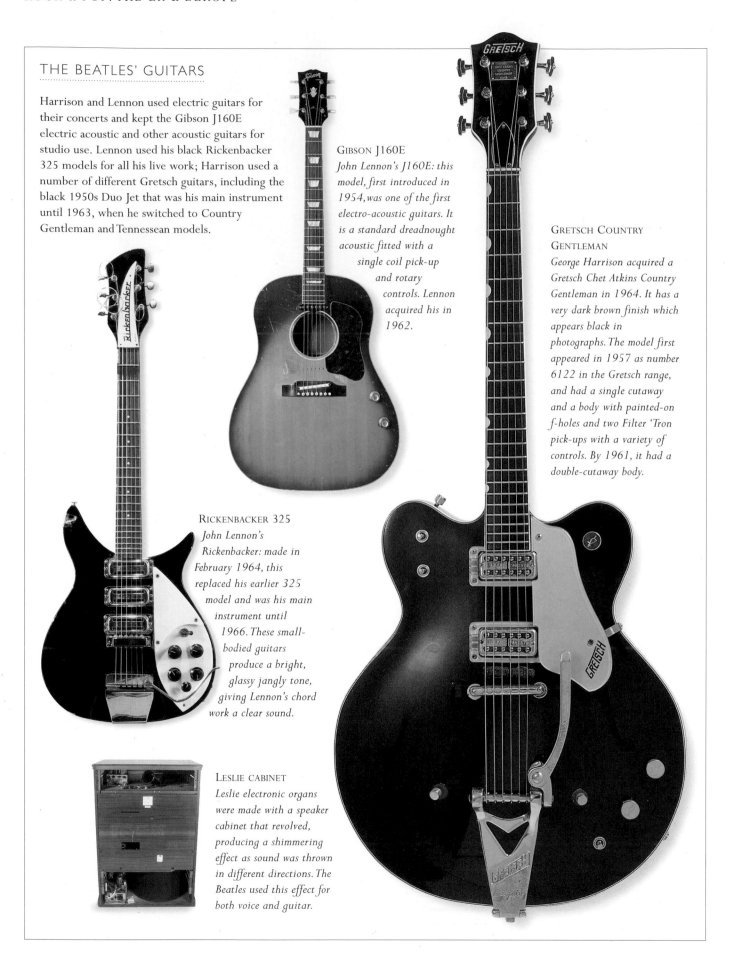

GIBSON J160E
John Lennon's J160E: this model, first introduced in 1954, was one of the first electro-acoustic guitars. It is a standard dreadnought acoustic fitted with a single coil pick-up and rotary controls. Lennon acquired his in 1962.

GRETSCH COUNTRY GENTLEMAN
George Harrison acquired a Gretsch Chet Atkins Country Gentleman in 1964. It has a very dark brown finish which appears black in photographs. The model first appeared in 1957 as number 6122 in the Gretsch range, and had a single cutaway and a body with painted-on f-holes and two Filter 'Tron pick-ups with a variety of controls. By 1961, it had a double-cutaway body.

RICKENBACKER 325
John Lennon's Rickenbacker: made in February 1964, this replaced his earlier 325 model and was his main instrument until 1966. These small-bodied guitars produce a bright, glassy jangly tone, giving Lennon's chord work a clear sound.

LESLIE CABINET
Leslie electronic organs were made with a speaker cabinet that revolved, producing a shimmering effect as sound was thrown in different directions. The Beatles used this effect for both voice and guitar.

"YESTERDAY"

Recorded in June 1965, Paul McCartney's "Yesterday" has a hauntingly beautiful melody with fingerstyle accompaniment using alternating bass notes and strumming on an Epiphone Texan steel-string acoustic guitar. This was tuned down so that McCartney could play certain types of full voicings with easy fingerings in the key of F major. After a two-bar intro, there are unusual bar lengths for the sections and beautiful, mesmeric harmonies with bass movements. The seven-bar verse repeats and a string quartet enters to give flowing support as the song moves to a poignant eight-bar chorus with bars of close voicings and contrary voice movements. The guitar is tuned down a tone to give F major.

"DAY TRIPPER" RIFF

Put down in October 1965, this is one of The Beatles' best-known early riffs. It builds from the first two bars in which Harrison and Lennon together play a long, sinuous bluesy unison line, based on an E pentatonic minor scale, with an added G♯ and upper F♯, and using a strong metallic tone. McCartney joins in on bass, doubling the line from the third bar onward and Lennon adds ringing two- and three-note chords from the fifth bar, backed by the rattling of Ringo Starr's tambourine.

LONDON R&B

While The Beatles' dominance of the pop world was growing, a vibrant music scene based around blues, folk, jazz, rock 'n' roll and R&B was flourishing in and around London. From this creative milieu, many fine guitarists emerged who had a considerable influence on popular music.

In the early 1960s, at London venues such as the Marquee, the Crawdaddy Club, the 21s, Klooks Kleek, Eel Pie Island and the Ealing Club, musicians were able to play and develop compositional and instrumental techniques in a free-flowing, creative atmosphere. Guitarists regularly took part in jam sessions, and a core of musicians played blues, jazz and pop in a small number of important, influential groups. These musicians were led by pioneering figures including Alexis Korner, Graham Bond, Georgie Fame, Zoot Money, Manfred Mann and John Mayall. Of the many fine and talented players who are now overlooked or forgotten, Dick Taylor of the The Pretty Things stands out, as does Mick Green from Johnny Kidd and the Pirates – a guitarist whose muscular style filled out the sound of the group and impressed many young guitarists around London.

hard-edged and rough-sounding, yet blended with a quirky subtlety. Their best early work is represented by a succession of hit singles.

Chuck Berry's "Come On", the group's first single, was recorded at Olympic Studios, London, in May 1963 with unremarkable strummed guitar parts. For their next single, The Stones took Lennon and McCartney's "I Wanna Be Your Man" (1963) – an unlikely choice for a group considered to be the very antithesis of The Beatles.

THE ROLLING STONES

One group who did not sink into obscurity was The Rolling Stones, founded by Mick Jagger and Keith Richards (b.1943) in 1962. With Bill Wyman in place on bass and Charlie Watts on drums, Jagger and Richards added Brian Jones (1942–69) as a second guitarist. From their beginnings as a primitive and undeveloped R&B act, the group evolved to become one of the most inventive and influential groups worldwide. Based around Richards' and Jones' traditional roots approach that combined various elements of black American music, The Stones' sound quickly developed its own unique identity –

ALEXIS KORNER
One of the early British singers and blues guitarists, Alexis Korner (1928–84) worked in several genres before concentrating on blues. He encouraged many players, and influenced the music scene with his recordings, concerts and broadcasts. He worked with harmonica player Cyril Davies from 1955, forming the seminal group Blues Incorporated in 1961. Korner's legendary Ealing Club was a fertile meeting place for young musicians.

BRIAN JONES
Mick Jagger and Keith Richards first heard Brian Jones at London's Marquee club and thought his guitar style sounded like Elmore James. Jones' slide playing and wide range of musical influences added greater range and depth to The Rolling Stones' music, and provided an effective contrast to Keith Richards' sound.

Featuring a screaming, distorted solo, the recording includes slide guitar that adds a colourful, textural undertow. With the recording of "Not Fade Away" (1964), the group explored 1950s pop and rock elements. Here, an acoustic guitar plays a Bo Diddley-type rhythm groove (*see page 179*).

At an early stage, The Stones recorded material at Chess Studios in Chicago – a location that undoubtedly affected their approach. Here, and at other recording studios, the band created a unique group identity by recording their own workings of American songs. The imaginative soul number "It's All Over Now" (1964), for instance, contains two contrasting guitar parts recorded with echo and reverb. The song is arranged with arpeggiated chords set against passages of sustained staccato chords leading to an intense rock 'n' roll-style solo. More traditional material such as "Little Red Rooster" (1964) highlights Brian Jones' quizzical slide phrases in answer to the vocal line.

When Jagger and Richards began writing their own songs, the group further developed their instrumental ideas and techniques. "The Last Time" (1965) features Brian Jones' infectious, repeating blues riff played across Richards' chordal rhythm and overdubbed fills. "Satisfaction" (1965) finds Keith Richards experimenting with a fuzz pedal – an effects unit pioneered in America and Britain by studio players – to mimic a sustained brass riff.

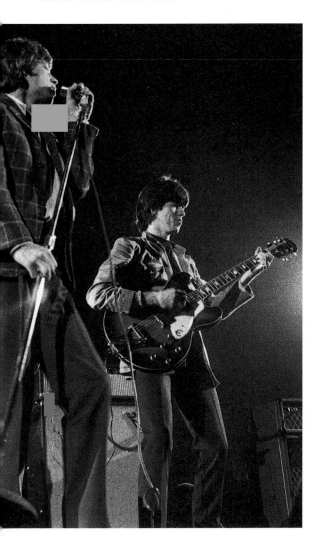

SESSION PLAYERS

Mainstream pop groups and those playing R&B and blues comprised only part of the guitar world. Behind the scenes, many fine players were working, including Vic Flick, who recorded "The James Bond Theme" (1962), and the outstanding Big Jim Sullivan, a top session guitarist who played for many artists and featured on hundreds of records. He was also a pioneer in the use of effects, such as fuzz, which he used on P. J. Proby's "Hold Me" (1964). Through his live appearances in pubs and clubs in the 1960s, Albert Lee also made a big impression on guitarists. Although one of the few country-influenced virtuoso guitar players in Britain, he was largely unknown to the general public. In the mid 1960s, he worked with Chris Farlowe and the Thunderbirds.

VOX MK. VI
Brian Jones acquired his Vox Mk. VI guitar in 1964. With its teardrop-shaped body and matching headstock finished in white, this seductive guitar has become an icon of the 1960s. While Brian Jones' own guitar had two pick-ups and a Fender bridge, Vox launched their commercial model with three pick-ups, a standard bridge and tremolo unit, and a plain, unpainted wooden headstock.

The raw power of Jagger/Richards' "Get Off Of My Cloud" (1965) represents a move toward a heavier, more rocky sound. Here, the energetic rhythmic strumming, backed by emphatic drums, is played with a distorted sound and a gritty edge. Opening with bright and clipped guitar figures, "19th Nervous Breakdown" (1966) contains rough, somewhat destabilizing guitar rhythm parts, as well as some colourful, emotional guitar fills.

ERIC CLAPTON

Eric Clapton (b.1945) has become the most prominent guitarist to emerge from Britain. One of the first to play with a strong, electric-blues soloing style, he soon developed a distinctive identity characterized by well-balanced, melodic phrasing played with verve, self-assurance and precise intonation.

At an early stage, Clapton's playing integrated elements from differing blues styles, including those of Big Bill Broonzy, Robert Johnson, Muddy Waters and, later, Freddie King (*see pages 49–56*). In 1963, Clapton joined R&B group The Yardbirds. His distinctive finger vibrato, note sustain and expressive, upper-register string bending can be heard on *Five Live Yardbirds* (1964), recorded at London's Marquee, and on the single "Good Morning Little Schoolgirl" backed by "I Ain't Got You". Early in 1965, Clapton decided to leave the group after the melodic, original pop single "For Your Love" was released with his guitar sidelined by other instruments, including a harpsichord. The B-side features a showcase for his blues soloing, the instrumental "Got To Hurry", recorded at the end of 1964; it brought him to the attention of John Mayall.

GIBSON LES PAUL
When The Rolling Stones toured America in 1964, Keith Richards acquired a guitar then considered unfashionable — a Gibson Les Paul Standard. He became the first high-profile pop artist to use a Les Paul in Britain. The guitar was used in the hit "Satisfaction" (1965), along with a fuzz pedal.

ERIC CLAPTON
At the start of his career, Eric Clapton, seen far right of Keith Relph in The Yardbirds, saw himself as a purist and distanced himself from the lighter side of British pop music. He worked hard to develop as a serious and expressive instrumentalist.

ROCK & PSYCHEDELIA

During 1964, developments took place that would shape the course of guitar playing and broaden its role. Increased volume, distortion and greater tonal colour made the instrument more effective in an age of unfettered creativity in Britain, and stylistic boundaries were broken.

The Kinks' 1964 single "You Really Got Me" marked a decisive move toward the raw power of rock by a group who wanted to convey emotional intensity. The track has a rough, aggressive edge and an earthy excitement, featuring two-chord motifs throughout. Played by Ray Davies (b.1944), these distinctive chords have a stark sound and strong rhythmic attack; brother Dave Davies (b.1947) added an anarchic solo. The torn abrasiveness of the chords on The Kinks' following single, "All Day And All Of The Night" (1964), has a similar quality. Here, the guitar's broken, distorted sound was achieved by playing through an amplifier driven to the limit.

PETE TOWNSHEND

While The Kinks were enjoying their first chart success, a group was emerging who would play a much greater role in shaping the style of guitar playing, backed by a powerful rhythm section, now termed rock. Although Pete Townshend (b.1945) originally played jazz, he turned to pop to express himself. He had an emphatic and dynamic approach, and felt that emulating American blues players was not artistically valid. It was with singer Roger Daltrey (b.1944), bass player John Entwistle (b.1944) and drummer Keith Moon (1947–78) that Townshend found his ideal vehicle in The Who, essentially a trio plus vocalist. He filled the sound and gave the group weight by using high volume and a heavy, chordal style as a backdrop for his compositions – The Who's early records often feature chordal breaks with few linear solos.

On The Who's first single, "I Can't Explain" (1964), Townshend's guitar has a terse edginess with its opening staccato chords and chordal solo breaks. The innovative single "Anyway, Anyhow, Anywhere" (1965) moves from an opening that uses flamenco-style strumming into an explosive, crashing, distorted sound.

POP INNOVATIONS

The Kinks' songs played an important part in the development of pop music in Britain. The group experimented with sound and structure, using a surprising range of chord voicings, tonal colour and dynamic level. The arpeggiated opening and chord slides on "Tired Of Waiting For You" (1965) are a distinctive part of the group's sound. The gentle, flowing harmonies of "Set Me Free" (1965) move to contrasting, driving chords that build to points at which tension is released. "See My Friend" (1965) is unusual in its use of a repetitive, mesmeric twelve-string drone chord in the main sections. The Kinks' sardonic humour and theatricality is evident on "Dedicated Follower Of Fashion" (1966). A phased opening lends depth to the beginning and, as the vocal enters, a contrastingly dry and rattling acoustic guitar rhythm supports colourful electric overdubs.

THE KINKS
Ray and Dave Davies produced clever and subtle guitar parts that enhanced some of the best tracks in British pop. Ray Davies wrote the majority of the songs and played rhythm guitar; Dave Davies added guitar solos and fills. Often quirky and characterful, their instrumental work is highly effective as an added part to the vocal line in their arrangements.

EARLY WHO

Pete Townshend was one of the first British musicians to use amplifiers from Jim Marshall's shop in West London. He pioneered the use of 100-watt heads to produce volume distortion and feedback, and led the way in generating a forceful projection of power.

PHYSICAL EXPRESSION

At live performances, The Who often built songs to a climax with noise and chaos, Townshend sometimes destroying his guitars. With acrobatic energy, he would rotate his right arm, smashing his hand against the strings with violent physicality. His aggressive showmanship, however, was tempered with humour — "We never let the music get in the way of our stage act".

The early use of feedback, added noise, pick scrapes and level fluctuations prompted the record company to send the tape back, assuming mistakes had been made in recording.

The brooding, powerful intensity of "My Generation" (1965) is derived from Townshend's use of simple chordal elements with a biting, rhythmic edge that were to become his hallmark. With alternating bass and pithy guitar breaks, the track modulates upward and ends with exuberant drum fills interweaving with guitar feedback.

Townshend's use of distortion and high volume caused him to adopt voicings using roots and fifths without thirds, to give a clearer, less muddy sound. In the studio, he started to use steel-string guitar against a heavy rhythm section, to great effect. "Substitute" (1966)

opens with a steel-string guitar intro that leads into a heavily strummed pattern played over the rhythm section. The song features a chordal break in which the group stops playing behind the guitar, to add poignancy.

Overall, Townshend broadened the effectiveness of the guitar with his high-volume, textural contrasts and emphatic chord playing with the rhythm section.

JEFF BECK

Jeff Beck (b.1944) is an outstandingly talented guitarist with a gifted musical imagination. His work bridges melodic playing styles and experimental concepts. An individualistic player, Beck's early influences include classical music, blues and the sophisticated melodiousness of Les Paul, Cliff Gallup (see page 181) and others. Early live recordings of Jeff Beck with The Tridents from 1964 reveal his well-established elliptical soloing and expressive sensitivity.

In February 1965, Beck replaced Eric Clapton in The Yardbirds, and his surprising touches and pioneering work in the use of tone, fuzz and distortion added a sense of suspense and a thoughtful intelligence. "Heart Full Of Soul" (1965) was Beck's first single with them. It had been recorded unsuccessfully with sitar, and he re-recorded it with guitar. The result is an unusual, effective Indian-style sound.

Other early recordings further reveal Beck's versatile and interesting playing. The heavy-rock riff on "I'm Not Talkin'" (1965) is an early approach to the type of distorted guitar that became highly popular in later years. The thematic slide solo on "Evil Hearted You" (1965) shows another side to his playing, and "Shapes Of Things" (1965) combines sinuous phrasing with colourful distortion and feedback. Beck makes the guitar sound unfamiliar on "Over Under Sideways Down" (1966). Here, he mimics the sound of an Islamic shawm by adjusting tone settings and playing legato in the upper register. His instrumental twelve-bar "Jeff's Boogie" (1966) also features unusual touches: harmonized lines, melodic phrases played with a tremolo bar, fast hammering, muted string sounds and harmonics.

After Jimmy Page (see page 154) joined The Yardbirds in 1966, the group recorded "Happenings Ten Years Time Ago" (1966). This inventive single includes a chaotic interlude in which guitars simulate crash sounds. The B-side, "Psycho Daisies", is also distinctive for its metallic, hard-edged rhythm.

NEW SOUNDS

In the mid 1960s, a few guitarists stepped beyond accepted boundaries. Steve Marriott, for example, develops a wild sonic interlude instead of playing a conventional solo on The Small Faces' "Watcha Gonna Do About It?" (1965). Eddie Phillips with The Creation uses clashing harmonies, feedback and a violin bow on groundbreaking singles such as "Painter Man" (1966).

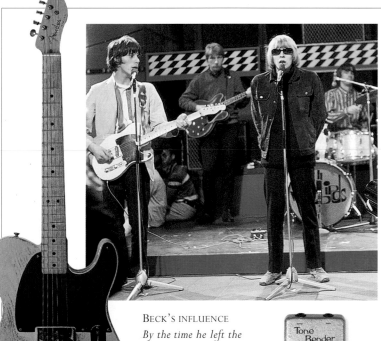

THE SOUND OF THE YARDBIRDS

One of Jeff Beck's main equipment combinations in The Yardbirds was a Fender Esquire or Fender Telecaster with a Vox AC30 amplifier. He also used the amplifier's Top Boost circuit and a Tone Bender fuzz unit to enhance the tone. This set-up gave his guitar a great deal of sustain and a singularly penetrating, electrifying sound. When recording in the studio, Beck often used other guitars, including a Fender Jazzmaster and a Gibson Les Paul.

BECK'S INFLUENCE
By the time he left the band in November 1966, Beck had helped to lay part of the groundwork for modern rock. His range of skills and imagination set him apart from his contemporaries.

Fender Esquire

Tone Bender

Vox AC30

REVOLVER

The Beatles recorded *Revolver* between April and June 1966 at Abbey Road Studios in London. Although there is no clear point of transition in The Beatles' music, *Revolver* represents an important stage in their musical evolution. Evident on the album are classical influences, and a wide range of instruments are used, including a string quartet, sitar, tablas, organ, brass, piano and harpsichord. Although the guitar work on *Revolver* is often scintillating, some of the finest tracks are not guitar-based, although guitar is often somewhere in the mix. Geoff Emerick was brought in as engineer, and studio techniques and effects included stereo, reverb, echo, compression, Leslie speaker cabinet, microphone placement, pioneering work with the development of artificial double tracking (ADT), and the use of flanging. During the production process, tapes of recorded guitar were played backward and at different speeds. Some tracks needed many takes – more than ten-hours' work were spent on some of the more experimental pieces.

TAXMAN (Harrison)
George Harrison's crunching, electric-guitar chordal rhythm based on simple harmonies, and the track's count-in, give this opening number a live feel. Paul McCartney plays two short fuzz-guitar solo fills that have an exotic, almost Oriental flavour.

ELEANOR RIGBY (Lennon/McCartney)
One of the few tracks to be recorded without guitar. The arrangements for two string quartets were written by George Martin, whose influences include the work of composer Bernard Herrmann.

I'M ONLY SLEEPING (Lennon/McCartney)
John Lennon plays a rhythmic chordal accompaniment with a steel-string acoustic guitar. The track features reverse

electric-guitar tape fills, a short reverse solo and a fadeout section. It took up to six hours to work out a guitar part, write it backward, and then record it and reverse the tape. Fuzz and clear, unprocessed guitar tracks were also laid down for this song.

LOVE YOU TO (Harrison)
Early takes of "Love You To" show George Harrison singing to his own acoustic guitar accompaniment. With the addition of sitar and tablas, the song was developed into an arrangement that conveys impressions of India and Eastern religions. Electric guitar is used for background additions to add layering to the drone effects.

HERE, THERE AND EVERYWHERE (Lennon/McCartney)
This track has an attractive electric chordal accompaniment, and a flowing, scalar harmonic sequence. The short fill is played by a processed guitar through a Leslie speaker cabinet.

YELLOW SUBMARINE (Lennon/McCartney)
The steel-string guitar strummed chord accompaniment on "Yellow Submarine" is played by John Lennon.

SHE SAID SHE SAID (Lennon/McCartney)
John Lennon plays jangling and inventive rhythm guitar on a song that has bars of 3/4 time. George Harrison's opening fuzz lead-guitar line, recorded with a swirling Leslie cabinet effect, is a quote from the vocal melody.

GOOD DAY SUNSHINE (Lennon/McCartney)
One of the finest tracks on *Revolver*, dominated by piano and other instruments, the background guitar chords are low in the mix.

AND YOUR BIRD CAN SING (Lennon/McCartney)
This has one of The Beatles' most original and distinctive guitar riffs, played with harmonized parts and a coruscating, distorted-fuzz tone.

FOR NO ONE (Lennon/McCartney)
A beautiful and haunting song, with the famous horn solo by Alan Civil, this is one of two tracks on *Revolver* without any audible guitar.

DOCTOR ROBERT (Lennon/McCartney)
This song has a chopped, off-beat rhythm. The interlocking guitar parts are a typical feature of The Beatles' music. The number features country-style fills played with two-note chords – often referred to as double-stopping.

I WANT TO TELL YOU (Harrison)
This Harrison song starts with a fadeup into an opening melodic riff that has a clear, twangy sound with reverb. It is one of the few parts on the album with an unprocessed sound, and is a highly compelling feature.

GOT TO GET YOU INTO MY LIFE (Lennon/McCartney)
The brass arrangement influenced by American soul dominates this song. George Harrison added electric chordal overdubs toward the end of the recording sessions to build the song to a climax.

TOMORROW NEVER KNOWS (Lennon/McCartney)
With its drone feel and repeating bass figure, this track has an Indian flavour similar to "Love You To". There are short guitar fills with an unusual sound. The latter part of the instrumental break includes the solo from "Taxman", but cut up, looped, slowed down so that it drops a tone, and played backward.

THE BEATLES 1965–67

During the period in which The Beatles recorded the album *Revolver*, they also put down the single "Paperback Writer", which John Lennon referred to as "Son of Day Tripper" because it is based around a distinctive guitar riff. The innovative and psychedelic B-side, "Rain", has a drone-like sound with resonant chiming guitars.

With the recording of "Strawberry Fields Forever" at the end of 1966, The Beatles moved further toward a style that created atmospheric, other-worldly dreamscapes. On this song, the guitar is used for arpeggiated fills, and the track includes touches such as an extended trill and processed, single-note sounds for effect. In contrast, the lighter and optimistic singles "Penny Lane" and "When I'm Sixty-Four" (the latter recorded for the forthcoming album) use very little guitar. This approach was indicative of the varied role the guitar was to play in The Beatles' music during 1967.

At this time, The Beatles were radically altering the function of the guitar in their music. Although partly a gradual evolution, there is undoubtedly a shift toward an increasingly introspective and sometimes dark philosophical mood in the music after the group stopped touring in 1966. With time on their hands, all the members reinvented the way in which they wrote and approached music. As a result, the guitar was no longer tied to the conventional role of playing chords, solos and melodic additions.

MAGICAL MYSTERY TOUR

In 1967, having completed *Sgt. Pepper's Lonely Hearts Club Band* (*see page 140*), The Beatles recorded some singles and the *Magical Mystery Tour* EP that continued the style developed in the *Sgt. Pepper* sessions. The single "Hello Goodbye", for instance, features characterful, distorted melodic riffs and expressive, single-note descending slurs with fuzz. Acoustic guitar underpins "Magical Mystery Tour" and "The Fool On The Hill", and electric overdubs add rhythmic elements and sonorous fills, while the unusual instrumental twelve-bar "Flying" sees George Harrison playing raked two- and three-note fills with a strong tremolo effect.

DEVELOPING SONGS
In 1966, while The Beatles were concentrating on writing and recording, they began to put the guitar into a more textural role, increasingly layering it with other instruments.

"AND YOUR BIRD CAN SING"

Recorded in April 1966 and played by Harrison with either Lennon or McCartney, this is an eight-bar break with attractive classical-style phrases in E major. It is composed of two bright distorted guitar parts playing the same phrases rhythmically with predominantly diatonic parallel thirds and sixths, and distinctive bending in three places. Four bars are used for the intro. It occurs twice in the song and is used again at the end.

SGT. PEPPER'S LONELY HEARTS CLUB BAND

One of the greatest albums in popular music, *Sgt. Pepper's Lonely Hearts Club Band* (1967) marked a further move by The Beatles toward experimentation and complexity. During the recording process from late 1966 until 1967, The Beatles spent 129 days in the studio. Tracks on the album often segue into each other, heightening the strong contrasts in mood and expression. In guitar terms, it is a deceptive album: the instrument being apparently sidelined, not often heard as a prominent component. In fact, The Beatles asked the studio production team to process and specially treat the guitar to make it sound unfamiliar or even unrecognizable. Songs on the album often do not rely on the instrument for harmonic support and, unlike virtually all The Beatles' other albums, *Sgt. Pepper's Lonely Hearts Club Band* contains few guitar-based highlights. Yet, although the arrangements appear to be dominated by the presence of other instruments, the guitar is often in the mix in an unfamiliar guise.

SGT. PEPPER'S LONELY HEARTS CLUB BAND
(Lennon/McCartney)
The opening track is exciting and atmospheric, managing to create the illusion of a live concert. In contrast to the album as a whole, the guitar parts here by Paul McCartney are conventional and engaging. McCartney plays straightforward rock guitar with a distorted, fuzz sound. At the beginning, broken chords and a swirling distorted riff with shaking, upper-register notes give way to the vocal.

WITH A LITTLE HELP FROM MY FRIENDS
(Lennon/McCartney)
As the opening track fades, this song opens with swooping glissandos on descending harmonies. Under the vocal, the guitar plays staccato chords, and there is a push-pull rhythm effect in the arrangement, with added, processed fills for colour.

LUCY IN THE SKY WITH DIAMONDS
(Lennon/McCartney)
On a song evoking a surrealistic landscape, the guitar stays in the background and merges into a kaleidoscopic soundfield. This contains electric keyboards and other instruments recorded with effects processing, such as Leslie speaker, varispeed, echo and reverb.

GETTING BETTER (Lennon/McCartney)
This has an uplifting, positive feel, partly provided by rhythmic guitar. It opens with two guitars playing simple, chopped staccato chords, juxtaposing octaves and chords. Typically, The Beatles are rhythmically subtle and mix metronomic and lilting, swing-feel beats. The parts shift emphasis harmonically and sound unresolved. This keeps the momentum and holds the song in a taut framework. The two-note descending countermelody provides an attractive addition to the vocal line, and the guitar has a range of interesting, muted tonal colours.

FIXING A HOLE (Lennon/McCartney)
A good balance is produced on this track with guitar chords masked by harpsichord. There are attractive passages of gliding, two-note fills. On the short, out-of-phase double-tracked solo, Harrison's playing has a fuzz sound and functions as a contrast to the vocal melody.

SHE'S LEAVING HOME
(Lennon/McCartney)
One of the finest songs on the album, supported by string parts, and the only track without guitar.

BEING FOR THE BENEFIT OF MR KITE!
(Lennon/McCartney)
With its recreation of a burlesque, circus atmosphere, "Being For The Benefit Of Mr Kite!" is a complex track that includes ambiguous harmonies produced by a range of unusual instruments. Guitar elements on the track are kept in the background.

WITHIN YOU WITHOUT YOU (Harrison)
Dominated by Indian instruments and strings, acoustic guitar can be heard in the background on this track.

WHEN I'M SIXTY FOUR
(Lennon/McCartney)
This song is not based around guitar chords. Toward the end of the track, there are almost indiscernible, and humourous, country-style guitar fills.

LOVELY RITA (Lennon/McCartney)
A schmaltzy, rollercoaster feel is achieved with dry, metallic-sounding acoustic steel-string guitar chords. These lighten the song and give it an optimistic feel.

GOOD MORNING, GOOD MORNING
(Lennon/McCartney)
The swirling, fuzzy guitar solo and exotic fills that have an iridescent tone add lift to "Good Morning, Good Morning". The track keeps guitar chords low in the mix.

SGT. PEPPER'S LONELY HEARTS CLUB BAND
(Reprise) (Lennon/McCartney)
Although similar to the opening track, this reprise opens with heavier guitars and has short fills that answer the vocal. It segues into the last track.

A DAY IN THE LIFE (Lennon/McCartney)
At the beginning of this track, the guitar is heard on its own for the first time on the album. With its beautiful, haunting acoustic chord sequence played by John Lennon, the song gradually builds, with piano and bass. By way of contrast, the dreamy, contemplative mood switches to a section by Paul McCartney in which the guitar creates a hurrying effect with a muted rhythm before returning to the first section.

SYD BARRETT WITH PINK FLOYD

The music of this period has been described as psychedelic. Science fiction, mythology and mysticism infuse the music with colour and rich harmonies, and effects conjure up dream-like soundscapes. In this era, the guitar was used to create unusual sounds, which can be heard on recordings by emerging "underground" groups who saw themselves as developing outside the pop mainstream. The early Pink Floyd with Syd Barrett (b.1946) were figureheads of this new scene.

From the beginning, Syd Barrett took an uncompromising approach to the guitar, as can be heard on the group's second single, "See Emily Play" (1967), with its strange slide effects, featuring huge echo and reverb, passages of soaring sustain and sparkling, high-register additions.

At the end of The Beatles' *Sgt. Pepper's Lonely Hearts Club Band* sessions, Pink Floyd started recording their debut album *Piper At The Gates Of Dawn* (1967) at Abbey Road Studios in London. On this album, Barrett's work is often derived from a conceptual approach that avoids clichés, and he proves himself adept at placing familiar elements in unusual contexts. His playing shows the influence of players from the avant-garde comtemporary (London) scene. Although Barrett's guitar parts are sometimes dissonant, he often conjures up soft, drifting harmonies. He uses a clear guitar sound with a great deal of echo and reverb, as well as feedback and sound effects, partly created by

using the volume and tone controls. Effects are used inventively, and pick scrapes and noises on the body of the instrument are combined with atonal passages. There are disconcerting mood shifts, from twangy, melodic riffs to other-worldly sonic explorations, and the guitar often has a voice of prophetic grandeur. The album's opening track, "Astronomy Domine", has unexpected harmonic shifts, pulsating rhythmic crosscurrents and see-sawing, high-register elements. "Interstellar Overdrive", with a dirge-like riff and chaotic passages of free-form improvisation, is one of the most unusual and advanced instrumental tracks in 1960s pop.

SYD BARRETT

A visionary pop songwriter, Barrett used the guitar for harmony and colourful touches. His songs often feature sharp, acidic electric chords and further layered elements, with echo and sustain in all registers.

PINK FLOYD

Not so much a band, more a collection of creative individualists: with Roger Waters on bass, Rick Wright on keyboards and Nick Mason on drums, Syd Barrett's playing is often set against an unconventional backdrop.

PSYCHEDELIA

In this period, many groups moved toward a visionary, atmospheric music. With tracks such as "2000 Light Years From Home" (1967), The Stones produced music totally out of character with their roots influences. Groups who had paved the way for innovation recorded some of their best work. The Kinks' "Waterloo Sunset" (1967) is built on laconic strumming on steel-string guitar and catchy electric melodic figures with echo. On The Who's "I Can See For Miles" (1967), Pete Townshend combines many of these elements to build excitement using overdubbed parts with shimmering electric and acoustic guitars over a pedal tone. This leads to a provocative solo — he controls just one note to produce swelling movement.

ERIC CLAPTON

The growing enthusiasm for the guitar in Britain in the 1960s led to its widespread adoption. Guitarists were greatly admired and a generation was ready to embrace a guitar hero. Although many pop instrumentalists were inventive, it was Eric Clapton who fired the imagination.

In April 1965, Eric Clapton replaced Roger Dean in John Mayall's Bluesbreakers. Multi-instrumentalist and singer, Mayall was a key figure in the development of electric blues in Britain. Shortly after Clapton joined, the group recorded the single "I'm Your Witchdoctor" with the B-side "Telephone Blues". After touring with the group for a few months, and absorbing a broad range of ideas, Clapton recorded the album *Blues Breakers – With Eric Clapton* in April 1966 at Decca's West Hampstead studio.

A confidence and maturity within the blues idiom is clearly evident on the album, and on certain tracks Clapton demonstrates his influences. Although "All Your Love" by Otis Rush is similar to Rush's original 1958 recording, there is a clutch of outstanding instrumentals. Freddie King's "Hideaway", for instance, contains a variety of sounds with strong finger vibrato, and a sweet tone contrasting with passages of broken, distorted chords. "Steppin' Out" is marked by a muscular, expressive riff and a powerful solo with string bending and sustain. John Mayall's own compositions "Have You Heard" and "Key To Love" also feature exceptional guitar solos and fills that incorporate soaring bends, trills, vibrato, distortion and hammer-ons and pull-offs. On "What I'd Say", Clapton suddenly inserts The Beatles' "Day Tripper" riff, which he plays with great verve and assurance.

BLUESBREAKING
On Blues Breakers – With Eric Clapton, *Clapton was backed by a tight, driving rhythm section made up of John Mayall on Hammond organ, John McVie on bass and Hughie Flint on drums. Brass was added on tracks such as "Key To Love".*

CLAPTON WITH CREAM

In the summer of 1966, Cream were formed with Eric Clapton, bass player and vocalist Jack Bruce and drummer Ginger Baker. Comprising three strong instrumentalists with a tremendous reputation, Cream was one of the first line-ups to be termed a "supergroup". They recorded their debut single "Wrapping Paper" in July 1966 and started putting down tracks for their first album, *Fresh Cream*, which was recorded in London. This material marked an important step in the development of pop music – Cream played blues covers, featuring Clapton working within a familiar framework, as well as innovative compositions by Bruce. At this time, they evolved a new musical landscape in which Bruce and Baker worked with the sophistication of a jazz rhythm section – the bass often playing countermelodies and the drums using a variety of fills and African elements. Above this rhythm section, Clapton's distinctive, high-powered, searing, vocalized electric-blues style established him as a key figure in the genre.

FRESH CREAM

On *Fresh Cream*, Cream's first album, the group forged a new style of sophisticated rock. "I Feel Free" features distorted guitar playing rhythmically with the bass and drums. "N.S.U." opens with arpeggiated chords and switches to an emphasis on the upbeat with driving power. The two Baker compositions "Sweet Wine" and "Toad" have simple and effective riffs, harmonies and rhythms. On many tracks, all members freely contribute to the structure of the music and interact effectively. As a result, Clapton's solos start to move away from a conservative blues style toward an extended improvisational melodiousness. The lengthy version of Skip James' "I'm So Glad" typifies the direction in which the group was moving.

THE BLUESBREAKERS' SOUND

In 1965, Eric Clapton started using a Gibson Les Paul Standard guitar with a Marshall 1962 2x12" Combo amplifier with KT 66 output valves. This combination of guitar and amplifier enabled Clapton to produce a thick-textured, rich, overdriven sound. On the *Blues Breakers* album, the instrumental "Hideaway" is stunningly effective. Clapton's *tour de force* playing soars above the group with the help of this type of equipment, which projects his rhythmic control and phrasing. Clapton's use of guitar and amplifier at this time was an important breakthrough in the development of blues rock guitar and many guitarists decided to emulate his sound.

Gibson Les Paul Standard

IN THE STUDIO
With producer Mike Vernon and engineer Gus Dudgeon, Clapton insisted on recording his guitar at a very high, "live" volume. Not a normal procedure at the time, this approach to recording gave his sound a great intensity and immediacy. Soaring sustain and distortion add an extra edge to his riffs and solos.

Marshall 1962 2x12" Combo amplifier

Evident on *Disraeli Gears* (1967), Cream's second album, is a wider range of progressive rock and folk influences. "Strange Brew" sounds like psychedelic pop with Stax blues. Inspired by Jimi Hendrix, Jack Bruce wrote the album's "Sunshine Of Your Love", a seminal track containing one of the most popular guitar riffs of the 1960s. *Disraeli Gears* also shows Clapton's development toward new sound textures, including wah-wah breaks on "On Tales Of Brave Ulysses", distorted and sound-processed playing on "Swablr", wah-wah chords

on "World Of Pain" and an Oriental-style solo on "Dance The Night Away".

Wheels Of Fire (1968), a double-album comprising one live disc recorded in America and a studio disc, features one of the 1960s most popular guitar solos. The live take on "Crossroads", based on Robert Johnson's "Cross Road Blues" (*see page 144*), finds Clapton playing an inspired solo with waves of climaxes and tension-release phrasing — a style that is a hallmark of his playing. In the studio recordings, Clapton's brooding, atmospheric

"CROSSROADS" SOLO

"Crossroads", based on Robert Johnson's "Cross Road Blues" (1936), was a regular part of Cream's live repertoire. It is a standard three-chord, repeating twelve-bar form, but the opening riff on Cream's version is not part of Johnson's original, and they play it in A and keep it within a controlled framework. It became a highly effective vehicle for Clapton as a soloist, and one of the high points of blues-rock soloing. Clapton takes two solo breaks, building up from a measured melodiousness to an intense, driving climax on the second break.

GIBSON SG STANDARD
Acquired by Eric Clapton not long after he lost his original Les Paul in 1966, this was painted in the psychedelic style by a group of Dutch artists known as The Fool. It was modified by the removal of the vibrato unit, and used by Clapton for the "Crossroads" solo, recorded at Winterland in San Francisco in March 1968, that can be heard on Cream's Wheels Of Fire *double album (1968).*

"CROSSROADS" RIFF

a three-note A-block chord with roots and a fifth is played with a distorted sound and leads to a bluesy riff dropping to a C and back to the root

the D chord has a broken, arpeggiated effect

the note C is bent upward to get a bluesy sound throughout

the E chords are played with roots and fifths

there is a slide up to the note E, and Clapton plays three bars of open improvisation over the chords before his vocal enters power sets off "White Room", on which he uses distortion, sound processing and wah wah for fills and soloing. "Politician" contains a stark riff with two interweaving melodic blues solos using overdubs. Clapton uses acoustic guitar very effectively for rhythm and colour on "Deserted Cities Of The Heart" and "As You Said". Highlights of the album are the traditional songs "Sitting On Top Of The World", with its distorted blues playing, and "Born Under A Bad Sign", on which Clapton plays a melodic solo.

Goodbye Cream (1969) was released shortly after Cream split in 1968, with one of

Clapton's most inventive solos on the live "I'm So Glad". "Badge", featuring George Harrison playing a distinctive, arpeggiated figure, sees Clapton adding fills with tasteful string bending. These differing tracks sum up Clapton's career with Cream, showing his ability to bridge blues and progressive rock and pop.

GIBSON FIREBIRD 1
Eric Clapton continually searched for a Gibson guitar that would give him the type of sound he wanted. He used a Gibson Firebird 1 toward the end of the 1960s.

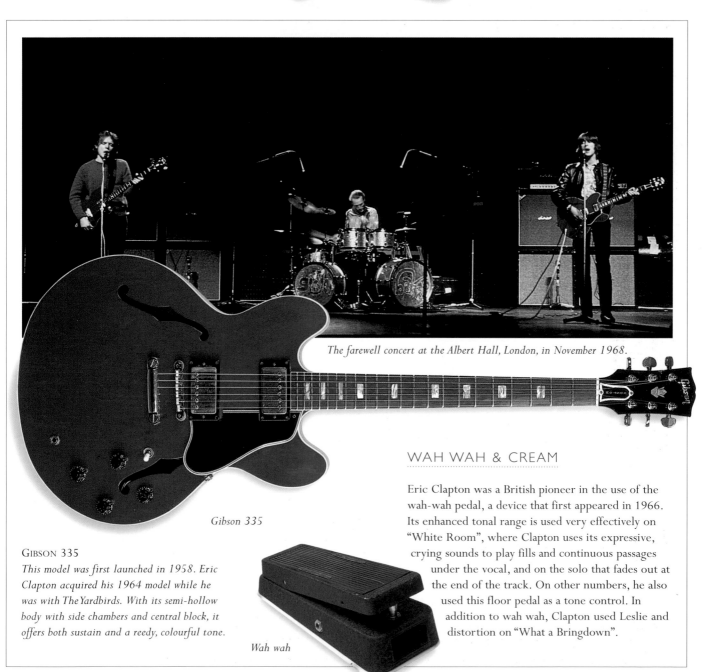

The farewell concert at the Albert Hall, London, in November 1968.

Gibson 335

GIBSON 335
This model was first launched in 1958. Eric Clapton acquired his 1964 model while he was with The Yardbirds. With its semi-hollow body with side chambers and central block, it offers both sustain and a reedy, colourful tone.

Wah wah

WAH WAH & CREAM

Eric Clapton was a British pioneer in the use of the wah-wah pedal, a device that first appeared in 1966. Its enhanced tonal range is used very effectively on "White Room", where Clapton uses its expressive, crying sounds to play fills and continuous passages under the vocal, and on the solo that fades out at the end of the track. On other numbers, he also used this floor pedal as a tone control. In addition to wah wah, Clapton used Leslie and distortion on "What a Bringdown".

PETER GREEN

An individualist who enjoyed a short period of incandescent creativity, Peter Green was one of the most talented musicians to emerge in Britain. Although inspired by the blues, his music has originality and a personal, introspective quality, and reveals a diverse range of influences.

Following the departure of Eric Clapton, Peter Green (b.1946) joined John Mayall's Bluesbreakers in July 1966. He is featured on the album *A Hard Road* (1967), recorded in October 1966, on which he displays an uncommon sensitivity and melodiousness. He approaches Freddie King's "The Stumble" (*see page 56*) with his highly original touch and sound, and idiosyncratic timing. His composition "The Supernatural" looks forward to the arrangements he was later to develop with his own group, Peter Green's Fleetwood Mac. After *A Hard Road*, one of the highlights of his career is "Greeny", the instrumental on which he displays astonishing tonal variety and delicate fragility as he reaches for expressive phrases.

Peter Green's Fleetwood Mac, formed in 1967, consisted of ex-Bluesbreakers Mick Fleetwood on drums and John McVie (b.1945) on bass, with Jeremy Spencer (b.1948) on guitar. They started recording in the autumn of 1967, working alongside American blues artists. Adding a third guitarist, Danny Kirwan (b.1950) in 1968, the group went on to develop their finest material around Green's compositions and arrangements.

With the supportive interplay of the other guitarists, Green's vocals and guitar solos are showcased on "Black Magic Woman" (1968). Beginning with a shimmering three-note chord played with vibrato, this composition features a tasteful and emotional melodic solo using expressive string bending and arpeggio motifs. His understated melodic sensitivity can also be heard on traditional material such as Little Willie John's "Need Your Love So Bad", in which short guitar phrases play a counterpart to Green's heartfelt vocal.

Green often used reverb to position musical elements and set moods. On the instrumental "Albatross" (1968), gently strummed chords, high-register lines, and mellifluous slide are mixed to produce a dream-like instrumental with underlying mesmeric bass and cymbals.

In one of Green's most personal songs, "Man Of The World" (1969), the guitar parts are carefully layered and arranged. It opens with folk-style fingerpicking on steel-string guitar chords with nylon-string fills, and breaks into rhythm with electric guitar and additional background elements.

Green finally left the group he founded in 1971. His 1970 solo album, *The End Of The Road,* has an appropriate title for an outstanding artist who was unable fully to concentrate on music again for some time.

PETER GREEN
A soulful, intuitive, and expressive player, Peter Green's music has a timeless beauty. His compositions juxtapose harmonies with riffs in simple and unusual combinations in which individual parts are often formally arranged to create atmospheric backdrops.

"OH WELL"

"Oh Well" (1969) parts 1 and 2 was one of the most original singles to chart during the 1960s. With over nine minutes of music, it is built around differing sections that reveal contrasting moods. It features the use of a classical guitar and opens with an infectious rhythmic riff that is joined by distorted electric guitar with bass in octaves; further melodic figures lead to a dramatic vocal, suspended in space. Intense passages of acoustic and electric guitar are followed by a long instrumental section that has a wistful sadness. Here, strummed acoustic chords are juxtaposed against thick-textured electric guitar lines, and there is an acoustic solo over bowed bass.

LATE BEATLES

During 1968 the Beatles brought the guitar back to the forefront in many of their songs as developments in blues and rock began to have a greater influence on their music. Their approach to composition and arrangement came to rely on sophisticated and intricate guitar parts.

In their last major period of change and development, The Beatles used more straightforward stylistic arrangements for many of their songs and cut down on the use of certain added instruments; the result gave a harder edge to their music. At the same time, early in 1968, they recorded the single "Lady Madonna". This blues-piano based boogie, with its distorted rocky guitar fills, points toward the future and indicates the direction the group were taking with the increased use of keyboards with guitar. "Across The Universe" (1969) was also recorded at this time and it harks back to their middle period, with Lennon's phased acoustic harmonies and an extra beat in bars of 4/4 giving an out-of-kilter, floating, unresolved quality.

THE WHITE ALBUM

The double album *The Beatles*, almost universally known as the "White Album", was recorded between May and October 1968. It is a varied and fragmented work in which the separate members of the group often record their own compositions without any contribution from the others. The guitar varies from heavy modern rock with sound processing to attractive acoustic ballads on which the guitar supports the vocal melody. Among the heavier tracks are the rocking rhythms and soloing on "Back In The USSR", the cutting riff of "Birthday" and the staccato introductory chords and fast-driving rock figures of "Everybody's Got Something To Hide Except Me And My Monkey". In contrast, the version of "Revolution" on the album is slow and relaxed in comparison with the single, and is supported with acoustic guitar.

The Beatles attempted to parody prevalent trends and John Lennon's characteristically irreverent approach is particularly evident on "Yer Blues". This has a groaning, stretched-out repetitive riff and overblown blues phrasing. The screaming, adventurous "Helter Skelter",

with its chaotic dissonance, sees Lennon, Harrison and McCartney playing different parts on a song that anticipates later trends with a metallic, acerbic sound. Complex metre changes are juxtaposed on "Happiness Is A Warm Gun" and this helps to convey its jaunty sarcasm. The guitar on "Savoy Truffle" also paints the scene with its flat, fuzzy chords and short, rasping solo.

The White Album also gave the Beatles the space to write tracks that convey humour and colour with a pastiche of guitar styles. There is an unexpected flamenco opening to "The Continuing Story Of Bungalow Bill" and country-style accompaniment on "Rocky Raccoon". "Wild Honey Pie" has a short passage of jazz soloing with a rolled-off treble that is rare in the group's output.

One of the most famous guitar pieces is "Blackbird", on which McCartney draws on acoustic folk-guitar music. Using fingerstyle, he plays a delicate melodic part based on an open

"REVOLUTION" ON STAGE
In 1968 The Beatles started to change their music by drawing on current blues, rock and folk styles. This can be heard on their single "Revolution" (1968) which uses a distorted guitar sound. The effect was created by plugging the guitars directly into the mixing desk, termed a DI technique (direct injection), which overloaded the signal.

tuning that stands on its own instrumentally. He also uses acoustic for "Mother Nature's Son" and "I Will". Lennon plays acoustic folk style on the hauntingly beautiful "Julia" which has two separate guitar tracks.

One of the highlights of the album is George Harrison's "While My Guitar Gently Weeps". Eric Clapton was invited to play fills and an expressive melodic solo, which was processed to give a rich, sonorous tone.

After this album, the single "Get Back" (1969) stands out for its rhythmic groove, where the guitar meshes well with electric piano. John Lennon plays short phrases that answer the vocal line and solo breaks that create an unusual sound by mimicking country steel guitar-styles and adding a bluesy feel.

ABBEY ROAD

The Beatles decided to work together again as a cohesive unit with producer George Martin for their album *Abbey Road*, which was recorded between July and August 1969. Harrison makes a tremendous contribution to the recordings, returning to some of the material that moulded his early playing, with country-style guitar fills on "Maxwell's Silver Hammer", "Octopus's Garden" and "She Came In Through The Bathroom Window". The parts on "Oh Darling" stand out, with rock-guitar chords, slides and staccato arpeggiation through the chord sequence.

Harrison continues to play creatively, revealing an original voice as he puts down a harmonized slide solo using overdubs on "Come Together". Similarly, "You Never Give Me Your Money" displays a thoughtful variety of sounds and touches, including chiming, processed chords, and sections with arpeggiation and blues-rock fills.

On "I Want You", there is a distinctive arpeggiated opening typical of his approach at this stage and highly effective compositionally. It returns at the end of a section before a passage of warm, sensitive melodic playing with the vocal line.

The opening to "Here Comes The Sun" is the most well-known acoustic intro from The Beatles' last period, but one of Harrison's most memorable greatest moments is his outstanding, melodically original composition, "Something" (*see opposite*).

EPIPHONE CASINO
In 1965, John Lennon acquired a sunburst Epiphone Casino, which he started to use for recording and public appearances. He stripped it of its finish, revealing the natural wood, and in The Beatles' last years together he is frequently seen with the instrument.

GEORGE HARRISON
As an instrumentalist Harrison played a crucial role in the sound of The Beatles and wrote some of their finest songs.

JOHN LENNON
Toward the latter stages of The Beatles' recordings, Lennon forged his own version of a number of guitar styles (folk, country, rock) and used them (as he did his composing) to convey his feelings. His guitar-playing reflects an outlook ranging from a gentle philosophical beauty to sardonic aggression.

John Lennon's song "Because" features an arpeggiated cyclical chord sequence, inspired by Beethoven, in unison with electric harpsichord and moog synthesizer; in contrast, the gently strummed, atmospheric chords on "Sun King" are similar in approach to those on Peter Green's Fleetwood Mac instrumental "Albatross" (*see page 146*).

With an appropriate title, "The End" provides a telling insight, revealing the three Beatles' differing personalities as guitarists. Harrison, Lennon and McCartney exchange solos in two-bar breaks. There is a wonderful contrast between McCartney's bright, metallic melodiousness, Harrison's contemporary, vocalized blues influences and Lennon's aggressive, rhythmic, distorted sound.

The Beatles' last single together, "Let It Be" (1970), has gospel overtones and a elegiac feeling, yet Harrison plays an optimistic melodic solo using a sound produced by a mixture of Leslie and distortion that blends in well with the organ.

THE END

"Let It Be" was released in the UK just before The Beatles finally acknowledged that they had split up in April 1970. In less than a decade, The Beatles had recorded the most extensively varied body of guitar work by any group in popular music. They cast fresh and inventive roles for the instrument and created guitar parts that are often both melodic and startlingly original.

After The Beatles split up, George Harrison developed a highly personal quality in his slide playing. This can be heard on his solo albums, including *All Things Must Pass* (1970), and on John Lennon's album *Imagine* (1971). He played a crucial part in the group and left a large body of outstanding work.

GIBSON LES PAUL
Harrison started playing and recording with a Gibson Les Paul in the late 1960s. This guitar was originally a gold top from the 1950s which was refinished in red. It was used for "Something", where its sustain helped Harrison create a supple, smooth-flowing solo.

"SOMETHING" SOLO

George Harrison plays a beautiful solo on his composition "Something". The song is made up of a repeating ten-bar verse in C major and a middle eight that modulates to A-major. Harrison agonized over his solo, putting it down a number of times before he was satisfied. It is characterized by slides between notes, expressive bending and rhythmic variety. It has unusual turns of phrase, following the chord sequence and ending on a high C.

ROCK & BLUES

Toward the end of the 1960s, many guitarists moved away from the diffuse eclecticism of psychedelia and the lighter side of pop. Innovations in rock and a renewed interest in blues and related genres created new styles and directions in guitar playing.

From 1966 onward, Eric Clapton and Jimi Hendrix brought a fresh impetus to guitar playing and a re-evaluation of the blues that changed the way guitarists used phrasing for fills and solos. This was combined with different structural styles, with an emphasis on forceful riffs and chords, high volume to convey power, and a more developed rhythm section.

JEFF BECK

After leaving The Yardbirds in 1966, Jeff Beck recorded Jimmy Page's instrumental "Beck's Bolero" (1967). A piece that reveals his fresh and innovative textures, it opens melodically with cascading echo effects and then breaks, with an exciting change of mood, into a heavy-rock riff before returning to the opening section. In 1967, Beck put together The Jeff Beck Group with Rod Stewart on vocals.

Although often remembered for the frivolous single "Hi-Ho Silver Lining" (1967), they became one of the first groups to take rock and blues strands and meld them into a powerful and effective hybrid form. Their modern-sounding rock music often has a minimalist, stripped-down hard edge and a direct, emotional projection. In comparison with his previous Yardbirds recordings, Beck here shows a more blues-influenced style.

The group's second album *Beck-Ola* (1969) moves further into the funky, rock-blues style outlined on their first album *Truth*, recorded in 1968. *Beck-Ola* contains heavy versions of traditional material with a faster edge to some of the soloing. Studio overdubs shape the music, and certain tracks feature two interweaving guitar parts. In this period, Beck's lines have a sharp, modern-sounding focus and attack played over heavy, distorted chords.

KEITH RICHARDS

Following The Rolling Stones' period of colourful pop arrangements in which the guitar was not always a key component, the group swung back toward the music that had originally shaped their sound and approach. The period from 1968 marks the growing dominance of Keith Richards. A number of factors led to this, including the increasingly peripheral role of Brian Jones.

On the album *Beggars' Banquet* (1968), Richards demonstrates his ability to juxtapose

JEFF BECK
During this period, Beck used a Gibson Les Paul, a guitar that gave him a richer sound with more sustain. His playing shows a strong blues influence and an adventurous approach to sounds and tone. In certain instances, the guitar amplifier was recorded inside a cupboard with the microphone placed outside to achieve a special, muted quality.

TRUTH

The Jeff Beck Group's first album, *Truth* (1968), played a part in defining the dynamic sound of modern rock, with the soloing on "Rock My Plimsoul" featuring high-register notes and string bending and the vocal expressiveness of "I Ain't Superstitious". The Yardbirds' song "Shape Of Things" is reworked with a heavier approach, and the arrangements of this and other material, including Willie Dixon's "You Shook Me" with its wah wah, unusual tonal variations and echo, caused many to regard this music as a precursor to Led Zeppelin. The album is diverse, however, also containing characterful versions of "Ol' Man River" and "Greensleeves".

HYDE PARK, 1969
Mick Taylor's blues lyricism contrasts starkly with Keith Richards' playing. On recordings he often plays fills and does not feature extensively. His solo on "Dead Flowers" (1971) is a high point, and on the album Exile on Main Street *(1971), his soloing on "Ventilator Blues" and slide work on "Stop Breaking Down" are among the few moments he emerges from the background.*

blues phrases to create original passages of soloing. This can be heard on "Stray Cat Blues", and "Sympathy For The Devil", with its bright, edgy and fractured quality. Richards also starts to experiment and to use open tuning for compositional inspiration. One of the most important elements in his playing is the use of fretted open tunings to create chordal riffs that often act as catchy figures and rhythmically drive the songs along.

His outstanding textures and colourful and distinctive chordal introductions with open tunings are used at the beginning of "Street Fighting Man" and on the single "Jumpin' Jack Flash" (1968), both recorded on small tape machines using steel-string guitars. The distorted overloading and unevenness in the tape gives the music a singular identity and a feeling of colourful authenticity. On the beginning to "Gimme Shelter" (1969), Richards uses harmonics on an open tuning with a tremolo effect to create an eerie atmospheric edginess.

Richards' skill and ability to stand out from other rhythm players is exemplified in the introduction to "Midnight Rambler" (1969), where he manages to make standard chords sound new and fresh, and on "Honky Tonk Women" (1969). Here the terse introductory notes sound as if they have been "squeezed" from the instrument. The Stones play sparse blues and country fills over simple rock chords, making musical allusions to the song's raunchy narrative.

During this period, Richards' adoption of an elementary open tuning with the bottom string removed can be heard on the hard-edged, driving chord riffs of "Brown Sugar" (1971). Keith Richards further expands his guitar vocabulary with the use of "Nashville" tuning on the country-rock number "Wild Horses" (1971). In this guitar tuning, the bottom four strings are tuned up an octave.

MICK TAYLOR

Replacing Peter Green in John Mayall's Bluesbreakers in July 1967, Mick Taylor (b.1948) features on a number of albums, including *Crusade* (1967). He often plays in an angular yet rhythmically loose style with a full tone, using short phrases and long, sustained notes. After *Crusade*, his playing with Mayall shows contemporary influences, including feedback, wah wah and tremolo-bar effects. After the departure and accidental death of Brian Jones, Mick Taylor joined The Rolling Stones, debuting on "Honky Tonk Women" (1969). He left in 1974 and was replaced by Ron Wood.

KEITH RICHARDS
Since the late 1960s, Keith Richards has played many of The Rolling Stones' chordal riffs using an open-G tuning with five strings – the bottom sixth string is removed, giving the chords a more incisive clarity by excluding the boomy lower end. With minimal left-hand technique, Richards often plays relaxed grooves and bluesy fills.

JIMMY PAGE

With the formation of Deep Purple and Led Zeppelin in 1968, a style of heavy rock emerged that was based on new rhythmic and harmonic approaches, characterized by a synthesis of blues, rock, classical and jazz structures and driven by high-powered amplification and effects.

SKILLED WRITING
Page's linear melodic riffs display a finely controlled execution. His tense, explosive solos contrast with reflective, carefully arranged elements in the music. Composition and soloing are well thought out, creating excitement with fast tempo breaks and acceleration.

Jimmy Page (b.1944) is one of the key figures who emerged in the 1960s to play a major role in defining the sound of progressive heavy rock. A versatile player, originally inspired by figures including James Burton (*see page 183*) and Scotty Moore (*see page 180*), Page played blues, folk and country styles and established himself as a top session musician, recording parts for groups including Them and The Kinks.

He also acted as a producer, working on John Mayall's "I'm Your Witchdoctor" (1965), which featured Eric Clapton. He joined The Yardbirds in 1966 (*see page 137*) and toward the end of his period with the group he decided to put his own line-up together with singer Robert Plant, bass player John Paul Jones, and drummer John Bonham. Page drew on ideas he had developed with The Yardbirds and put together one of the first modern-sounding heavy-rock bands in which the guitar was supported by a rhythm section with low, thick-textured bass and drum sounds. The band started playing gigs in the autumn of 1968 and after briefly appearing as The New Yardbirds they were renamed Led Zeppelin, and Page used his talents as an arranger and producer to create a fresh synthesis of blues and rock.

In October of that year, the band went into the Olympic Studios in London and the first album, *Led Zeppelin*, was recorded. The playing is hard-edged and driving, with intelligent arrangements and a variety of original guitar sounds. Page puts together combinations of effects, including a distortion unit, wah wah and a Leslie speaker cabinet with a small Supro amplifier. The innovative recording and mixing uses reverb, echo, backward echo and delays. "Good Times, Bad Times" has metallic power chords and a fast, bluesy solo with cascading lines with a violin-like sound, and repetitive, hypnotic rhythmic motifs drive "Communication Breakdown". With the soloing on other songs, Page uses muted sounds, slide and call and response phrases between guitar and voice. A violin bow is employed to play some guitar parts on "Dazed And Confused" and "How Many More Times?". "Dazed And Confused" is a particularly interesting track that develops through differing sections with a wide range of colours before going into a fast up-tempo section with a solo.

GIBSON LES PAUL STANDARD
Gibson Les Pauls were among Jimmy Page's main studio and stage guitars. The original series, produced in 1958–60, have tremendous sustain, and are ideal for creating a rich, seamless blues-rock sound.

"HEARTBREAKER"

"Heartbreaker"'s hypnotic opening riff on *Led Zeppelin II*, is played at a tempo conveying a magnetic sense of tension and expectation. It is based on an ascending pentatonic motif with an added flat fifth that suddenly drops down by a sixth; this motif is repeated with a touch of rhythmic propulsion, rises by a tone and drops back to the starting note. Page takes an inspired unaccompanied solo that he plays with abandon, using phrases with vocal inflections and wide bending. It is rhythmically unfettered and loosely based around pentatonic blues ideas, spiked with bursts of fast passages in which hammering and pull-offs alternate with picking. When the group comes back in, Page changes emphasis and overdubs a further expressive solo which has a richer harmonic character.

Acoustic guitar is used for "Your Time Is Gonna Come" and "Babe I'm Gonna Leave You". The instrumental "Black Mountain Side", a British, folk-influenced composition, features acoustic guitar in an open tuning and a background of tabla percussion.

LED ZEPPELIN II

The second album, *Led Zeppelin II*, recorded in 1969, has some acoustic numbers but is substantially built around a number of tracks that are characterized by heavy electric riffs. The rhythmic "Whole Lotta Love" riff features innovative sounds – overdubs of slide guitar with a special studio effect to add an extra touch – before moving into a free soundscape section that ends on dramatically powerful chords with lead breaks. "Bring It On Home" starts with a blues, then crescendos to a climax with orchestrated heavy-rock overdubs. Page takes an inspired unaccompanied solo on "Heartbreaker".

Following on from this important, highly rated album, Page continued to use much acoustic instrumentation, including 12-string, on *Led Zeppelin III*. Here, some of the tracks are influenced by the work of traditional acoustic blues artists; others have country and folk elements.

On *Led Zeppelin (IV)*, "Stairway To Heaven", with its memorable arpeggiated opening, builds up through sections of strummed

electric chords and an increase in tempo before breaking into the powerful chords that usher in one of the most lyrical solos in rock (*see page 156*). Heavy rock is represented by the popular riff of "Black Dog".

On subsequent albums, Page continued to expand the group's repertoire, producing material built on the styles that he had developed, and he also expanded his vocabulary, integrating new sounds and styles within the group's approach to progressive heavy rock. On *Houses Of The Holy* (1973), guitar is used for the arrangements on the powerful "The Song Remains The Same"; on *Physical Graffiti* (1975), "Kashmir" has dark multi-layering with acoustic guitars in unusual tunings and an Indian flavour, and "Bron-Y-Aur" is an acoustic folk piece.

GIBSON EDS-1275
Jimmy Page often performed with a Gibson EDS-1275 doubleneck guitar, using the 12-string sound for shimmering arpeggiation and chords and the 6-string neck for chords and soloing. The guitar was used in live performances to play songs including "Stairway To Heaven", giving it a different sound to the original studio version.

"STAIRWAY TO HEAVEN"

One of the most popular tracks in the history of rock, "Stairway To Heaven" (1973) has a whole range of elements that give it depth and variety. It starts seductively, drawing in the listener, and moves through distinct sections with melodies, textures, changing tempos and one of Page's finest solos.

PAGE & PLANT
Led Zeppelin was one of the world's most exciting stage acts in the 1970s.

INTRODUCTION

Using a steel-string acoustic guitar, the introduction to "Stairway To Heaven" starts with an A-minor chord that is arpeggiated with a descending bass and ascending top melody notes. This is followed by a series of chords that lead the piece into a repeat before the vocal enters.

attractive triads

A-string pedal tone

MELODIC VARIATION

After the first part of the vocals, the rhythm section enters and Page uses a Fender XII electric 12-string to play a sonorous chord melody. This is structured around A minor 7, moving to D major and an attractive upper series of triads, mainly supported by a ringing, open D-string pedal tone.

D major chord

FANFARE

The melodic variations on 12-string, with acoustic guitar mixed in, open out to a dramatic fanfare effect. Starting with a declamatory D major and a short, ascending motif, Page plays a series of chordal variations that go through complex metrical changes before he moves to the solo.

note bending

SOLO

Page plays a lyrical rock solo which has a natural, organic feel. Based on the A minor pentatonic scale, the solo sweeps over simple harmonies and the tempo accelerates to add excitement and energy. Page's ideas unfold towards a climax with repeating motifs before a short series of powerful chords punctuate the end.

HEAVY ROCK

The type of music that has come to be termed "heavy rock" encompasses a rich diversity of guitar styles. The development of this music was shaped not only by Led Zeppelin, but also by Deep Purple and Black Sabbath, groups whose guitarists had markedly differing personalities.

RITCHIE BLACKMORE
Deep Purple's Ritchie Blackmore will always be associated with the simple opening riff to "Smoke On The Water", one of rock's best-known guitar introductions. Blackmore was one of the first rock-guitarists to develop a distinctive style utilizing scales and melodic patterns.

TONY IOMMI
Black Sabbath developed a type of physical, stream-of-power music. Tracks such as "Paranoid" (1970) are based on driving, repetitive hypnotic riffs that have a flat, colourless texture. Iommi uses simple power chords and some sombre harmonies. His soloing style is fast and blues-based with effects.

Developments in rock and blues during the 1960s brought about the formation of Deep Purple, a group whose signature was high volume combined with fast tempos and a highly arranged combination of rock and classical music. Ritchie Blackmore (b.1945), who had a background working on sessions and backing pop singers, brought an unusual range of influences to Deep Purple. In contrast, the music of Tony Iommi (b.1948) of Black Sabbath has a much narrower focus – his soloing with the group is essentially based on the blues.

RITCHIE BLACKMORE

With Deep Purple, formed in 1968, Ritchie Blackmore developed a style that has superficial affinities with Jimi Hendrix but, in fact, draws heavily on classical phrasing. At one extreme, he is a theatrical soloist, using the tremolo arm for a shaking vibrato effect and to move the pitch of notes by large intervals. His concentrated playing is improvisatory and scalar in approach, and his solos are often fiery and imbued with a fast, nervous energy. His innovative use of repeating arpeggiated motifs has been very influential in rock soloing.

On Deep Purple's first album, *Shades Of Deep Purple* (1968), "And The Address" demonstrates Blackmore's distorted riffs and the surging solo features vibrato and wild leaps over large intervals. The solo on "Mandrake Root" uses classical arpeggiation and scalar lines before breaking into a free section with distortion. On their

second album, *Book Of Taliesyn* (1969), the group move further into a neo-classical vein with extended instrumental sections. "Anthem" features a classically influenced electric solo over strings. The highlight of the album is "Wring That Neck", an instrumental showcase for Blackmore's individual voice in which jazz influences merge with rock and blues.

The album *Deep Purple* (1969) showcases a simpler, heavy-rock style within which Blackmore plays heavy-rock chords and riffs using a strong vocal projection with effects. On *Deep Purple In Rock* (1970), the flamboyant "Speed King" features a wide range of tone and colour, and "Child In Time" shows articulate and controlled blues influences and note-bending. During the 1970s, Blackmore went on to produce inspired solos on *Machine Head* (1972), particularly on "Lazy" and "Highway Star", a track with a harmonized opening and a solo containing classical motifs.

PROGRESSIVE ROCK

Progressive ideas gave the guitar more interesting roles as a harmonic component and as a solo voice for improvisation, sampling from a further range of influences. Groups expanded their vocabulary, writing with adventurous structures and unusual rhythms and time signatures.

Throughout the 1960s classical and jazz influences shaped pop and rock music. There was a whole range of varied material, from the orchestrated mystical grandeur of The Moody Blues to the flippant pastiche of The Move, who spiked their psychedelia with classical quotes. Love Sculpture's recording of Khatchaturian's "Sabre Dance" (1967) with Dave Edmunds (b.1944), and US guitarist Mason Williams' "Classical Gas" (1968) both became hit singles. A band without a guitarist, The Nice (with Keith Emerson on keyboards), was one of the most significant groups to forge a classical rock hybrid. Rock bands also experimented with the orchestral sound: in 1970, Deep Purple recorded *Concerto For Group And Orchestra* with the Royal Philharmonic Orchestra.

ROBERT FRIPP

Robert Fripp (b.1946) is the most innovative guitarist to emerge from progressive rock. He was a founder member of King Crimson. Their first album, *The Court Of The Crimson King* (1969), features the sophisticated and musically complex "Twenty-First Century Schizoid Man". Fripp's solo uses long sustain and he plays unison ensemble parts to create one of the most original guitar pieces in rock music. The contrasting "Moonchild" opens ethereally, and the rounded tone of the guitar in free-form open passages contrasts with reflective arpeggiated chords. On subsequent albums, Fripp continued to put together dynamic structural devices and original lines, sometimes in the context of unusual time signatures.

One of Fripp's instrumental highlights is "Sailor's Tale" from *Islands*

MIKE OLDFIELD

With advancing technology and multi-track recording, guitarists developed within the studio, taking advantage of layering parts to build music using overdubs. Stylistic barriers were broken down and the instrument was used within a new type of orchestration. Mike Oldfield (b.1953) is a guitarist who was able to make the transition from instrumentalist to composer with *Tubular Bells* (1973). On this album he made up a tapestry with loops of repeating passages that often use the guitar.

(1971), but it is on *Larks' Tongues In Aspic* (1973) that his structural organization of time elements comes into the ascendent. For example, the album's title track (Part One) juxtaposes a combination of menacing fuzzy rock riffs, a solo with a continuous stream of intervallic atonal motifs, and a

ROBERT FRIPP
Robert Fripp's controlled cerebral approach is built on concepts concerning form and vocabulary, tunings and an original playing style. Solos and passages range from melodic and lyrical to atonal and are devoid of commonplace phrasing. He uses carefully planned, highly organized lines and often processes harmonies to create unusual sounds and textures.

frenzied rhythmic passage against classically based violin sections. The album shows off a variety of original approaches: Fripp using a plectrum on electric and steel guitar to play parts that sound like classical guitar; the hissing, rasping guitar sound that opens the mocking "Easy Money"; and an exploration of rhythmic rock-guitar figures on the title track (Part Two).

Two albums were made with "non-musician" Brian Eno, *No Pussyfootin'* (1972) and *Evening Star* (1976). On both these recordings, Fripp plays in conjunction with tape machines and synthesizers to create ambient sounds. He devised "Frippertronics" using tape recorders and effects to play live and to record further musical experiments. A number of pop singers, including David Bowie on *Heroes* (1977), booked Fripp to work on their sessions, and he often added unexpected elements to their tracks.

MICHAEL KAROLI

In avant-garde Germany, guitarists such as Michael Karoli (b.1948) of the group Can were adopting electronics and an experimental approach. Members of the band had studied with the composer Karlheinz Stockhausen and been influenced by Berio and Ligeti. Can's first album, *Monster Movie,*

was recorded in 1968 and their conceptual framework often offsets the guitar against the background of a rigid rhythm section playing cyclical elements with synthesizer and electronics. On *Tago Mago* (1971), Karoli plays in a blues-based style on "Paperhouse" and "Halleluhwah", yet familiar elements sound strange in a setting based around long, free-improvised passages, and he often puts in surprising elements to produce an alienating effect. On the extended "Aumgn", the opening effects lead into a cohesive soundscape that avoids pastiche. With an improvised group-interplay system and what was termed instant composition, Karoli tried to sidestep the standard guitar vocabulary and create new soundscapes different from the Anglo-American popular-music paradigm. Can's music became an influence on later ambient and progressive compositional thinking.

STEVE HACKETT

Steve Hackett (b.1950) played with Genesis from 1970 until 1977. A great deal of his recording with the group consists of harmonic layers and textures with the keyboards. Hackett used guitar synthesizers in the early 1970s, and many of his guitar lines feature sound processing, including fuzz. He plays harmonized parts, with dropped-in backward tapes of solos. Away from his use of 12-string, he is one of the few guitarists in popular music who uses a nylon-string guitar with a normal-sounding classical technique that shows a range of influences, including J.S. Bach. "Blood On The Rooftops" on *Wind And Wuthering* (1977) opens with a well-executed passage of classical guitar and the song has extensive arpeggiated parts that work very effectively with the vocals.

FENDER STRATOCASTER
With its penetrating sound and clarity, the Fender Stratocaster was ideal for musicians who wanted to play lines in the upper register that would have colour and separation. By the late 1970s, black pickguards and knobs were a standard option, producing a striking effect against a black body and maple neck.

MICHAEL KAROLI
Within the context of the band Can, Karoli took the guitar into new realms, where he was able to break away from tradition and modernize the sound and role of the instrument.

PINK FLOYD

David Gilmour (b.1944) joined Pink Floyd in January 1968 and worked alongside Syd Barrett (*see page 141*) during his last few months with the group. Gilmour is a blues-influenced, melodic player with a concise and tasteful compositional approach that uses space and long, sustained lines. His solos are often powerful and intense with expressive upper-register playing using bending and vibrato. Pink Floyd's original approach to rock developed partly through live-performance settings and writing film soundtracks, and Gilmour's guitar is often placed in the context of gently paced extended pieces. On *Meddle* (1971), the group creates a continuum of sound and the guitar provides one of the bands of colour. Among his best work is "Shine On You Crazy Diamond" from *Wish You Were Here* (1976); in the context of sustained keyboard harmonies, Gilmour's opening phrases are played in a strong blues style with a sweet, full sound leading to his plangent solo. "Comfortably Numb" on *The Wall* (1979) is another track with powerful soloing, and on this album Gilmour creates high acoustic tunings. He sometimes works by laying down a number of solos and then taking the best parts from each and merging them into one.

DARK SIDE OF THE MOON

Recorded between June 1972 and January 1973 at Abbey Road Studios, London, *Dark Side Of The Moon* is one of the most popular albums ever made by any group. Tracks segue into each other, and the full, vibrant sound, given extra richness and depth by engineer Alan Parsons, conveys a powerful sense of atmosphere and presence. Dave Gilmour spent a lot of time setting up sounds for the guitar. Apart from expanding the dynamic range, the textures and timbres developed in the studio help to create contrasts in mood. There are effects on a number of tracks, including tremolo, Leslie and a Uni-Vibe. The guitar is used for arpeggiated chords in combination with such effects, as can be heard on "Any Colour You Like". There is fuzz and echo on "Time", backward chords on "Speak To Me", and "On The Run" uses train and explosion

effects created with synthesizers and guitar feedback. "Breathe" features slide on a magnificently powerful lap steel, with a volume pedal and a number of guitar overdubs to give separate colours. One of the best-known tracks, "Money", adopts a 7/4 time signature and the guitar with a tremolo sound plays the riff with the bass. There are effective echo and dry, flat sounds. This track moves into 4/4 for the driving guitar solo that features a Stratocaster followed by a Lewis guitar with a two-octave neck for high notes.

JAZZ INFLUENCES

Toward the end of the 1960s, jazz increasingly came to be appreciated for its technical content and rich vocabulary compared to blues. The stylistic barriers between jazz and rock were being broken down in America by Miles Davis. The work of British guitarist John McLaughlin (*see pages 114–15*) in America, fusing jazz with rock and modal ethnic music with Lifetime and The Mahavishnu Orchestra, had a profound effect on the way guitarists improvised and worked with instrumental composition and form.

Guitarists who had leanings toward a more sophisticated style of improvisation based on jazz were able to work in progressive rock, and they started to emerge at the beginning of the 1970s. The group If featured jazz-guitarist

JAN AKKERMAN
As jazz combined with classical music came to be appreciated, Dutch band Focus became one of the most successful groups in 1973 with their popular singles "Sylvia" and "Hocus Pocus" and albums that briefly established Akkerman as a well-known and highly regarded guitar player.

STEVE HILLAGE
A guitarist who combines melodic psychedelia with blues and jazz is Steve Hillage with Gong. On his solo album, Fish Rising (1975), Hillage explored interesting areas and went on to develop his own type of ambient music.

Terry Smith, who adapted his style to combine bebop phrasing with notes using more sustain at a higher-volume level. One of the most overlooked talents of this era was Ollie Halsall (b.1949), an outstandingly fluent and inventive guitarist who combined blues with jazz playing in Patto and with Kevin Ayers. A whole host of groups appeared with jazz-influenced guitarists working in a particularly English style of melodic progressive rock; it included Pye Hastings with Caravan, Andy Latimer of Camel, and Phil Miller with Hatfield and The North. In 1970, Gong were formed in France with Australian guitarist Daevid Allen (b.1941) and they developed an original type of psychedelic fusion. Steve Hillage (b.1951) joined the group in 1972 and played on the

NEW STRUCTURES

At the beginning of the 1980s, Robert Fripp formed a new King Crimson and recorded the groundbreaking *Discipline* (1981) with American guitarist Adrian Belew. The overall sound is close to jazz rock, and some of the core motifs owe their origin to fusion lines and classical minimalist composers. The music has highly arranged interweaving guitar parts with unusual time signatures in strictly organized pieces that appear repetitive yet move forward through a subtle shifting of patterns. There is a mechanical torsion in the strophic ostinato figures, and accents fall in unusual places, producing fast, rippling effects and shifting sheets of sound.

album *Flying Teapot* (1973) before releasing his own album *Fish Rising* (1975). Fred Frith (b.1949) on Henry Cow's debut album *Legend* (1973) is far more experimental, drawing on the pioneering work of musicians on the free side of jazz and avant-garde techniques.

Alan Holdsworth, perhaps the most influential improviser to emerge in Britain during the 1970s, joined Soft Machine and recorded *Bundles* in 1975. He went on to work on Bill Bruford's solo album *Feels Good To Me* (1977) and the with jazz-rock fusion group UK. On the album *UK* (1978), his tremendous solo on "In The Dead Of Night" brought him to the attention of mainstream audiences. Around this time, Brand X, one of the most successful British fusion groups, were formed. Their debut album *Unorthodox Behaviour* (1976) features John Goodsall, who plays with a fast jazz-rock style and a brittle tone.

Some rock players who had jazz leanings moved across to fusion bands. In the mid-1970s, Gary Moore (*see page 166*) played with a tangled density and a highly individual harmonic flavor with Colosseum II. On his solo album *Back On The Streets* (1979), he plays instrumental jazz-rock fusion on the track "Hurricane" with effervescent linear speed.

Jazz-influenced soloing in rock largely disappeared from the mainstream in Britain with changes in pop fashion and the decline in the role of the guitarist as a high-powered soloist. One talented player was Alan Murphy (1954–89) whose style drew from blues, rock, and the innovative sound of Alan Holdsworth. He appeared at the end of the 1970s with the group SFX, but went largely unrecognized.

STEVE HOWE

The best-known player in rock to use jazz influences in the 1970s was Steve Howe (b.1947) who joined Yes in 1971. He stands apart from most high-profile rock players in this period through his frequent use of undistorted sound and a markedly eclectic approach, incorporating virtually every type of guitar style. Throughout the 1970s he recorded and performed sophisticated arrangements that called for a wide range of techniques. Howe's versatility is demonstrated on his first album with the group, *The Yes Album* (1970), on which he uses effects and different types

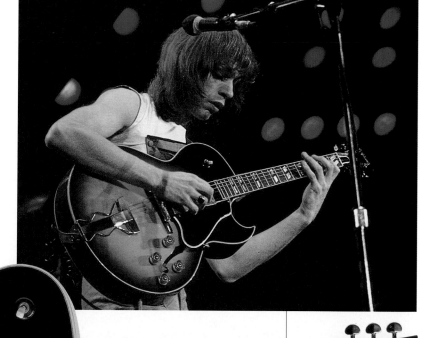

of electric and acoustic guitar to generate a range of sounds. The solo fingerpicking on the steel-string acoustic instrumental piece "Clap" combines country, ragtime, and folk elements. Howe is inventive, with an individual style and a liquid tone that fuses jazz with other areas of influence. On extended solos his rhythm and structural phrasing has a European feel and sounds classically influenced, and his colourful addition to songs can be heard on the harmonics on the opening to "Roundabout" (1972). Yes recorded long instrumental passages both live and in the studio. On the live *Yessongs* (1973), Howe has room to stretch out and solos on "Siberian Khatru," "Close To The Edge" and "Yours Is No Disgrace." In this context he uses classically influenced arpeggios and plays a torrent of seamless, fast scales, often propelled by his right-hand technique.

"YOURS IS NO DISGRACE"

"Yours Is No Disgrace" on *The Yes Album* (1971) is a stylistic *tour de force*. It opens with Howe playing riffs with the controlled distortion typical of his style with the group. The track next has a distinctive passage of attractive, flowing arpeggio lines, moving to harder-edged sounds and passages of steel-guitar fadeup background effects. The guitar plays a lone rhythmic metallic blues-rock break before the band comes back in and there is melodic chordal vamping before a short section of nylon-string riffs. An exotic fuzzy guitar line enters, then Howe plays a jazz-guitar solo, switching to steel-string backing for part of the song before restating earlier sections. The track ends on an ascending glissando dominated by keyboards that fades to silence.

GIBSON ES-175
Steve Howe is one of the few rock guitarists to be clearly associated with jazz and an archtop guitar. He used this 1964 Gibson ES-175 for a large part of his early work on stage and in the studio with Yes.

RAMIREZ 1A
Steve Howe occasionally used a nylon-string guitar, and its sound stands out on passages and dropped-in parts that broaden the palette of colors used in Yes's sophisticated arrangements.

Ramirez 1A

JEFF BECK

STICKING WITH THE BLUES
In a period in which strong jazz-fusion influences dominate, Beck has an unmistakable blues and rock sound. He improvises quite unlike a jazz soloist and is able to take tasteful, extensive solos with great economy and a controlled use of the expressive powers of the electric guitar.

Jeff Beck's albums *Blow By Blow* (1975) and *Wired* (1976) are among the freshest and most melodic instrumental albums to be recorded with a jazz-rock rhythm section. Beck stamps his personality on the genre, partly because he works to his strengths as a rock improviser. With Beck's strong thematic playing and the help of producer George Martin, *Blow By Blow* became a best seller. In this period, Beck produced a variety of sounds by using different touch techniques to give the electric guitar an intensely musical quality. His guitar ranges from a vocal immediacy to sounds that conjure up other instruments. Volume effects create a woodwind sound and Beck simulates synth-wheel "keyboard bends". He tends not to use heavy block voicings, instead laying down light, funk-influenced rhythm parts.

Beck takes a lyrical approach to Lennon and McCartney's "She's A Woman" and uses a voice-box effect to give strange, synthetic resonance to his words. His solo on "Scatterbrain" is bubbly and positive with glistening runs, and contrasts with one of his finest and most popular solos on Stevie Wonder's composition "Cause We've Ended As Lovers". This has an opening with sustained, keening calling notes followed by a delicate solo that builds up to an effusive climax featuring trills, sustained notes and bending, and call-and-response phrasing. On *Wired,* Beck continued in the same vein, with tracks such as "Sophie" displaying his abilities as a virtuoso rock-influenced improviser in exuberant exchanges with the keyboards. Following these albums, Jeff Beck has gone on to produce other highlights on albums such as *There And Back* (1980) in a guitar career that has seen continual evolution.

"GOODBYE PORK-PIE HAT"

This complex twelve-bar blues by Charles Mingus is simplified for Beck's solo: the section below is based on simplified harmonies. The solo has an expressive range of tones, achieved by "dropping-in" short sections and notes on successive recordings. Apart from standard slides and finger vibrato, Beck uses a volume fade-up in bar two and in bar 17, where he reintroduces the theme. Vibrato and tremolo vibrato are used in bars eight and 20, and bending on a pair of notes with a ring-modulator effect in bars 14 and 15.

ANDY SUMMERS

In 1977, Andy Summers (b.1942) joined the Police, with Gordon "Sting" Sumner on bass and Stewart Copeland on drums. In this setting, Summers moves away from standard rock approaches and tends not to take extended solos. Instead, he constructs arpeggiated sheets of sound with multi-layered effects that emphasize chorus and echo. He also uses phasing, reverb, delay and controlled distortion. A controlled textural player who uses the guitar to add colour to songs using harmonics, artificial harmonics and muted percussive figures to fill space, his vocabulary owes very little to any particular guitar style. Chords are often voiced minimally with upper

POLICE WORK
Andy Summers was one of the first players to develop a highly original approach to the guitar within a trio by using layered, arpeggiated lines instead of block chords and pioneering the development of new effects.

sections anchored by roots from the bass guitar, and rhythmically he positions them inventively in relation to accents and beats. Minimalist ideas and repetitive motifs with lines and sparse voicings are processed to create interesting backdrops within a subtle rhythmic framework, often using displacement.

The Police recorded their first single, "Roxanne", and album *Outlandos d'Amour* in 1978. Their early music combines elements of punk with reggae, and highlights Summers' individual approach to chords that are picked and voiced without roots, and the use of block power chords for solidity.

On "Message In A Bottle" (1979), he creates a dry timbre using unusual voicings combined with his own effects. "Walking On The Moon" (1979) has shatteringly bright opening chords and spatial effects with echo. A guitar synthesizer further enlarges the sonic horizons on "Don't Stand So Close To Me" (1980).

"Every Breath You Take" (1983) bears the hallmarks of his ground-breaking innovations, and in the 1980s he developed his ideas further on albums with Robert Fripp, *I Advance Masked* (1982) and *Bewitched* (1984).

CHORUS & PHASING

A new generation of portable effects, including phasing and chorus, started to arrive during the 1970s, adding to established effects such as echo and reverb. Chorus and phasing pedals, such as the Tube Echoplex, Boss Chorus CE1 and MXR Phase 90, create a thickened texture by splitting a sound signal into two parts and then merging them so they are out of phase. With different settings, this creates a swirling effect and thickened textures with more body and a different type of sustain. Andy Summers

created an unmistakable voice by using such effects with echo and reverb to play chords and arpeggiated figures.

MXR Phase 90

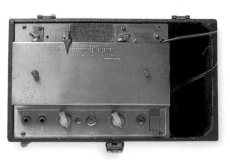

Tube Echoplex

Boss Chorus CE1

MARK KNOPFLER

When Knopfler (b.1949) started the group Dire Straits in 1977, their relaxed instrumental approach was a complete break from styles prevalent at the time. With a smooth, flowing technique and laid-back rhythms, Knopfler established a synthesis unusual in Britain by reworking traditional material and integrating blues and country techniques. Playing fingerstyle, he gives the impression of restrained finesse with understated fills that are often played with excellent dynamic control. With a light, relaxed feel, he uses bending for solos and intricate chordal elements with hammering and bends to create rhythm fills and solos; for added detail he combines harmonics and picked notes for chords and arpeggios.

The band's first album, *Dire Straits* (1978), features his tasteful chordal playing and slide guitar. The rhythm-guitar playing is melodic and percussive and he creates a clear, ringing sound for solos. There are occasional effects, such as a volume pedal to mimic steel-guitar sounds, and subtle use of delay and echo. The song "Sultans Of Swing" has a fine country-influenced solo with chordal elements, arpeggios and hammer-ons and pull-offs for the single-note passages. "Wild West End" displays a wide range of sounds with rhythm played on a resonator, chords played with harmonics, electric additions with a volume, and single note and chordal fills. On subsequent albums, Knopfler develops his range and depth as a player with skillful work on solos such as "Tunnel Of Love" (1980) and long instrumental passages on tracks like "Telegraph Road" (1982). By the time he recorded *Brothers In Arms* (1985), Knopfler had broadened his range, producing tracks on which the guitar floats across dreamy reflective landscapes. Away from Dire Straits, Knopfler has played in The Notting Hillbillies and worked extensively with other artists.

FINGERSTYLE
Mark Knopfler is influenced by country players as well as blues and 1950s rock, and integrated traditional elements to create a synthesis unusual in the British pop and rock world. He uses fingerstyle on electric and acoustic instruments and his technique is smooth and flowing.

RESONATOR GUITAR
Mark Knopfler often uses resonator guitars, including a mid-1930s Style O with a distinctive "chicken foot" pattern coverplate. With a metal body and resonating cone, it produces a very distinctive tone that is ideal for both slide and fingerpicking.

ROCK & HEAVY METAL

The 1970s saw an increasing interest in heavy metal, a style characterized by high volume and fast tempos. Groups record and perform with a dramatic physicality channelled into the music, characterful vocals, and a multitude of riffs, often with unison parts. Guitar solos form a high point in the music as it reaches the peak of its crescendo, and the content is made up of fast, blues-based licks, scales and hypnotic, repeating motifs. One of the finest players in this intense, high-powered genre is the German guitarist Michael Schenker (b.1955) He played with The Scorpions, recording albums from 1973 onwards, and worked with UFO in the 1970s. Schenker formed his own group, producing albums such as *One Night In Budokan* (1982). His playing has depth and taste and manages to be effective across the board.

During the 1970s, Status Quo, with guitarists Francis Rossi (b.1949) and Rick Parfitt (b.1948), played unpretentious music with straightforward rocking rhythms and riffs. Driving boogie rhythms, honest and infectious simplicity, and a good-time feel made "Rockin' All Over The World" (1977) and "Whatever You Want" (1979) enduringly popular.

At the end of the 1970s, the archetypal heavy metal band, Iron Maiden, were formed, with Dave Murray (b.1955) as guitarist. Among their most popular work is the melodramatic riff for "The Number Of The Beast" (1982). Def Leppard, with Steve Clark (1960–91) and Phil Collen (b.1957) on guitars, recorded albums that were painstakingly put together over long periods in the studio, with elements such as power chords being recorded one note at a time.

DIVERSITY IN STYLE

Over the last 20 years there has been a proliferation of different styles in the rock-guitar genre. During the 1980s, sonic innovation became a key progressive element, while in the 1990s, major figures have often reworked music from different periods to create new styles.

THE EDGE
Using layers of sound, Dave "The Edge" Evans sets up atmospheric backgrounds and a sense of space. He uses unusual voicings and open tunings. Commonplace techniques on the instrument, such as harmonics, slide, tremolo-bar movements and muted strings, are processed electronically to enhance their sound.

During the 1980s, extended soloing and linear virtuosity fell out of vogue in the mainstream pop world. One approach to working within songs was explored by Dave "The Edge" Evans (b.1961) of U2, whose intuitive musicality led him to develop his own techniques, adding layers of electronically altered guitar with a mechanical logic.

DAVE EVANS

Evans' playing is based on a sonic approach with a highly creative, sophisticated sound produced by a series of intelligently thought-out applications of effects. Notes are used sparingly, and he does not often produce improvised linear solos but uses touch and color with an individual and original voice. During the late 1970s and 1980s, a new generation of sound-processing units was developed that enabled guitarists to conjure up new sounds. Evans is one of the pioneers in this field and has had devices custom-built to expand his range. His guitar repertoire ranges from bold rhythmic figures to delicate timbres and nuances.

Evans runs chords and single notes through delay units, resulting in a cascade of sound which has a synthetic texture. This is often combined with echo and reverb as well as devices to create continual sustain. Individual notes are used to create a pedal tone throughout a song, and repeating arpeggiated motifs set up a sense of continuous rippling movement. Standard techniques, such as muting and harmonics, are processed so that they become virtually unrecognizable.

These effects can be heard on tracks throughout the 1980s, such as "I Will Follow" (1980), with its synthetic folk effect, and "Gloria" (1981) with a repeating melodic riff. "Sunday Bloody Sunday" (1983) opens with light arpeggios before moving to cutting acoustic sounds and incisive harmonics.

GIBSON EXPLORER
Evans employs a range of guitars including Fender Stratocasters and the futuristic Gibson Explorer, which first came out in 1958. Vox amplifiers are used on stage.

JOHNNY MARR

Johnny Marr (b.1963) formed the Manchester-based band The Smiths in 1982 with singer and lyricist Morrissey. Their first album, *The Smiths,* was recorded in 1983.

Marr has a distinct identity and is influenced by a wide and diverse range of music, from pop and soul to folk and African styles. One of the exceptional players in pop, he pays great attention to detail and has developed a variety of techniques and approaches to sound. During his time with the band, Marr wrote The Smiths' music, and the songs have a subtle, harmonic approach with unusual chord voicings and progressions. His guitar parts are arranged with delicate two- and three-note chords and countermelodies, and he uses arpeggiated motifs, lines, and fragments of harmonies. He often plays with his guitar tuned up a tone to create a brighter sound, and he also uses open tunings.

Instead of taking solos, Marr adds overdubs and delicate touches to enhance the mood of a Smiths' song with passages of subtle variations on repeating sections and linear melodic motifs played in different registers. He also combines electric and acoustic guitar sounds and makes use of a large number of rack-mounted effects and pedals.

"This Charming Man" (1983) uses many overdubs with harmonized two-note passages and melodic additions. On other outstanding pieces, such as "How Soon Is Now" (1985), the guitar has a vibrato sound and layered overdubs that include open tunings with harmonics, slide, and a part with an electronic harmonizer set to an interval.

Marr left the group in 1987 and went on to work extensively on his own and with other artists, ranging from Bernard Sumner to Paul McCartney, using his singular gifts as one of the finest guitarists in the history of pop.

THE QUEEN IS DEAD

On the outstanding album *The Queen Is Dead* (1986), Marr plays with controlled understatement, yet his work is varied and creative. He uses acoustic guitar on many tracks, layering it beautifully with added electric guitar. "Bigmouth Strikes Again" has an effective, lilting rhythm and there are attractive melodic chords on "The Boy With The Thorn In His Side." Subtle and interesting harmonies can be heard on "Some Girls Are Bigger Than Others."

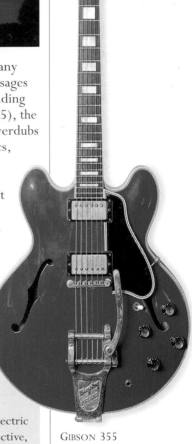

GIBSON 355
Although he performs live with a Gibson 355, Johnny Marr uses a wide range of instruments, put through Fender amplifiers for a clear sound.

TOWARD THE 1990s

Another Manchester band, The Stone Roses, was formed in 1985 with John Squire (b.1962) on guitar. Their debut album, *Stone Roses* came out in 1989. With swirling sustain and effects, arpeggiation and infectious melodic motifs, Squire's controlled playing on tracks such as "I Wanna Be Adored", "One Love" and the powerful "I Am The Resurrection" made him one of the most highly regarded figures of the early 1990s. Another important current of development came from the Indie movement that had been building up during the 1980s with players such as William Reid of The Jesus And Mary Chain and Kevin Shields of My Bloody Valentine, whose style of loud, distorted guitars with effects constructed a trance-like, high-energy wall of sound.

OASIS

One of the best songwriting groups to emerge after this is Oasis with Noel Gallagher (b.1970). The group's guitars have a crashing excitement and a large, full sound. On "Rock 'n' Roll Star" from *Definitely Maybe* (1994), guitars play plangent, distorted chords in a chord sequence that moves around typical

Britpop harmonies blended with rock riffs and breaks. Gallagher takes bluesy melodic solos and a large proportion of the material has a 1960s Beatles' sound, including "Shakermaker" with its arpeggiated distorted chords and "Up In The Sky", using a repeating riff and mix of electric and acoustic parts. The group reworks the boogie-riff rock sound of the early 1970s on "Cigarettes & Alcohol" and achieve a grainy, minimalistic edge to the strummed acoustic and thin bluesy electric sound on "Married with Children". On the following album *(What's The Story) Morning Glory?* (1995), Oasis continue to build material around a strong guitar sound on songs such as "Hey Now", "Some Might Say", and "Morning Glory" that have erupting, distorted sounds and a driving intensity. One of their best tunes, "Wonderwall", starts with a catchy acoustic chord sequence that drives the rhythm as the drums and strings enter and the song builds up.

NEW DIRECTIONS

Of the major groups to have emerged in the 1990s, the most interesting are Radiohead with guitarist Jon Greenwood (b.1971), whose music is innovative and futuristic. Their album *The Bends* (1995) opens with "Planet Telex"

which has shaking, pulsating guitar chords and strange tone effects that convey alienation. Greenwood often uses smooth, strummed acoustic parts, such as on "High And Dry" with its attractive acoustic chords and melodic solo breaks. "Fake Plastic Trees" reveals sustaining electric layers and on "(Nice Dream)" there are background ambient sounds and electric arpeggios. Fluctuating levels and normal distorted chords create tension and release on "Bones", and on "Just", a dramatic ascending figure alternates with softer, colourful textures before ending with abrasive soloing. On "Street Spirit", classical-style arpeggiation is played on electric chords.

During the 1990s there was a rich diversity, with both pop and blues-rock melodiousness and experimentation. Groups such as Jason Pierce's Spiritualized on *Laser Guided Melodies* (1992) create trance-like, altered-state music. On Ocean Colour Scene's "The Riverboat Song" (1996), guitarist Steve Cradock uses a repeating blues-rock riff with fundamental harmonies before playing an incisive, bluesy, wah-wah solo. In pop, Blur with Graham Coxon (b. 1969) produce a bright, hard-edged sound. The opening track on their album *Parklife* (1994), "Girls & Boys", features funky distorted rock guitar with a dissonant edge. "End Of A Century" has overlayed acoustic and electric parts, and chords played with a hard downbeat. Coxon adds characterful parts in an exuberant punk style on "Trouble In The Message Centre" and contributes tangled parts to "Jubilee".

Among other popular acts are The Manic Street Preachers, with James Dean Bradfield (b. 1969) on guitar. On their album *Everything Must Go* (1996), Bradfield reveals an intense, serious style with muscular guitar parts, dry acoustic and electric distorted chords and riffs. This hard-edged approach is taken further by Kelly Jones of The Stereophonics on *Performance And Cocktails* (1999), on which "Roll Up And Shine" starts with explosive guitar sounds and features attacking, tonally sharp, rough-edged rock-guitar chords and riffs. In a thriving music scene, the guitar continues to be a focal point for shifting trends and is still a major voice in contemporary popular culture at the beginning of the 21st century.

JON GREENWOOD
Radiohead guitarist Jon Greenwood applies effects that have their own individual colour and different functions. As well as using standard harmonies, he positions elements to move through the music, conjuring up a three-dimensional soundscape.

GRAHAM COXON
Playing in Blur, one of the most popular groups of the 1990s, Graham Coxon draws from the theatrical side of pop, new wave and punk. His style of playing is imaginative, yet at the same time traditional and straightforward with a non-technical approach, adding rhythms and melodic figures in a light, accessible fashion.

BERNARD BUTLER

One of the most imaginative guitarists of the era, Bernard Butler recorded progressive music with Suede on their album *Dog Man Star* (1994). His tonally powerful guitar has a mellow depth with tasteful effects, and his inventive vocabulary combines melodic pop chords and lines with folk lyricism to create a modern psychedelic sound. Among the standout tracks are "We Are The Pigs", which has sinuous, sustaining melodic lines, and "Heroine", with its shimmering chords, bluesy high-register additions and crunching rhythms. Butler also uses acoustic effectively, as on the haunting "Daddy's Speeding" and the atmospheric "Black Or Blue".

ROCK
& POP

NORTH AMERICA

AMERICA IS THE HOME OF POP AND ROCK 'N' ROLL GUITAR MUSIC. THE STYLES THAT UNDERPIN POPULAR MUSIC AROUND THE WORLD HAVE THEIR ROOTS IN AMERICAN BLUES, JAZZ, COUNTRY, AND FOLK MUSIC, AND THE URBAN DEVELOPMENTS WITHIN THESE GENRES THAT TOOK PLACE IN TOWNS AND CITIES ALL OVER THE COUNTRY.

JIMI HENDRIX *was a brilliant guitarist, singer, and composer who played with passion and dramatic power and became a key figure in the development of popular music.*

ROCK 'N' ROLL & POP

The convergence of many vibrant styles gave birth to rock 'n' roll, a watershed in the development of popular music. The strong rhythms of the first rock 'n' roll music conveyed a sense of the energy and explosive excitement that were to electrify the 1950s.

It is virtually impossible to point to one figure specifically or a particular recording as the beginning of rock 'n' roll. A whole range of developments was taking place in the 1940s, and early rock 'n' roll, as we understand it today, may have been performed in various types of black venues by the early 1950s.

Before the advent of rock 'n' roll, popular music did not necessarily focus on the guitar, but the rising interest in blues and country music, combined with the development of the electric guitar in the 1930s, ensured that the instrument would become a powerful voice in the postwar period.

The complex derivation of the genre is hard to unravel, and it is just as difficult to pinpoint the day that rock 'n' roll was born as it is to identify its parents for certain. There are innumerable recorded antecedents before rock 'n' roll became firmly established around 1955. Jackie Brenston's "Rocket 88" (1951) is among early recordings that point the way.

Early on, the medium had a tendency to absorb and simplify earlier musical ideas. The blues of Robert Johnson (*see page 49*), Muddy Waters (*see page 53*) and John Lee Hooker (*see page 54*), the country of Hank Williams (*see page 68*), the melodic experiments of Les Paul (*see page 106*), jump blues and the styles and rhythms of R&B – all play a part in shaping the music. The label "rock 'n' roll", used as a new generic term in the early 1950s, comes from a song title of the 1930s and dates back even earlier.

Bill Haley (1925–81) was an early figurehead on the scene, presenting material that mixed country and R&B elements. His recordings feature guitarist Danny Cedrone (1920–54) on tracks such as "Rock The Joint" (1952), a precursor to "Rock Around The Clock", and hits such as "Crazy Man Crazy" (1953) paved the way for commercial rock 'n' roll success. After Cedrone's untimely death, Fran Beecher (b.1921) joined the group and his work can be heard on the scintillating short breaks on "Razzle Dazzle" (1955).

Rock 'n' roll was not always based on the guitar, but as the 1950s progressed, the instrument came to dominate the genre and increasingly replaced the parts that were once played by piano and saxophone.

CHUCK BERRY

The key figure in the development of the guitar in rock 'n' roll is Chuck Berry, born Charles Edward Anderson Berry in St. Louis Missouri in 1926. He grew up singing in the Baptist Church tradition and took up guitar while in high school. As a singer, guitarist and composer, he has become one of the architects of rock guitar and master of a freewheeling, three-chord driving boogie guitar style based on the I, IV and V three-chord blues (*see page 178*). His completely distinctive instrumental style integrates blues, jazz and country elements, and his solos reflect the influence of figures ranging from Robert Johnson, Charlie Christian (*see pages 102–03*) and T-Bone Walker (*see page 52*) to Muddy Waters. Berry was also

HALEY'S COMETS
Bill Haley started out as a country-influenced player, singing to an acoustic guitar. He formed his group The Saddlemen (renamed The Comets by 1953), laid down heavier rhythms and added electric guitar solos, often a major feature in his work. His appearance in the film The Blackboard Jungle *(1955) made him a star and to many heralded the start of the rock 'n' roll age.*

"ROCK AROUND THE CLOCK"

A major hit in the US and UK, "Rock Around The Clock" was recorded in New York in April 1954. Parts of the song are similar to Hank Williams' "Move It On Over" (1947). Featuring Danny Cedrone, it highlights R&B-style electric guitar rhythm played with slides and distortion, and a high-energy solo mixes fast jazz scales with blues licks using string bending.

"MAYBELLENE"
Chuck Berry's first hit "Maybellene", with the B-side "Wee Wee Hours" was released in July 1955. It reached number one on Billboard's Rhythm & Blues *chart and number five on the* Cashbox Top 100 *chart, establishing Berry as a major new figure on the music scene.*

THE CHUCK BERRY SET-UP

Chuck Berry used the classic combination of a Gibson guitar and a Fender amplifier to record and perform his music. He produced a distorted, dry sound with a lot of volume and good projection.

In 1955, at the beginning of his recording career, he used a Gibson ES-350TN with P90 pick-ups, which had just come out. He also used Fender amplifiers, and one of the models he used when performing live was a Fender Twin, which first went on sale in 1952.

Fender Twin amplifier

Gibson ES-350TN

BERRY'S GIBSONS
After the launch of the Gibson 335 in 1958 and the luxury models 345 and 355 in the following year, Berry adopted this line of instruments (in a red finish) as his main guitars for the rest of his career. Their construction, combining the features of thinline hollow-body and electric solid-body guitars, give him sustain and a deep, powerful tone. He is seen here with a 345.

influenced by boogie-woogie piano styles, which partly moulded the shape of his dry, punchy, percussive rhythm style. He started his recording career at Chess Records in Chicago in 1952 and his breakthrough came with "Maybellene", recorded in May 1955. This was based on his own adaptation of the country tune "Ida Red", modifying the form and rhythm and using a throaty, distorted sound. The distorted edge to the guitar, with its sense of stirring energy, and the short solo with repeating motifs and smoky urgency have tremendous appeal. Berry alternates one twelve-bar, three-chord I-IV-V section with a section held on the I chord to build tension. He uses a pronounced alternating root to fifth bass movement on the chords (*see below*). The solo opens with a figure derived from T-Bone Walker that was to become a Berry hallmark: he plays a note and runs another against it by sliding it up to the same pitch to give a sense of rhythmic propulsion. His second single, "Thirty Days" (1955), uses a similar style of distorted rhythm playing and root movement.

Berry was able to create his own types of chord backing with great control and subtlety.

CHUCK BERRY TWELVE BAR

Berry assimilated a range of influences and put together a style of backing for his vocals that projected the clearly defined and well-executed rocking rhythms derived from boogie piano styles. Most of Berry's material is based on twelve-bar forms, and the sequence below shows one of his progressions. Starting with four bars in A, it moves to two bars of D then back to two bars of A, followed by two bars of E before finishing on two bars of A. The major characteristic is the use of a pair of fifths, where the upper note is moved to a sixth to give boogie-woogie movement. This is the basis for the most widely used sequence in rock 'n' roll, where E in bar nine moves down to D in bar ten. The upper sixths are often held longer, and there are different bluesy triplet rhythms. A final bar of E is often used to link back to the beginning. (*See pages 234–35 for musical terminology.*)

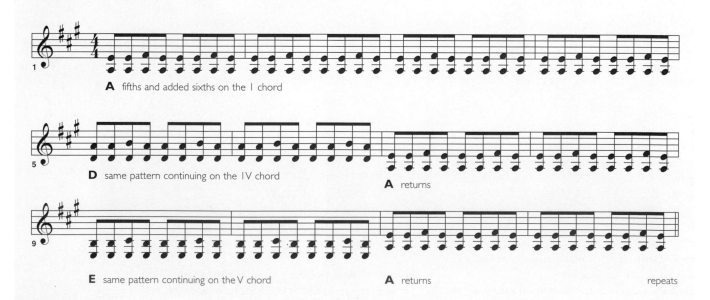

A fifths and added sixths on the I chord

D same pattern continuing on the IV chord   **A** returns

E same pattern continuing on the V chord   **A** returns   repeats

"JOHNNY B. GOODE"

The opening to "Johnny B. Goode" (1958) is one of the most famous in popular misic. Using a similar approach to the beginning of "Roll Over Beethoven", it benefits from superior overall construction. Berry stretches the idea out and lets it breathe melodically, adding his sliding technique of playing pairs of notes at the same pitch. The solo contains echoing excerpts from the opening. The song's simple, short fills, repeated, with slight variations, in a rhythmic framework, generate a spirited and infectiously joyous sound.

On the atmospheric "Downbound Train" (1955), he creates a rhythm that gives the feeling of a train moving, and "Havana Moon" (1956) has its own peculiar Caribbean flavour. "Roll Over Beethoven" (1956) is an important track on which Berry introduces one of the key elements in his playing. The song has a driving, incisive rhythmic opening with single lines, double stopping and chords with slides. This acts as an independent melodic passage that prefaces the song. In contrast, the solo break uses similar elements but has a simpler overall conception.

Berry's music is full of simple, well-executed ideas put together with great effectiveness. "School Days" (1957) opens with a chord that mimics the school bell, and in the song he answers his own vocal lines with chord breaks that restate the melody and provide variety. On "Carol" (1958), Berry plays both bluesy, single-line bending and chordal responses to his vocal lines and takes a short, inventive chord solo. "Memphis Tennessee" (1958) achieves its special character with sliding chords, offbeat staccato fills and an understated chord solo that conveys the bleak emotion of the song.

In a long and productive career, Berry produced dozens of rock 'n' roll classics. In addition to his rhythm playing, his riffs, breaks, fills and solos have become templates for all rock 'n' roll guitar players. They are often elliptical variations on the same ideas, but clever, offbeat positioning lifts them and gives a fresh urgency. Still working in the 21st century, Chuck Berry is undoubtedly the godfather of rock 'n' roll guitar.

BO DIDDLEY

Born in Mississippi, Bo Diddley (Elias McDaniel, b.1928) grew up listening to Muddy Waters and John Lee Hooker, and his work has affinities with Chicago blues music. Diddley signed to the Checker label, a subsidiary of Chess records, and developed his own rhythmic style with minimal use of linear solos or chordal harmony. He uses an open-D tuning and simple, expressive techniques, including slides as well as effects, to enhance the feeling of exotic power in his music.

After the success of the unique beat behind "Bo Diddley" (1955), he used the same approach for "Pretty Thing" (1956), on which the guitar opens with a similar colourful and highly effective pattern. The jiving, echo-laden "Who Do You Love" (1957) has twangy breaks and a rocky solo by guitarist Jody Williams, while "Road Runner" (1960) features wild pick scrapes and is driven by a strong, rocking figure in a low register.

Diddley's unique urban sound and style is very different from his contemporaries and has been described as having a "jungle" feel. Succeeding artists have used his hallmark beat as a staple variant to support their songs.

BO DIDDLEY
With his gritty voice and charismatic stage presence, Bo Diddley played the part of a rock 'n' roll star to perfection, projecting a distinctive image, including strange-shaped Gretsch guitars. He formed a group that included his half-sister, "The Duchess" on guitar, Otis Spann on piano and Jerome Green on trademark maracas.

"BO DIDDLEY"

Two of Diddley's compositions were released on one single in 1955. "Bo Diddley" introduced the distinctive rhythm specifically associated with him. This rhythmic pattern, sometimes rendered onomatopoeically as "shave-and-a haircut-six-bits", suggests an African character. The chords have strong tremolo effects and volume fluctuations that enhance the feel. The raw, direct B-side "I'm A Man" is a particular type of blues minimalism based on one chord with a driving, repetitive riff that is both hypnotic and compelling.

SCOTTY MOORE

In 1954 Scotty Moore (b.1931) started working with Elvis Presley (1935–77) in Sam Phillips' Sun Studios in Memphis, Tennessee. Moore had grown up in Tennessee idolizing country players Chet Atkins and Merle Travis (*see pages 68–71*) and assimilating the blues. He considered Elvis' music to be "honky-tonk" in style, with its rock 'n' roll mixed with country and blues

ELVIS & MOORE
Elvis Presley bought his Martin D-18 in 1953 and used it for recording and performing until 1956. It appeared on his first single "That's All Right, Mama" and the B-side, "Blue Moon Of Kentucky", released in 1954. He is seen above using a Martin Dreadnought while Scotty Moore plays his Gibson L-5CES.

Martin D-18

elements; it was sometimes referred to as "Hillbilly Cat", cat signifying the blues element. In their early recording sessions, Presley strums energetic chords on acoustic guitar to give backing to his great vocals. Bill Black on double bass underpins this, while Moore adds driving figures and inventive solos, the vital elements to give a modern electric sound; his slides and staccato add further lift and incisiveness to the music. At the beginning of Elvis' career, Moore plays riffs, fills and solos with a chordal style that implies fuller harmonies and dispenses with the need for arrangements with added instruments; he also limits his passages of single-line soloing.

THE SCOTTY MOORE SOUND

Scotty Moore plays with a thumbpick with fingers and occasionally a standard flatpick. He uses Gibson archtop models, starting with the ES-295 played on the early recordings. His guitar sound was often treated with a slapback tape echo-effect created in the studio. Later, he was seen with a natural-finish Gibson L-5CES, using Alnico pick-ups that produce a colourful, deep tone. In 1955, Moore started using an EchoSonic amplifier, specially built by Ray Butts to include an echo unit, which enabled him to produce the sounds he wanted directly in the studio and on tour.

On the first Elvis sessions, recorded in July 1954, the Arthur "Big Boy" Crudup blues, "That's All Right, Mama", features a Moore solo mixing chords and melody. Moore often used echo, and this can be heard on "Mystery Train" (1955), a timed-echo effect conjuring a feeling of movement. At the end of 1955, Presley signed to RCA, the sound and arrangements were developed, and guitarist Chet Atkins was brought in sometimes to add further parts to Moore's work, as he does on Elvis' first big hit "Heartbreak Hotel" (1956). This shows distinctive emphasized chords and chord breaks using slide. One of the highlights of Moore's playing in this era is "Hound Dog" (1956), on which his guitar has a shatteringly bright tone for the strumming patterns and he produces a captivating lilting solo.

Scotty Moore left Elvis in 1958; his legacy was his contribution to a sound that is one of the main constituents of "rockabilly", a term coined after the 1950s to describe rock 'n' roll with country influences.

CARL PERKINS

Another major Sun Records artist of the mid 1950s was Carl Perkins (1932–98). Born in Tennessee, he absorbed blues from local musicians, and country music through listening to the Grand Ole Opry radio show. He released a number of country singles before "Blue Suede Shoes" (1956) marked a shift towards rock 'n' roll and became a huge hit with its driving rhythm and melodic chordal breaks. The B-side, "Honey Don't", has a distinctive intro with a bluesy, sliding, descending figure played against open-string, jiving boogie riffs, offbeat rhythms with earthy acoustic and electric guitar textures and a chord solo with a catchy, rhythmic edge.

With his writing, singing and playing abilities, Perkins was set to become a major star, but a car accident in 1956 removed him from the burgeoning rock 'n' roll scene at a crucial time. He returned to record significant numbers that display a wide range of sounds; they include "Matchbox" (1957), that opens with an abrasive, tremulous intro, and "Dixie Fried" (1957), with its minimal staccato guitar rhythm, and solo breaks using expressive slides.

His playing veers from a snarling rocky modernity to a sensitive elliptical melodiousness and his sound, using slides, bends and staccato, is bright and resonant. In a long career, Perkins was a key figure who pioneered rockabilly, wrote songs that became standards, and produced guitar parts that were often imitated and helped to shape later styles of pop and rock music.

CLIFF GALLUP

Cliff Gallup (1930–88) was one of the most talented backing guitarists of the 1950s. Based in Nashville, he worked with Gene Vincent and the Blue Caps in 1956. With a liquid tone, often with echo, his playing uses jazz chords and his solos switch between unexpected elements, creating a sense of surprise. The most well-known track is the classic "Be Bop A Lula" (1956), in which a flowing solo is followed by a declamatory break mimicking the vocals. The wonderfully mad "Bluejean Bop" (1956) opens with impressionist jazz harmonies and moves on to solo breaks that juxtapose short, melodic quotes and interesting phrases with a verve and panache quite unlike anything in mainstream rock 'n' roll. "Race With The Devil" (1956) features a solo break with sharply defined, precisely executed ideas that dovetail into each other, and a second break in which Gallup plays in a steel-guitar style.

Gibson ES-5 Switchmaster

After working with Gene Vincent, Gallup carried on playing but languished in obscurity for the rest of his career. An individual with a capacity to produce virtuosic cameos on which his humour and individuality shine out, and which are hard for succeeding players to copy and fully assimilate, he is perhaps the most overlooked guitarist in 1950s rock 'n' roll.

CARL PERKINS
The dry, metallic-sounding rhythm and soloing style of Carl Perkins was produced on a Gibson ES-5 Switchmaster, which first came out in 1955. This is a modified upgrade of the earlier ES-5, with three pick-ups, a four-way switch, and pairs of volume and tone controls for each pick-up which gives the Switchmaster an unprecedented electric tonal range.

CLIFF GALLUP
Rock 'n' roll records of the 1950s often feature beautifully executed, well-thought-out parts. Cliff Gallup (far left) produced some of the greatest cameo solos in the genre.

COCHRAN'S GRETSCH
*Eddie Cochran's main
electric guitar was a
Gretsch 6120, which
first came out in 1955.
It was fitted with a
Gibson P90 pick-up
in the rhythm position.*

DON & PHIL EVERLY
*Both Everly brothers
sing harmony vocals and
play acoustic guitar, and
their recordings feature
a full acoustic sound,
with additions from a
backing band and
extra electric parts
from session guitarists.*

EDDIE COCHRAN

A straightforward style and a harder edge can be heard in the work of Eddie Cochran (1938–60), who developed his career in California. Starting from a country-music base, he evolved a rock 'n' roll style with a modern urban sound that has depth and maturity.

Boosted by the powerful tone, presence and percussive urgency of his guitar, Cochran's seemingly limited harmonic and melodic vocabulary didn't stop him performing with considerable versatility. He played a major part in establishing the use of strong, powerful steel-string chordal-style acoustic rock guitar. Cochran's approach was popular and has proved to be perennially influential on succeeding generations of players, his guitar working effectively with his vocals to convey youthful frustration and direct emotional expressiveness. This can be heard on his first hit, "Sittin' In The Balcony" (1957), while "Sweetie Pie" (1960) has a loose, scrappy low-register chords style with effects that shows originality.

Cochran's solos are always memorable, ranging from "Twenty Flight Rock" (1957), which has a short, scratchy chord solo full of understated character, to "Jeanie, Jeanie, Jeanie" (1958), featuring stinging rhythm sounds and a short, raunchy chordal solo with a rasping tone.

Cochran's high emotional input is evident on "Eddie's Blues" (1964). Released posthumously, this instrumental features wild, shaking tremolo-bar chord sounds and a frenzied emotional solo. Cochran vibrates the pick to convey impassioned energy and plays extended, fast hammered phrases that bristle with hypnotic energy.

ROCK 'N' ROLL TOWARD POP

As rock 'n' roll and popular music unfolded in the 1950s, different stylists appeared, adopting a variety of approaches to the guitar. The fiery side of rock 'n' roll started to wane in the popular mainstream, and compositions with a lighter approach used the guitar in a harmonic

"SUMMERTIME BLUES"

One of the great tracks from the 1950s, Eddie Cochran's "Summertime Blues" (1958) derives its power from the emphasis on steel-string guitar with electric bass. Simple strummed chords punctuate the vocals and carry the song. The follow-up, "C'mon Everybody" (1959), is also fuelled by the powerful combination of driving electric bass and strummed chords. In an effective use of space, the guitar drops out in sections, which helps to give it impact when it comes back in.

and rhythmic role to produce varied sounds that paved the way for pop styles in the 1960s. The Everly Brothers, Don (b.1937) and Phil (b.1939), had a country background and a father, Ike, who was an accomplished guitarist. One of their characteristics is the use of catchy, acoustic chordal intros, and this can be heard on their first big hit "Bye Bye Love" (1957) with its chord riffs with muted rhythms. "Claudette" (1958) and "Bird Dog" (1958) also demonstrate acoustic guitar intros.

Buddy Holly (1936–59) and his group The Crickets used light, melodic chord rhythms. "That'll Be The Day" (1957), recorded in New Mexico, has memorable parts: a country-style blues intro and understated, sparse rhythm with echo moves into a chordal break using a typical rock 'n' roll driving figure followed by boogie riffing. "Peggy Sue" (1957) is built on strumming with a dull tone running alongside drum fills before a contrasting, fast-strummed melodic chord-break on which the tone suddenly becomes trebly.

Holly's career was cut short when he died in a plane crash in 1959. His legacy, in guitar terms, was a highly personal style that often uses open-string chords and simple chords as melody parts, which gave his playing great appeal to aspiring guitarists.

BUDDY HOLLY
His ability to create a fresh approach with the guitar in a trio setting allowed Buddy Holly to record numbers that shaped the future of pop-guitar rhythm playing. "Not Fade Away" (1957), for example, features a distinctive rhythm and strummed-chord melody parts that complement the vocal. Holly was the first major figure to be seen using a Fender Stratocaster.

Fender Stratocaster

Fender Bassman amplifier

STRATOCASTER & BASSMAN

The Stratocaster first came out in 1954; with its futuristic design and three pick-ups, it became an icon of modern design that produced a range of transparent sounds ideal for rhythm and lead playing. Buddy Holly often combined his guitar with a Fender Bassman amplifier to give a full-bodied projection.

JAMES BURTON
Appearing as a gifted teenager on the Louisiana Hayride show, James Burton worked with a wide range of acts until he had an early break as a session guitarist, playing a solo on Dale Hawkin's single "Suzie Q" in 1957.

JAMES BURTON

One of the greatest young session players to emerge in the late 1950s was James Burton (b.1939). He took over from guitarist Joe Maphis in Ricky Nelson's band in 1957. His beautifully executed short cameo solos stand out for their ideas and musical taste. "I Got A Feeling" (1958), "It's Late" (1958), "Believe What You Say" (1958) and "Travelin' Man" (1961) demonstrate Burton's ability to play concise and well-balanced phrases. He had tremendous influence on pop guitarists in the 1960s, and went on to have a career as one of the industry's most prolific session and backing-band guitarists, playing with Elvis Presley, and many others.

DUANE EDDY

With the rise of rock 'n' roll and pop and the tremendous new interest in the guitar, Duane Eddy (b.1938) broke into the mainstream and changed the musical landscape with a powerful twangy sound, in which bass strings are used to pick out the melody. On "Rebel Rouser" (1958), the guitar has an astonishing bottom end and the strings sound like heavy-duty cables. Eddy's guitar retains a balance and clarity as it moves from a bright metallic to a percussive muted sound on tracks such as "Because They're Young" (1960), and on the well-known "Peter Gunn" (1960), a repeating guitar riff easily holds its own with a throaty tenor sax. Eddy's guitar work and commercial success cleared the way for the guitar to become an instrumental pop voice in its own right.

INSTRUMENTAL STYLISTS

Distortion and raunchy "power chords" distinguish the work of Link Wray (b.1930), which stands out as historically significant in that it predates heavy-rock guitar. His first important record, "Rumble" (1958), was followed by atmospheric muscular playing with heavy-rock style effects on "Rawhide" (1959), "Jack The Ripper" (1962) and many other tracks.

A rather overlooked figure is Lonnie Mack (b.1941), who, in 1963, produced instrumentals such as a version of Chuck Berry's "Memphis", and "Wham", that combined elements of 1950s rock and country styles with blues soloing using bends and effects.

Some of the most exciting group guitar work was recorded by The Ventures, started in 1959, with Bob Bogle (b.1937) playing the lead parts and Don Wilson (b.1937) playing rhythm. Their work is a playful take on the popular guitar vocabulary of the late 1950s. They take Duane Eddy's

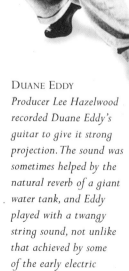

DUANE EDDY
Producer Lee Hazelwood recorded Duane Eddy's guitar to give it strong projection. The sound was sometimes helped by the natural reverb of a giant water tank, and Eddy played with a twangy string sound, not unlike that achieved by some of the early electric country players.

SURF GUITAR

At the end of the 1950s, Surf appeared as a musical label in Los Angeles. The Surf sound has a manic energy and a peculiar melodiousness, partly in the tradition of instrumentals of the Californian country scene. There is a strong Fender flavour and a smooth sophistication in studio production quality, with echo and reverb effects. Dick Dale (b.1937), "The King Of Surf Guitar", recorded "Let's Go Trippin'" (1961) and "Miserlou" (1962) with a flamboyant intense approach, and displays a precise technical control that enables him to play melodic lines and double stops with a cutting staccato.

twang a stage further in the context of precise arrangements. "Wailin'"(1960), a steaming rocker, shows a variety of guitar sounds, and their version of jazz guitarist Johnny Smith's "Walk Don't Run" (1960), with its classical melodic lines, is spirited and characterful.

STEVE CROPPER

Booker T. and the MGs was the name given to the informal band made up of a talented group of studio musicians who worked for the Stax label in Memphis. The guitarist, Steve Cropper (b.1941), initially inspired by 1950s soul-guitarist Lowman Pauling (d.1973) and a wide range of other influences, has built up a history of fine guitar recordings. Cropper's tone has a metallic ferocity, yet his playing is always sparse and pervaded with a feeling of suspense. On "Green Onions" (1962), his precise, understated work and a solo based around short phrases help to generate a rolling sense of excitement.

MEMPHIS SOUND
Cropper's sensitive use of dynamics, controlled volume, economy, and fine sense of rhythmic positioning enhance rhythmic grooves and draw the listener in.

POP DEVELOPMENTS

At the beginning of the 1960s, pop music in America was defined by melodic pop, rock 'n' roll guitar and a whole range of black popular styles. With the advent of British pop and rock, America was spurred to build on its musical heritage and create fresh sounds.

In Los Angeles, the Surf-music scene with its sunny optimism and energy was the matrix from which emerged a group that was to become one of the major forces in popular music. The Beach Boys were formed in 1961 by the three Wilson Brothers, Brian, Carl and Dennis, together with Mike Love and Al Jardine. The group were shaped musically by the prodigious talent of Brian Wilson (b.1942), who sang and played bass. His major contribution was writing, arranging and producing. Carl Wilson (1946–98) sang and played guitar, but a large part of the group's music was played by session musicians, with guitar parts by a host of studio players. In the early days, the guitar sound was often highly derivative. The breakthrough second single "Surfin' Safari" (1962) has a dry, muted rock 'n' roll rhythm and a twangy chordal solo. "Surfin' USA" (1963), based on the Chuck Berry number "Sweet Little

Sixteen", reveals a Beach Boys' arrangement, yet the guitar parts mirror Chuck Berry's guitar style, a homage also evident on the "Johnny B. Goode"-style intro to "Fun Fun Fun" (1964). Nevertheless, the group often used guitar very effectively, as on the chordal parts that offset the beautiful harmony vocals on "In My Room" (1963).

ROGER McGUINN

One of the first influential pop groups with a distinctive guitar sound to emerge from Los Angeles in the 1960s was The Byrds. Members of the group had a pronounced leaning toward folk and, with the style revolution taking place in pop music, they started creating their own synthesis of folk and pop, which has affinities with the work of Bob Dylan, The Searchers and The Beatles. The major figure in the group is Roger McGuinn (b.1942), whose playing shows harmonic sensibilities and takes strands from folk as well as jazz. With David Crosby, he created a chiming sound with jangling, sonorous chords that became one of the hallmarks of 1960s pop. The Byrds' captivating version of Dylan's "Mr. Tambourine Man" (1965), with its bright, swirling opening of two guitars playing

THE BEACH BOYS
Guitar parts on The Beach Boys' songs are often played in various styles with a controlled approach that supports the tunes. "I Get Around" (1964) has a raunchy rock 'n' roll feel, and "Don't Worry Baby" (1964) features jangly strumming and clean, chipped fills with reverb that lift the arrangement. As the group developed, the guitar became increasingly harmonic and textural.

PET SOUNDS

Late in 1965, Brian Wilson started putting together tracks for what would become one of the great albums in pop music, *Pet Sounds* (1966). Virtually all the guitar parts are by experienced studio players, including Barney Kessel (*see page 105*), Glen Campbell and others. On some of the most effective tracks, the guitar is almost invisible, woven into a collage of sound, yet it has an essential role in the creation of textures within innovative arrangements. Apart from some strummed chordal rhythms, the guitar is treated as part of a plucked string ensemble with various combinations of harpsichord, mandolin and even ukelele on "Wouldn't It Be Nice", "Caroline No" and "Sloop John B".

melodies and chords and a hypnotic mixture of rolling and staccato rhythm figures under the vocal, became a major hit in 1965. One of their most interesting arrangements is Pete Seeger's folk song "Turn, Turn, Turn" (1966), which opens with a simple melodic theme and features arpeggiated figures and a 12-string solo that progresses to state the melody. With guitar lines inspired by John Coltrane, The Byrds'

composition "Eight Miles High" (1966) opens with a bass riff and the guitar vibrates a note before playing a short theme and taking off into a passage of tangled improvisation with unusual lines using unfamiliar intervals. This returns for a solo interlude and is reintroduced at the end. With such approaches, The Byrds' music became an important part of the foundation of the "West Coast" sound in the 1960s.

Rickenbacker 370/12RM

ROGER MCGUINN
George Harrison inspired McGuinn to take up the Rickenbacker electric 12-string guitar. Some of McGuinn's early textures were created with the help of a Vox Treble Booster to add edge, and studio compression for added sustain. The effect, combined with his pick and fingerstyle technique, forged a distinct identity that has influenced the sound of pop guitar.

SOUL & FUNK

During the 1950s, pioneers such as Lowman Pauling with The 5 Royales paved the way for a style of soul music that was based on R&B and Gospel. A fresh sound was created in the context of strong vocal arrangements in which guitar combined with other instruments to form a backdrop. In 1959, Berry Gordy founded the important studio and recording company that came to be known as Tamla Motown. During the 1960s, a large body of great pop songs were produced there with the help of a group of session guitarists, including Robert White, Joe Messina and Larry Veeder. Their work can be heard on tracks by many artists: Barrett Strong's "Money (That's What I Want)" (1960) sees distorted guitar playing riffs with saxophone. A seductive riff opens the Temptations' sublime "My Girl" (1964) and "I'm Losing You" (1966) has clipped rhythm parts. Stevie Wonder's "For Once In My Life" (1968) opens with two funky cross-rhythm patterns joined by a melody

part. One of the most attractive additions was the contribution of Marv Tarplin on Smokey Robinson's "The Tracks Of My Tears" (1969), where the guitar plays melodic chords.

At the Stax studios in Memphis, Steve Cropper (*see page 184*) worked as the main house session guitarist and as a producer; he also co-wrote material for recordings such as Wilson Pickett's "Midnight Hour" (1965) and Otis Redding's "Dock Of The Bay" (1968).

One of his most well-known guitar parts is that for Sam and Dave's "Soul Man" (1967), on which he plays a distinctive melodic part that opens the tune and contributes features made up of two- and three-note chords throughout the song.

A funkier, choppy rhythm that provided an insistent edge was developed by Jimmy Nolen (1934–83), who worked with James Brown from 1965. His funky parts are often based on holding down simple harmonies. Nolen plays bright chips and dry, strummed fills on "Papa's Got A Brand New Bag" (1965) and "I Got You (I Feel Good)" (1965). One of his classic and instantly identifiable chordal motifs is heard on "Get Up" (1970).

Another individual key to the creation of a funky, rhythmic soul style at this time was Leo Nocentelli (b.1946), recording with The Meters.

JIMMY NOLEN
Jimmy Nolen brings funky offbeats and steamy, rolling rhythms together with sharp focus on James Brown's "Cold Sweat" (1967).

THE LOS ANGELES SCENE

The Doors were formed in 1965, with Jim Morrison on vocals, Ray Manzarek on keyboards, John Densmore on drums and Robbie Krieger (b.1946) on guitar. The band has a sound and identity all its own, with the keyboards allowing Krieger the space to fill a thoughtful, original-sounding role. His playing is a complete departure from that of his contemporaries, drawing directly on classical and flamenco influences in addition to American popular music, and he often adds quite novel elements and melodic solos that have an almost compositional flavour. On *The Doors* (1967), the long version of "Light My Fire" moves towards jazz, with Krieger taking a solo with an altered scale. "The End" has an atmospheric setting with an Indian classical-music flavour, building to a chaotic climax. Krieger further developed his instrumental voice on the album *Waiting For The Sun* (1968).

Other Los Angeles groups explored progressive avenues. Love, formed in 1965 with Arthur Lee (b.1945) on guitar, put together an intricate, more blues-influenced sound that can be heard on *Forever Changes* (1968). In the same year, Spirit, with the young guitarist Randy California (*see page 198*), brought out their debut album *Spirit*, setting psychedelic folk, pop harmony and blues-rock guitar in adventurous compositional settings.

SAN FRANCISCO

The vibrant, multi-faceted and experimental music scene that grew up in 1960s San Francisco made the city a mecca for musicians and attracted guitar players from all over the Americas.

One of the first groups to gain prominence was Jefferson Airplane, formed in 1965 with Jorma Kaukonen (b.1940) playing lead guitar and Paul Kantner (b.1942) on rhythm. Their first album, *Jefferson Airplane Takes Off,* was released in 1966 and a series of popular albums followed, including *Surrealistic Pillow* (1967). With their fusion of different strands of music

and a distinctive sound, they became part of the psychedelic movement and one of the groups who created the "San Francisco sound". Kaukonen and Kantner play in a sonorous, chordal folk-pop style with attractive voicings. At their most effective, the guitar parts mesh to create a dancing interplay. An early acoustic instrumental highlight is Kaukonen's composition, "Embryonic Journey" (1967). On the group's stronger material, the lead guitar is often used simply for touches and additions. A feeling of mystery pervades the opening short guitar lines on the unusual "White Rabbit", for instance, and the rockier, driving "Somebody To Love" ends with a solo shrouded in background reverb and echo.

Kaukonen used blues and country music in his playing, and as Jefferson Airplane developed, he moved toward a heavier rock style using distortion and effects such as wah wah. The soloing sometimes meanders, but shorter passages and fills, and the acoustic playing, are highly effective. One of the group's finest pieces, "Wooden Ships" (1969), uses a muffled, sustained sound on acoustic and electric guitar parts to conjure the sound of the sea.

THE DOORS
As part of a group with the charismatic Jim Morrison and the classical keyboard playing of Ray Manzarek, Robbie Krieger could transcend the standard pop and blues vocabulary and pursue his own path as a player with an individual voice in a group that had its own unmistakeable sound.

JORMA KAUKONEN
Joining the powerful Grace Slick and Marty Balin on vocals, Paul Kantner on guitar, Jack Casady on bass and Spencer Dryden on drums, Jorma Kaukonen worked as part of a group that wrote strong material and in which all the individuals could be creative and build distinctive arrangements.

JERRY GARCIA

Contemporary with Jefferson Airplane were The Grateful Dead, formed in 1965 with Jerry Garcia (1942–95), and Bob Weir (b. 1947) on rhythm guitar. On their first album, *The Grateful Dead* (1967), Garcia shows the direction he is taking on "Viola Lee Blues", where he explores linear possibilities in an extended piece. One of the group's most famous albums, *Live/Dead* (1969), is compiled from different performances and demonstrates their jam-session approach on tracks such as "Dark Star", the rhythmic "Turn On Your Love Light", and "Eleven" with its long passages of improvisation. "Feedback" shows an avant-garde side, with free-form excursions, volume-level fluctuation and pitch effects. On the album *Workingman's Dead* (1970), there is a shift toward concise songwriting and pronounced country-guitar styles. "Uncle John's Band" shows acoustic rhythm and soloing; "High Time" is characterized by country-style electric soloing with effects; and "New Speedway Boogie" and "Cumberland Blues" have dry, twangy rock and country-guitar playing.

The Grateful Dead built a core of material which was performed with a concentrated power that held audiences.

"DARK STAR"

One of The Grateful Dead's most well-known pieces, "Dark Star", was originally released as a single in 1968. It became an important part of the group's live repertoire and by the time it was recorded for *Live/Dead* (1969) had mutated and become a vehicle for extensive improvisation. On this 23-minute version, Garcia builds around an ascending melodic motif and moves into a jazz-influenced area, with a full scalar vocabulary and interesting pentatonic lines. A rambling, exploratory piece, it depends on a great deal of interplay between the soloing Garcia and bass player Phil Lesh. Over the years, "Dark Star" became one of the major pieces in The Grateful Dead's extensive repertoire.

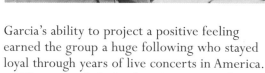

Garcia's ability to project a positive feeling earned the group a huge following who stayed loyal through years of live concerts in America.

The style of playing long instrumental jam sessions was also developed by Quicksilver Messenger Service, formed in 1965 by John Cipollina (1943–89) and Gary Duncan. *Happy Trails* (1969) has a 25-minute version of Bo Diddley's "Who Do You Love?" with a long, intense solo using effects and tremolo.

In a burgeoning Bay Area scene, other guitarists appeared, including Steve Miller and Carlos Santana (*see page 198*). Creedence Clearwater Revival, formed in 1967 with John Fogerty (b. 1945), played music utterly unlike the other mainstream groups, based partly on 1950s rock 'n' roll, with Fogerty taking short, punchy solos with a sharp tone and attack.

THE EAST COAST

Away from the West Coast, in music centres such as New York, guitarists were adding parts to singles and albums with very different musical identities. The addition of electric guitar to Bob Dylan's album *Bringing It All Back Home* (1965) and the move to a full group sound proved to be a historic turning point. Mike Bloomfield

(*see page 59*) plays electric guitar on the subsequent *Highway 61 Revisited* (1965). His electric rhythm, fragments of arpeggios and fills with the organ layer on "Like A Rolling Stone" (1965) gave it the edge that helped produce Dylan's first major hit.

The Lovin' Spoonful's Zal Yanovsky (b.1944) created a variety of melodic touches, tone colours and inventive rhythms. "Do You Believe In Magic?" (1965) has a full, yet light rhythm sound and relaxed, twangy, country-style fills. On "You Didn't Have To Be So Nice" (1965), the electric guitar plays chiming chords and a countermelody. "Daydream" (1966) features staccato electric and acoustic chords, muted lines with echo and volume pedal fade-ups, and "Summer In The City" (1966) sparkles and thrums with crunchy, bright strummed chords.

EAST-WEST

The Paul Butterfield Blues Band's second album *East-West* (1966) was an important breakthrough, opening doors and laying the cornerstone for a a progressive fusion between blues, jazz, rock and eastern music. It features Mike Bloomfield, one of the most outstanding blues-guitar soloists of the 1960s. He moves toward both jazz and Indian classical music, taking ideas from raga scales, phrasing and motifs. The title track "East-West" is a 13-minute instrumental that had a tremendous effect on guitarists all over the world.

EXPERIMENTALISM

THE VELVET UNDERGROUND
On the landmark album *The Velvet Underground And Nico* (1967), Lou Reed (Louis Firbank, b.1942) and Sterling Morrison (1941–95) used the guitar in differing contexts, ranging from vacuous arpeggiated chords through to a more nihilistic, bleak feeling with rough execution and a flat, driving rhythm on tracks such as "I'm Waiting For The Man", and the monotone drone of "Venus In Furs". The solo on "Run Run Run" has an edgy tension, and "The Black Angel's Death Song" has a strange and appealing repetitive dark rumble. The frenetic free-form passage on "European Son" sees the movements up and down the fretboard as it is furiously strummed. The overall effect is interesting and original, combining folk, pop and rock approaches with a conceptual sophistication that attempts to avoid cliché, although the guitar has an inescapable earthy authenticity. On their second album, *White Light / White Heat* (1967), the Velvets further develop their avant-garde drone and feedback style before moving on to the more melodic approach they were pursuing at the end of the 1960s.

CAPTAIN BEEFHEART
Some of the strangest and most bizarre guitar music in the 1960s came from Captain Beefheart (Don Van Vliet, b.1941) whose first album *Safe As Milk* (1967) introduced an irreverent and experimental approach to blues. The second album *Trout Mask Replica* (1969)

was produced by Frank Zappa and featured guitarists Jeff Cotton and Bill Harkleroad (Zoot Horn Rollo). This is a shattering type of irregular, avant-garde blues rock, with atonal sheets of sound and playing across the beat. It has a raucous intensity and, in spite of the clashing parts and dramatic madness, the music works as it rolls forward in a tangle of bizarre development. Inspired by experimental art, the jagged compositions sound shambolic but were, in fact, carefully structured and rehearsed.

VELVET UNDERGROUND
A group who were known for an experimental approach to popular music, The Velvet Underground produced music that did not need a strong technical guitar style. Their declamatory statements and introspective material nevertheless relied on effective guitar textures.

JIMI HENDRIX

One of the most revered figures in the history of popular music, Jimi Hendrix outshone his contemporaries in rock, displaying brilliant talent and imagination. He reinvented the sound of the electric guitar, redefining its voice to give it an elemental potency and expressiveness.

THE EXPERIENCE
The innovative sound, flair and intensity of The Jimi Hendrix Experience had a tremendous impact on both musicians and the general public. At an early stage, the group interplay is remarkable. There is a strong empathy, and the relationship between the guitar and drums dominates the overall sound of the band. The music has a spontaneous quality and Hendrix said at the time that the group had a "free form" approach.

One of the greatest guitarists, Jimi Hendrix created a completely new landscape of sound and colour, developed blues in a modern context, and opened out the structure of rock music. Hendrix was born in Seattle, Washington, in 1942. Drawn to blues and rock 'n' roll through radio and records, he acquired his first guitar at the age of 12 and was playing with local bands by the age of 16. In 1962, he turned professional, working with many leading figures in black music, including Wilson Pickett, The Isley Brothers, and Ike and Tina Turner. In 1965, Hendrix moved to New York City, where he played around the bars and clubs, eventually forming his own group, Jimmy James and the Blue Flames. A year later, Chas Chandler, bassist with The Animals, saw Hendrix playing in Greenwich Village at the Cafe Wha?, and persuaded him to move to England to develop his career.

UK SCENE

Jimi Hendrix arrived in England in September 1966, and within days was introduced to the London music scene and encouraged by Chas Chandler to sit in with bands. An extraordinary guitarist and a spectacular showman, he was an immediate sensation. Hendrix had absorbed stage gimmicks from his time on the black music circuit, playing the guitar behind his back and the strings with his teeth. His personality shone through in his playing, and he was able to convey humour as well as great depth. Many leading pop musicians, including The Beatles and the Rolling Stones, were fascinated by his elemental energy and intensity. With encouragement from Chandler, Hendrix began auditioning musicians for the rhythm section of a group that would feature him on guitar. He eventually chose bass player Noel Redding and drummer Mitch Mitchell. With Redding's bass as an anchor, and Mitchell's flamboyant, improvisational style combining jazz and rock techniques, they provided the perfect foil for Hendrix's guitar.

The new group was called The Jimi Hendrix Experience, and Chas Chandler persuaded Hendrix to sing and develop his own material. After rehearsing intensively they played their first live dates in France during

FIRST EXPERIENCE RECORDINGS

With Chas Chandler acting as their producer, The Experience went into De Lane Lea Studios in Kingsway, London, in October 1966 to record their first tracks. The group recorded a cover of "Hey Joe", a song with tragic lyrics by Billy Roberts that was planned as a single. It is a slow ballad featuring an emotional guitar solo using clean guitar sound with bluesy, vocal melodiousness. For the B-side, Hendrix wrote "Stone Free", a complete contrast to "Hey Joe", with distorted texture, a driving funky edge and an electrifying fast solo. "Hey Joe" was released in December as the group was playing its first major run of UK dates, and reached number six in the UK pop charts in January 1967.

October and started recording. Their debut single was "Hey Joe"; a second single, "Purple Haze", and its B-side "51st Anniversary", were recorded in January 1967. Just before this session, Hendrix had met Roger Mayer, an electronics engineer who had developed new sound effects for the guitar. These can be heard on "Purple Haze", a dramatic, powerful rock number defined by the overdriven, heavy sound of the guitar. The opening tritone motif is followed by sweeping melodic riffs, strong crunching chords, and octave fills. "The Wind Cries Mary", a haunting ballad with ascending chords and a sensitive, delicately transparent solo, was also recorded in January, and released as the group's third single.

ARE YOU EXPERIENCED?

Between October 1966 and April 1967, the band accumulated material for their first album *Are You Experienced?* (1967), which features Jimi Hendrix's varied and inventive compositions and inspirational playing. The recorded sound has a warm immediacy and is full of techniques and effects with extreme tremolo-arm pitch variations, sound processing – such as distortion, echo and reverb – and tape manipulation, including changes in speed and backward passages that give strange sounds and create a futuristic otherworldliness. "Foxy Lady" opens with rattling notes and simmering feedback before the chords crash in, bringing a warm power and sensuality. Sinuous, sustaining line-bending, and wailing tremolo-arm effects dominate "Love Or Confusion", and "I Don't Live Today" floats along over ethereal sonic excursions. Cut-off riffs build tension on the fast, complex "Manic Depression" that rides on a driving 3/4 rhythm, and Hendrix plays an ascending line that breaks into a wild, primeval solo. The slow "Red House" is full of expressive blues breaks

JIMI HENDRIX
A tremendous performer, Jimi Hendrix appeared to be physically at one with the instrument, playing with an astonishing agility and pumping the tremolo arm to create surging layers of undulating movement. His musical spirit and presence is timeless and his legacy of recordings, together with film footage from live concerts, continues to inspire succeeding generations.

FLYING V
The original Flying V was first launched by Gibson in 1958. In 1965, a second, redesigned version appeared with an altered headstock and large pickguard with new fittings. The guitar shown here was owned by Jimi Hendrix from 1967 and used extensively. He painted it with multi-coloured flowers, and it has recently been restored.

with a smoky sound and echo. The songs show that Hendrix was an individualistic writer with a keen awareness of the effectiveness of arrangements. Guitar overdubs provide extra parts and fill out the sound.

On the second album, *Axis: Bold As Love* (1967), Hendrix further extends his sound with electronic experimentation on the way-out "EXP", and uses wah wah on "Up From The Skies". Among the highlights is "Little Wing", which has beautiful melodic chords, often with added hammer-ons and pull-offs, and a dramatic detuning drop before the solo. Sliding figures, chordal backdrops and backward guitar define "Castles Made Of Sand", and "If 6 Was 9" is minimalist rock with episodes of open exploration. The acerbic "Little Miss Lover" features a churning funkiness with muting, and a variety of tones with screaming lines and vocal wah wah; chopped, rock-funk rhythms and fast strumming characterize "You Got Me Floatin'".

LEFT-HANDED PLAYING
Hendrix mainly played Fender Stratocasters. Although left-handed, he used a standard right-handed model but upside-down, and strung it in a normal way, detuning it down to E♭.

LIVE

When Hendrix returned to the US in June 1967 to play at the Monterey Pop Festival, he was virtually unknown and vowed to "pull out all the stops". One of his set's highlights was "Wild Thing", where Hendrix smashed his guitar against the amplifiers to generate chords and open atonal sections before pouring lighter fluid over the instrument and setting it on fire – then he smashed it to pieces and threw them into the stunned audience.

In August 1969, Hendrix played the Woodstock Festival with an extended line-up including Billy Cox who replaced Noel Redding on bass. Hendrix put in a stunning performance, full of improvisational brilliance, and his set contained one of the defining moments in pop culture. As a protest against the Vietnam War, he plays a savage version of "The Star-Spangled Banner", screeching, avant-garde interjections with feedback and whistling turning it into a mocking parody with a grotesque, surrealist edge.

Toward the end of the year, Hendrix formed a new group, called The Band Of Gypsys, with Billy Cox on bass and Buddy Miles on drums. They can be heard on the album *Band Of Gypsys* (1970) that features their debut concert, recorded live at Fillmore East in New York City on New Year's Eve 1970. With simplified, funky drumming, the overall sound is heavy and bassy in comparison to that of The Experience. The grim "Machine Gun" opens with solo guitar heavy with restrained foreboding and Hendrix plays a recurring chopped staccato figure to mimic gunfire. His solo is contorted and full of darkness and pain, with passages of flowing wah wah, wobbling notes and exclamatory phrasing. In contrast, the upbeat "Power To Love" has a nasal sharpness, with wah wah and shaking notes.

A few weeks after playing at the Isle of Wight Festival in England in August 1970, Jimi Hendrix died in Notting Hill, London, from a mixture of drugs and alcohol.

LATER ALBUMS

After Hendrix died, a number of records were released containing both finished and unfinished studio tracks. Collections of some of these tracks were released as the albums *Rainbow Bridge* (1971) and the *Cry Of Love* (1971). Highlights include "Freedom", exuberant with funky riffs, the cathartic "Room Full Of Mirrors", and the capriciously humourous "Dolly Dagger", with its fast fills, high-register melodic chord additions, and heavily processed solo sound. Hendrix's gentle, reflective spirituality can be heard on the gently breaking chords and melodic fills of the sublime "Angel", and on the soft, flowing "Drifting", that features colourful harmonic changes.

Among the outstanding live albums are *Hendrix In The West* (1972) and *Live At Winterland* (1987). There are many studio tapes that show he was always pushing the boundaries and developing with extensive jam sessions with various guests which move toward open-ended jazz. Hendrix left a large body of great work that sounds as vibrant and powerful today as it did back in his heyday.

Marshall head

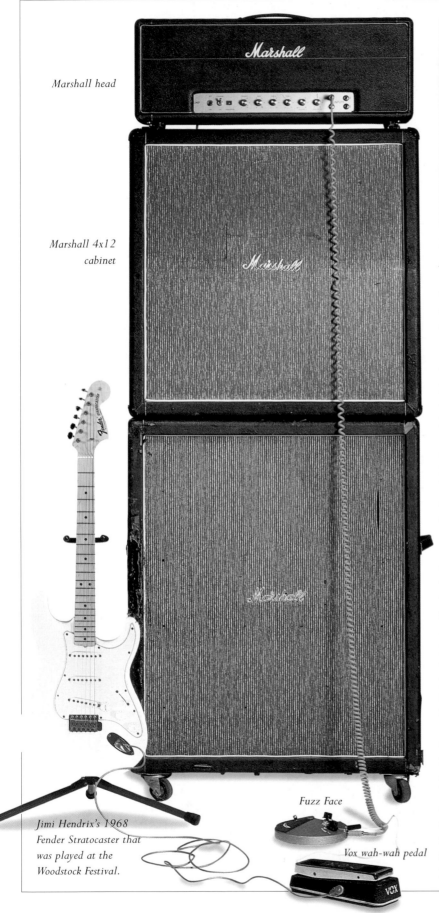

Marshall 4x12 cabinet

Jimi Hendrix's 1968 Fender Stratocaster that was played at the Woodstock Festival.

Fuzz Face

Vox wah-wah pedal

MARSHALL SOUND

Jimi Hendrix's main amplifier heads were Marshall 100-watt models, often modified to give a higher power output. There is no master volume control, and a full signal from the guitar with the volume fully up gives a rich, bright overdriven sound.

PLAYING SET-UP & APPROACH

His creative use of equipment enabled Hendrix to transcend genre and invent a new indefinable language. Although he mainly played Fender Stratocasters, he also used many other types of guitar, including the Gibson Flying V and Les Paul, steel-string acoustic guitars and electric bass. For effects, he used a fuzz pedal, wah wah and an Octavia and Uni-Vibe, with units built and modified by Roger Mayer.

Hendrix's revolutionary experimentation with sound-processing units, combined with overdrive, feedback, phasing, Leslie, stereo effects, and his unusual tremolo bar and tone and volume control techniques created a completely new, distinctive range of sounds and textures. He could create a soundfield with sustain and wailing feedback that pulsated and shifted with tone and colour. He also detuned strings to very low pitches, scraped the pick along the strings to give crying and shrieking sounds and hit the guitar body to simulate things ranging from storms to explosions.

He wrote creative chord sequences, used octaves, and his melodic and rhythmic riffs are inventive and original. His spontaneous solos have a powerful and expressive vocal quality, with string bending, trills, slides, glissandos and tremolo-bar movements, and his rhythmic skill enabled him to move effortlessly from a supple, laid-back feel to incisive attack. His pick technique was accurate and relaxed and his large hands enabled him to play extra bass notes under chords and fills.

STAGE & STUDIO
Hendrix was highly creative, both in live performance and in the studio, where he developed his own strong ideas. By the time he was working on the completion of Electric Ladyland *in the summer of 1968, he was acting as his own producer and felt that he had attained a level of artistic freedom.*

ELECTRIC LADYLAND

Tracks for this important and innovative album were initially laid down in London and produced by Chas Chandler before Hendrix eventually took over as producer with engineer Eddie Kramer and finished it in New York City in August 1968. On some tracks, Hendrix worked obsessively, recording over 40 takes. In addition to Mitchell and Redding, the album features guests, including Steve Winwood and Jack Casady.

AND THE GODS MADE LOVE (Hendrix)
Described by Hendrix as "a 90-second sound painting of the heavens", the album's opening track features backward tapes and echo with drum sounds and voice slowed down.

HAVE YOU EVER BEEN (TO ELECTRIC LADYLAND) (Hendrix)
This track has a spacey, effect-laden, drifting quality with short melodic fills, a languorous solo and backward guitar.

CROSSTOWN TRAFFIC (Hendrix)
One of the most exciting and focused tracks, this is driven by a tremendous rhythm and the guitar is mixed with a kazoo sound for the melodic riff.

VOODOO CHILE (Hendrix)
This track opens with a thick-textured, blues-guitar sound. With organ and relaxed groove from the bass and drums, Hendrix plays melodic fills around the vocal before going into a series of open-ended guitar solos that build in intensity.

LITTLE MISS STRANGE (Redding)
Redding plays acoustic guitar parts, and Hendrix adds slide fills and an unusual-sounding melody before going into a solo with varied sections, from dry sounds to a searing sustain, muted staccato, and a rhythmic wah-wah interlude.

LONG HOT SUMMER NIGHT (Hendrix)
This opens with a burning guitar sound followed by a vocal, backed by blues fills. Hendrix takes a blues solo and builds up

behind the vocals, before going out with a vibrating, picking solo.

COME ON (LET THE GOOD TIMES ROLL) (King)
This has abrasive, distorted rock riffs with a funky rhythmic drive and inspired uptempo solos with wah wah, and fast-strummed upper-register passages with chords and octaves.

GYPSY EYES (Hendrix)
The coruscating edginess of this track is created by a combination of searing downward slide and guitar lines with vocal and muted rhythmic fills. It goes into a heavy bass-and-drum backing with guitar rhythms and soaring fills before fading away at the end.

BURNING OF THE MIDNIGHT LAMP (Hendrix)
Featuring lines on wah-wah guitar with harpsichord, this track has a mandolin-like sound, created by using taped guitar fills speeded up from 7½ ips (inches per second) to 15 ips. There is a wah-wah solo with a wobbling surrealistic texture.

RAINY DAY, DREAM AWAY (Hendrix)
An open-ended loose shuffle sees Hendrix swapping phrases with organ and saxophone, producing a bright metallic sound and using funky chords. This moves to a descending chordal fill that suddenly breaks into a wah-wah sound, mimicking the human voice

1983 (A MERMAN I SHOULD TURN TO BE) (Hendrix)
Guitar sound effects move into a short, arpeggiated, chordal melody introducing the linear guitar theme that occurs throughout the song. In the background, guitar overdubs simulate water effects. There are passages on which the guitar builds up repeating scalar patterns and harmonized parts with the drums, solos over the theme, and free, open passages with detuned notes and spacey effects.

MOON, TURN THE TIDES. (Hendrix)
The previous track segues into this drifting piece, in which the guitar part is

made up of a short exploratory phrases, chords and backward tapes. It goes into sections, with a drum solo and a passage in which the bass is brought forward in the mix; the track ends with guitar solos and sonic effects.

STILL RAINING, STILL DREAMING (Hendrix)
On this continuation of "Rainy Day Dream Away", the guitar plays another expressive vocal wah-wah part that interweaves with the vocals before taking over and going into a powerful stream-of-consciousness exposition.

HOUSE BURNING DOWN (Hendrix)
Using shifts in phrasing, Hendrix creates a searing intensity on this track, which features a rhythmic uplift with explosive screaming guitar that has shattering intensity. The heavily processed solo has dynamic level changes and is mixed to create movement and field depth, giving a three-dimensional soundscape. At the end, pick scrapes produce growling and mechanical effects and there is panning between left and right stereo channels

ALL ALONG THE WATCHTOWER (Dylan)
With Dave Mason playing acoustic guitar, powerful electric chord overdubs and linear fills give this track a majestic beauty. Hendrix plays one of his greatest solos: four distinct eight-bar passages start expressive melodic lines, there is slide and wah wah, and funky chords climax with crying, ascending unison notes. The track finishes with a yearning guitar solo ending on one high note.

VOODOO CHILE (SLIGHT RETURN) (Hendrix)
One of the most interesting and complex tracks in rock, this opens with wah wah and leads to distorted chords and lines. There is a tremendous range of textures from the guitar over a deep rhythm-section groove with chopped passages, unfettered distortion and glissando effects. The solos have a cutting edge and a sense of notes being stretched to their limit, with tremolo and string-bending mixed with a range of touch and expression that is otherworldly.

FRANK ZAPPA

The most sophisticated and imaginative composer to emerge from the pop scene in the 1960s, Frank Zappa was also an inspired guitarist. Drawing from an unusual mixture of genres, he made up his own rules and forged a unique musical identity.

Born in Baltimore, Frank Zappa (1940–93) grew up in California. In 1964, he joined a Los Angeles band called the Soul Giants; a year later he had transformed them into the Mothers Of Invention, and a year after that, he recorded his first album, *Freak Out*. This introduces Zappa's humorous pastiche of popular genres, with avant-garde experimentalism supporting savagely humorous lyrics. The opening track, "Hungry Freaks", starts with raunchy electric riffs, and has a sneering, fuzzy guitar solo in a bluesy style. "Who Are The Brain Police?" buzzes with free-form passages, feedback and sonic guitar noise. He uses blues-rock playing for parody and social commentary on "Trouble Every Day" and strums humorous pop chords to offset "I'm Not Satisfied" and "You're Probably Wondering Why I'm Here".

On subsequent albums, the material does not always rely on guitar; instead Zappa uses tape manipulation and edits. *We're Only In It For The Money* (1968) is made up of wonderfully absurd juxtaposition, with scores of episodes that shift in content and style, but only tantalizing glimpses of guitar.

INSTRUMENTAL DEVELOPMENT

From the beginning, Zappa started to expand his vocabulary and develop his own type of original modern classical- and jazz-influenced harmony, combining odd time signatures, exotic instrumentation and studio techniques, including the use of speeded-up tapes. His compositional flair is evident on *Uncle Meat* (1969): he plays a long, jazzy solo on "Nine Types Of Industrial Pollution"; uses acoustic guitar to introduce the haunting beauty of the theme for "Dog Breath Variations"; and submerges the innocuous strummed guitar on "Project X" beneath other instruments, which seem disconnected. The album ends with a number of versions of the captivating linear number "King Kong", supported by jazzy guitar chord playing.

On the predominantly instrumental album *Burnt Weenie Sandwich* (1969), "Overture To A Holiday In Berlin" mixes steel-string guitar with other instruments playing the theme, and a similar texture is created for "Aybe Sea" which sees steel-string guitar playing lines with harpsichord and electric wah-wah guitar in certain parts of the background. "The Little House I Used To Live In" has an astonishing range of wah-wah guitar passages, including

FIRST STAGES
Zappa's characteristic approach to the instrument was already evident in his early work. Mainly playing a Gibson ES-5, he uses the guitar as an ensemble instrument, plays his own highly original raunchy blues style with rhythmic inventiveness and uses popular guitar styles imaginatively within his bizarre songs.

EARLY INFLUENCES

Zappa's primary early influences are the blues, 1950s rock 'n' roll and 1960s pop rhythms. In his playing, he manages to transcend the stylistic implications of these influences, reducing their importance to that of cameo roles within his compositional frameworks. Most importantly, he also absorbed ideas from modern and avant-garde jazz, and classical and experimental conceptual approaches. Sounds from around the world can be heard in his music and playing.

themes with mixed acoustic and electric guitars, a short calling-repeating motif, muted, raked melodic chords and a solo break with wah-wah inflections.

Zappa developed a way of playing long, directional solos with wah wah that unfold inventively as rhythmic and melodic ideas expand. This can be heard on "Theme From Burnt Weenie Sandwich" and "Holiday In Berlin, Full Blown".

GUITAR STYLE

Frank Zappa played drums at an early stage and this undoubtedly affected his guitar playing, which often incorporates unusual, inventive rhythmic passages. He uses both pentatonic and modal approaches seamlessly, and his melodic phrasing contains compositional ideas and unusual intervals. His legato phrasing has affinities with the articulation associated with the saxophone and violin, and, with hammering, pull-offs, bending, slides, grace notes, trills and a technique of tapping upper notes with a pick, Zappa's playing is full of detail.

Some of his solos are laid over straightforward modal vamps, repeating bass figures and pedal notes underpinned by electric bass and keyboard layering. Polyrhythmic drums, tuned percussion and interjections from brass and woodwind are used as added backdrops. With his imagination and intelligence, his complex ideas and his inimitable guitar playing, Zappa has created highly innovative material that has great depth and quality.

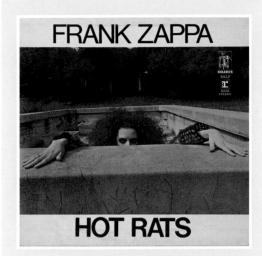

HOT RATS

On the album *Hot Rats* recorded in August and September 1969, Zappa composes extensive instrumental passages of music bursting with ideas and emerges as a fully-fledged guitar soloist. This music is jazz-rock fusion with classical ideas ahead of anything emerging from the jazz community at the time. Opening with the wonderfully exuberant "Peaches En Regalia", the guitar plays lines with keyboards and a passage that mixes wah-wah acoustic guitar with flute. Zappa's guitar cuts into "Willie The Pimp" with a tearing rock tone and plays around the vocals (courtesy of Captain Beefheart) using wah wah that sounds like the human voice, before taking an intense, lyrical solo featuring his characteristic slow trilling effects, double stopping and rhythmic vamps.

The outstanding "Son Of Mr. Green Genes" is a cleverly written sectionalized piece shot through with a commanding guitar solo and with theme-and-variations development. Zappa plays with the ensemble but emerges explosively at various points to play liquid guitar breaks, using overdrive and varying levels of wah wah, and displaying his melodic and rhythmic intelligence through both open and written sections. The lines move from sharply defined rhythmic phrases to lyrical expressiveness. At the end, Zappa's guitar plays a dramatic downward glissando on which every fret can be heard. On "Gumbo Variations", the guitar bubbles away beneath the violin in the mix, playing funky chords before gradually taking over with an overdriven, reedy sound played with driving incisiveness over the pulsating groove.

Gibson
SG Special

ZAPPA'S GIBSONS
First launched in 1961, Gibson's SG-series guitars became Frank Zappa's main instrument for a number of years. He played customized models, some of which had an additional contact pick-up placed on the bridge or the neck to make an extra range of tones available.

INTO THE SEVENTIES

At the end of the 1960s, a very diverse music world was reflected in the guitar styles of American popular music. Talented guitarists had emerged from various genres and the music became an exhilarating blend of different traditions, from folk and blues to jazz and Latin music.

SANTANA

As he rides over the superb Latin rock drumming, supported by simple modal harmonies on bass and keyboards, Carlos Santana builds his solos to a climax with a rich, sustaining sound and fluent melodic invention, using soaring double stopping and high-register bending.

RANDY CALIFORNIA

Inspired by the electric virtuosity of Jimi Hendrix and others, Randy California developed a surging, distorted lead style. An innovator, his ground-breaking solo on "Street Worm" (1970) features fast, sophisticated jazz phrasing.

One of the most important and influential new genres to emerge at the end of the 1960s was Latin rock. This was pioneered by Carlos Santana, born in Mexico in 1947, who formed the group Santana in San Francisco in 1966. Santana is a versatile player who has a command of blues and rock soloing with added jazz elements. He uses funky Latin rhythms and fills, gritty distorted chordal fills, and his playing is full of both clear and distorted tones, controlled feedback and a variety of textures. The band was a platform for his strong melodic arrangements and dominant sound. Their first album, *Santana* (1969), added a further dimension to rock, mixing extended Latin instrumentals with vocal

tracks. The instrumental "Waiting" demonstrates rhythmic chordal work, incisive double stopping and surging melodic blues-based playing, and the passionate soloing on "Soul Sacrifice" is given a lift by tight backing rhythms. On the album *Abraxas* (1970), the group's version of Peter Green's "Black Magic Woman" features a sensitive solo inspired by the melody, and one of Santana's best melodic compositions, "Samba Pa Ti" is also a vehicle for expressive improvisation. One of Carlos Santana's hallmark sounds – bluesy cries with pairs of bent notes – is heard on "Mother's Daughter".

HEAVY ROCK

America started to produce high-volume rock bands during the late 1960s. Vanilla Fudge, formed in 1967, with Vince Martell on guitar, was one of the first to use high volume and a powerful rhythm section. The anarchic Detroit group MC5, with Wayne Kramer and Fred Smith, unleashed a ferocious, primeval aggression on *Kick Out The Jams* (1969). Some players, such as Ron Asheton on the album *The Stooges* (1969), excluded blues and other primary influences, replacing them with a nihilistic irreverence and abandon. This type

of unbridled energy has a direct appeal and has shaped the course of popular guitar playing. Mainstream heavy rock at the end of the 1960s was personified by Grand Funk Railroad's Mark Farner (b.1948), who built his playing around distortion and heavy riffs, and the more interesting Mountain, with Leslie West (b.1945), whose style was influenced by British players, notably Cream (*see page 142*).

CSN&Y

The sound of Crosby, Stills & Nash, formed
in 1968 with David Crosby (b.1941), Stephen
Stills (b.1945) and Graham Nash (b.1942),
was a synthesis of folk, country and pop
songwriting and featured the expressive blues-
rock playing of Stephen Stills. On *Crosby Stills
& Nash* (1969), the group combine acoustic and
electric guitars, and their style is exemplified
by tracks like "Suite: Judy Blue Eyes" and
"Wooden Ships". Neil Young (b.1945), who
had produced material such as "Cinnamon
Girl" (1969), joined the group in 1969 and
the CSN&Y album *Deja Vu* (1970) sees Stills
and Young playing in contrasting styles.

The album includes a mixture of full-
bodied acoustic guitar sounds and a range of
electric riffs and solos. The first track features
highly effective guitar supporting the harmony
vocals and adding variety. "Carry On" opens
with mesmeric, deep, thrumming acoustic
rhythms and simple melody parts, backed by
electric solo breaks with overdrive, before
moving into a section with a spiky, rhythmic
wah-wah solo played against a repeating
electric bass pattern. The slow-paced "Almost
Cut My Hair" has gritty, distorted electric
staccato chords and fills with double stopping.
It features two interwoven guitar parts with
differing bluesy styles, forced against each
other with searing intensity. Joni Mitchell's

ROBBIE ROBERTSON

A departure from prevailing trends, the playing
of Canadian guitarist Robbie Robertson
(b.1945) is rootsy and eclectic. Robertson
played on Bob Dylan's album *Blonde On Blonde*
(1966) before forming The Band in 1967. They
released their debut album *Music From Big Pink*
in 1968 and developed their own blend of rock
'n' roll mixed with blues and various kinds of
folk and country music, including jug styles.
Straightforward guitar sounds are used in
arrangements with a variety of instruments.
Their album *The Band* (1969) has a tremendous
mixture of styles, from the clean, rock 'n' roll
guitar of "Jemima Surrender", via the acoustic
bluegrass soloing of "The Unfaithful Servant" to
the funky chords and fills of "King Harvest".

"Woodstock" is turned into a blues-rock
number with loose opening riffing and manic
guitar. The mesmeric acoustic guitar-playing
on "Deja Vu" and a muted electric guitar
improvisation with the treble rolled off,
conjures up a strange sound landscape.

Neil Young left the group in 1971 and
went on to produce fiery guitar playing on
his own albums, playing intense solos with
an emotional edge, such as that on "Cortez
The Killer" (1975).

MARTIN D-45
*The decorative top-of-the
range Martin D-45, that
first came out in 1939,
was often used by CSN&Y.*

CSN&Y IN ACTION
*A strong line-up featuring
Stills and Young playing
lead guitar parts, CSN&Y
combined folk and pop
ballad-style writing with
cutting electric-guitar solos.*

DUANE ALLMAN

Tennessee-born Duane Allman (1946–71) played authentic, gritty southern blues-rock. Imaginative and soulful within the constraints of a blues-based vocabulary, Allman used both standard and an open-E tuning, and developed his own type of slide sound using a glass bottle, combining it with a rocky overdrive and phrasing derived partly from harmonica players. His burning, Chicago-style guitar can be heard on "B.B. King Medley" (1968). In 1969, he formed The Allman Brothers band with younger brother Gregg (b.1947) on keyboards and Dickey Betts (b.1943) on second guitar. Their blues-rock is often based on traditional material, with Betts taking harmony lines and solos as well as rhythm. Allman plays with his right-hand thumb and fingers, and his particular intense, soft, sustaining melodiousness can be heard on "Dreams" (1969), where he mixes fingered notes with slide and arpeggiated slide motifs.

The album *Live At The Fillmore East* (1971) is a showcase for the band. On "Statesboro Blues" and "Don't Keep Me Wondering", Allman's sensuous, diffused slide phrases have a vocal quality, and his full, sonorous sound infuses the surging phrases in the high register. The 23-minute long "Whipping Post" has a funkier, jazzy feel, and Allman's inventiveness shines on the flowing, bluesy phrasing and lyrical passages. He develops lines by extending ideas, and uses interesting scalar concepts, double stopping, muting and harmonics.

"In Memory Of Elizabeth Reed" sets a sensitively played melody against violin-like effects, harmony lines and a rhythmic, improvisatory solo. Allman and Betts could also play attractive acoustic melodies, such as "Little Martha" (1972). After Duane's death, The Allman Brothers carried on, with Betts producing fine instrumentals, such as "Jessica "(1973).

DUANE ALLMAN

An exceptional player with a highly-charged sound, Duane Allman's idiosyncratic creativity is manifest in a body of outstanding recordings. His career was cut tragically short by a fatal motorbike accident in 1971.

SESSION MAN

Duane Allman worked as a sideman and session musician for Jerry Wexler at Muscle Shoals studio in Alabama, recording blues, pop and soul numbers with artists such as Wilson Pickett and Aretha Franklin. On Franklin's "The Weight" (1969), he plays resonant slide breaks with a buzzing, vibrant tone. The quirky personality of his acoustic slide playing can be heard on John Hammond's "Shake For Me" (1969), but his most famous work was his tremendous contribution to Eric Clapton's "Layla" (1970).

ROY BUCHANAN

One of the most overlooked guitar players during the 1960s, Roy Buchanan (1939–88), was finally able to put out his own album, *Roy Buchanan*, in 1972. His playing on the instrumental tracks conveys humanity and a dark intensity. "Sweet Dreams" starts with crying notes increasing in volume and moves into melodic steel-guitar style bending, with fast interjections taut with expressive tension. On the great "Pete's Blue", he is backed by a slow-paced rhythm section working off a repeating bass line and a fundamental Chicago-style bluesy harmony. Buchanan begins with full, upper-register bluesy phrases and moves into an astonishing episodic solo. Improvised passages, with a wailing guitar sound and altered scales, are inspired by Islamic music, and he extends the unusual phrasing up into a higher register, controlling the artificial

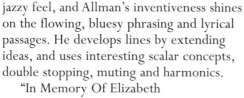

ROY BUCHANAN

Although rooted in blues, rock 'n' roll and country music, Buchanan's playing reveals a strong individual character and an emotional power that transcends the confines of the genre.

harmonics created by picking and using part of the right hand to create an ethereal sound. Constant inventiveness informs the solo, as Buchanan embarks on a musical journey consisting of melodic double stopping, short passages of cascading motifs, and a range of colour with bending, muting, detuning and broken-up, atonal exclamations. His depth and sensitivity can be heard on "The Messiah Will Come Again", with its sustained melodic lines giving way to a cathartic torrent of ascending notes, followed by seagull-like sounds.

JOHNNY WINTER

The fierce blues-rock style of Johnny Winter (b.1944) is based on electric and acoustic guitar with a simmering slide. In a trio format on *Second Winter* (1970), he plays with a distorted sound on "Memory Pain" and slide on "Slippin' and Slidin'" and "Highway 61". He formed a high-energy group with second guitarist Rick Derringer and a highlight album is *Johnny Winter And Live* (1971) on which the duo perform rock standards, including "Johnny B. Goode" and "Jumpin' Jack Flash".

LOWELL GEORGE

Lowell George (1945–79) was one of rock's outstanding slide players and a fine all-rounder who worked as a session musician with many artists, including Bonnie Raitt, throughout his career. After a stint with Frank Zappa, he formed Little Feat in Los Angeles in 1969. Their sound amalgamated country-rock and blues styles with idiosyncratic elements from folk and ethnic sources.

There is a edgy quality of suspense and warning with the guitars at the beginning of the title track on *Sailin' Shoes* (1972), on which the slide work and moments of dissonance pull restlessly at the vocal line. "Willin'" demonstrates acoustic chords and sensitive, country-style electric additions.

A second guitarist, Paul Barrere (b.1948), joined the band for their third album, *Dixie Chicken* (1973), which features some of George's best work, including the title track that merges repeating, melodic guitar lines with vocals, "Two Trains", on which rhythmic

chord textures support George's slide work, and "Fat Man In The Bathtub" with its suitably full-bodied sound. *Feats Don't Fail Me Now* (1974) moves toward a funky sound on parts of the title track and "Spanish Moon". "Rock 'n' Roll Doctor" with its stop-start, funky rhythm features smoky guitar textures and a short slide break with notes stretched out to create fresh phrases. George continued to produce high-quality music throughout the 1970s, but died on tour in 1979.

ROCK STYLES

During the 1970s, rock in America embraced a whole host of guitarists, many of whom have enjoyed great commercial success. Lynyrd Skynyrd, formed in 1973, featured three guitarists, Allen Collins, Gary Rossington and Ed King. The smoothly articulated phrasing of the solo on "Free Bird" (1973), that builds organically in an extended track with repetitive blues motifs, has become one of the most popular in rock, and their rocking "Sweet Home Alabama" (1974) stands out.

The Eagles, an important group with a distinctive sound derived from country-rock and blues, formed in 1971 with Glenn Frey (b.1948) and Bernie Leadon (b.1947) on guitars. Don Felder (b.1947) joined in 1974 and "One Of These Nights" (1975) features him on lead. With the departure of Leadon, Joe Walsh (b.1947) joined the group in 1975 and is featured on the album *Hotel California* (1976). The title track has an acoustic opening and multi-layered parts with a funky rhythm, and a section with harmonized guitars leads to a fade-out. "Life In

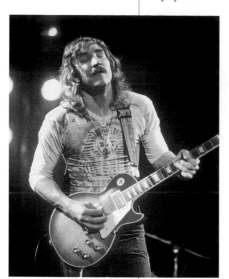

JOE WALSH
The Eagles' style of Californian rock, with Joe Walsh on guitar appears straightfoward, but is, in fact, often a collage with layers of guitar parts using overdubs.

The Fast Lane" offers a mean distorted riff, with Walsh playing a slide solo.

Heavy rock is represented by the popular riffs achieved by Joe Perry (b.1950) of Aerosmith on tracks such as "Walk This Way" (1975), and Ted Nugent (b.1948) with solos such as "Stranglehold" (1975).

STEELY DAN

The group who took their name from William Burroughs' *The Naked Lunch* was formed in Los Angeles in 1972. Their music was based on carefully arranged and finely produced songwriting that combined pop with jazz, soul and funk. In the early 1970s, the group featured a number of guitarists who displayed contrasting yet complementary styles, including the jazz-influenced Denny Dias and Jeff "Skunk" Baxter (b.1948). Elliot Randall plays one of the group's most popular solos on "Reelin' In The Years" (1972).

Steely Dan's third album *Countdown To Ecstasy* (1973) features creative, bop-style jazz soloing set in the context of an unusual and inventive pop song, "Bodhisattva". One of the highlights is "My Old School", which sparkles with Baxter's effervescent guitar breaks, played with fine control and great delicacy. There is a wonderful use of space and a stylistic leaning toward a type of linear funk in the blues and country-based phrasing.

FUNK STYLISTS

SLY AND THE FAMILY STONE
In the late 1960s, Sly And The Family Stone with Sylvester "Sly Stone" Stewart and his brother Freddie Stone on guitars developed a stripped-down, minimalist approach combining funk with rock fills. Freddie Stewart developed his own voice with abrasive wah wah on "Don't Call Me Nigger, Whitey" (1969) and brittle rhythm sounds on "Thank You" (1970).

FUNKADELIC
At the other end of the spectrum, Funkadelic, formed in Detroit in 1968, produced a rich psychedelic funk. Within this setting, Eddie Hazel (1950–92) is a strong and inventive improviser, producing one of the best recorded solos in the genre on "Maggot Brain" (1971), on

which his lyrical, soaring, rich blues-rock style is graceful and expressive.

CHIC
At the end of the 1970s, Nile Rogers (b.1952) emerged with his New funk band, Chic, to which he contributed an emotionally charged style with funky chordal riffs. His playing is aggressive and driving yet supple and technically assured. "Le Freak" (1978) has a catchy, repeating melodic rhythm figure with a gritty texture, and on "Good Times" (1979), assertive chopped chords are stamped across the track.

Other outstanding players include the Hendrix-influenced Ernie Isley (b.1952) and Curtis Mayfield (1942–99) with his wide range of soul and funk influences.

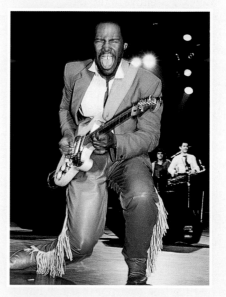

NILE RODGERS
Rodgers' bright, sharply executed chords dig into the beat with an incisive energy.

RY COODER

A great slide player with an unmistakeable voice, Ry Cooder (b.1947) worked on sessions and played in Captain Beefheart's Magic Band before releasing his first album, *Ry Cooder*, in 1970. This is a set of Cooder's versions of traditional material, from Woody Guthrie's "Do Re Mi" to the rough-edged, tumbling "Alimony", bristling with gutsy electric riffs and a slide solo. Cooder also has a tremendous grasp of acoustic traditional styles, playing dancing fingerpicking on "Police Dog Blues" and recreating one of his favourite pieces of music, Blind Willie Johnson's "Dark Was The Night", using slide with reverb.

On the album *Into The Purple Valley* (1971), he explores Caribbean music and reworks obscure material, integrating traditional styles with unusual instrumental arrangements to create his own identity. Calypso acoustic guitar and mandolin feature on "F.D.R. Trinidad", and the stately beauty of Bahamian Joseph Spence's instrumental "Great Dream From Heaven" harks back to a lost era. Burlesque electric guitar, full of angular character, and a slide solo that helps to convey a sense of ironic social commentary enlivens the traditional "Taxes On The Farmer Feeds Us All". "On A Monday" has wonderful textures, with dry, squawking electric guitar syncopations and melodic acoustic slide over the top. Cooder's masterful acoustic slide on "Vigilante Man" is evocatively magical; the guitar is measured and graceful but drops away dynamically, with intricate and vulnerable passages suggesting suspense.

Chicken Skin Music (1976) integrates Tex-Mex rhythms with Flaco Jiminez's accordion playing on "He'll Have To Go", and Hawaiian music on "Yellow Roses" showcases slack-key player Gabby Pahinui's luscious, dreamy sound against romantic acoustic guitar. "Chloe" is full of jazzy Hawaiian interchanges and slide melody passages, with Cooder and Pahinui playing together seamlessly, and gospel harmonies underpin "Always Lift Him Up/Kanaka Wai Wai".

Bop Till You Drop (1979), one of the first digitally recorded albums, brought Cooder to a wider audience in the 1980s.

J.J.CALE
The supremely reticent cult-figure Jean-Jaques Cale (b.1938) has a signature rootsy style that is characterized by a shuffling boogie and relaxed, loping rhythm. Naturally (1971) has laid-back grooves and an earthy, natural sound with tasteful bluesy breaks and country-style melodic fills.

MUSIC FOR FILM

From 1980 onward, Ry Cooder started to build up an extensive body of music for film and television. He has an uncanny ability to paint archetypal American scenes, often with a brooding sense of atmosphere, as on the title music for *Paris, Texas* (1984); here, Cooder plays acoustic slide over a shimmering background that conjures up a vast, hot, empty landscape. The unforgettable thematic slide phrases and gently plucked chords ride over elemental blues harmonies mixed with mysterious wind sounds, bowed bass and chiming arpeggios that suggest old shopfront signs moving in the hot breeze. *The Long Riders* (1980) has sentimental fingerstyle American-themed folk guitar working with an array of instruments, and a more modern sound is produced for "King Of The Street" from *Trespass* (1992), with hard-hitting rhythms and edgy slide guitar.

RY COODER
A multi-instrumentalist and researcher into traditional repertoires, Cooder also has a tremendous knowledge of tunings and stringed-instrument techniques. He has developed his own range of timbre, vibrato and microtonal control using acoustic and electric instruments, often with an open-D tuning and glass bottleneck. He invests material with voluble interjections, and his use of the guitar to extend the meaning and inference of lyrics is remarkable.

NEW WAVE & EXPERIMENTAL

In the mid to late 1970s, new wave and punk groups brought an acerbic edge to rock guitar, and experimental guitarists were looking for new ways to add unusual parts to rock and pop songs. This iconoclastic movement was centred on New York, home to many new-wave bands.

Precursors to punk were Johnny Thunders with the anarchic New York Dolls (formed in 1973) and rock poet Patti Smith, whose album *Horses* (1975) features the fractured, neurotic energy of Lenny Kaye and other guest guitarists.

The energy and raw primitive power of punk was harnessed by The Ramones. Their albums, *Ramones* (1976) and *Rocket To Russia* (1977), have a high-speed, hard-edged intensity and prove it is possible to create something vibrant around basic chord sequences.

TELEVISION

A more adventurous and constructive thinking lay behind the guitar playing in the group Television, originally formed in 1973. Featuring both Tom Verlaine (b.1949) and Richard Lloyd on guitar, the group's debut album, *Marquee Moon* (1977), presents intelligent and original compositions that move away from standard clichés. The focus is on assembling unusual arpeggiated harmonies and blocks of sound with imaginative melodic hooks and solos. Rock and a repeating folk-style figure are brought together on the guitars for "See No Evil", and "Venus" has a short, elliptical solo. "Friction" features themes, riffs and solos with unusual lines and an altered scale. Contrasting episodes with passages of tension and thematic sonority mark the extended track "Marquee Moon". It opens with juxtaposed rhythmic figures that move to a melodic passage. A short, flowing linear solo cascades from high points, contrasting with an exploratory, Oriental-style melodic solo that is supported by dry, abrasive chords; the track progresses into double stopping and then octaves, before ending with more sonorous chords and high-register touches that lead to the return of the opening figure.

FENDER JAZZMASTER
A guitar that was first available in 1958, the Fender Jazzmaster was often used as a studio instrument and did not catch on as a stage guitar in pop for a number of years. With its unusual pick-ups it has its own particular Fender sound.

TELEVISION
Adopting thoughtful guitar parts, Television stand out in their time for their inventiveness.

REMAIN IN LIGHT

A visionary individualist, Adrian Belew (b.1949) worked with Talking Heads and plays on *Remain In Light* (1980), an album on which the group put together a striking multi-layered collage to which Belew adds strange new sounds. A simmering tension is set up between Byrne's and Harrison's simple harmonies and funky cross rhythms and Belew's uncompromising sonic excursions. "Born Under Punches" showcases the group's coruscating jungle-funk. "The Great Curve" features astonishing solo breaks with see-sawing pitches, unusual lines, and phrasing the tremolo bar and harmonics.

TALKING HEADS

Talking Heads, with singer and guitarist David Byrne (b.1952), took an artistic approach to song forms, using repetitive ideas and allowing the guitar to provide atmosphere, tension, and subtle light and shade in their lyric-based conceptual frameworks. Their first album, *Talking Heads '77* (1977), shows funky, clipped guitar rhythm work with reggae and ethnic influences. With dancing punchy chords, a light touch and a non-linear soloing approach, Byrne anticipates the move away from highlight guitar solos and blues-rock distorted sounds in certain areas of pop. His guitar provides terse, angular melodic figures and strong, flat downbeat chords with the bass and drums. Rolling, clean rhythms sometimes jump to fast rattling funk fills. There are virtually no standard linear solos and where there is an instrumental break, such as that on "No Compassion", for example, it is played with a quirky slide sound. When the guitar is used for colour and timbre it is highly effective. One of the group's most well-known songs, "Psycho Killer", ends with the disturbing feeling enhanced by rustling notes, rock fills and textures.

Talking Heads continued to explore and integrate "world" music with their electro-mechanical modernism on the album *Fear Of Music* (1979), on which American guitar rhythms sit with African and ethnic input. The group's minimalist ideas, and powerful statements made through the use of unexpectedly juxtaposed motifs, tempo changes and other devices helped to move pop music away from its roots.

ADRIAN BELEW
An architect of new guitar soundscapes, Adrian Belew worked with Talking Heads and produced his own albums. He uses effects such as compression and controlled feedback, synthesizers, unusual techniques and the tremolo bar, and often simulates environmental noises and animal calls.

LATER ZAPPA

Zappa continued to explore new areas and produce a large body of important guitar work that integrated new musical ideas from around the world. By the time he recorded *Apostrophe (')* (1974), Zappa had incorporated jazz-rock fusion developments yet retained his bluesy style and humour, which can be heard on the manic guitar breaks thrown into "Nanook Rubs It In", "Uncle Remus" and the ultra wah of "Stink-Foot". The album *Zoot! Allures* (1976) features Zappa playing "Black Napkins", a live instrumental solo, on which he improvises intense flurries of notes. "Friendly Little Finger" shows soloing in which rock-blues, Indian, Arabic and world-music elements collide. "Zoot! Allures" is based around arpeggiated figures, feedback and shimmering chords combined with harmonics and tremolo-arm pitch variation, and Zappa takes a way-out, emotional solo on the fade-out. Material on the album *Joe's Garage* (1979) features the use of xenocrony, in which pieces are put together by assembling tracks from unrelated compositions and performances, and music is arranged around guitar solos. A series of three *Shut Up 'N Play Yer Guitar* instrumental albums released during the 1980s is a showcase for the tremendous variety in Zappa's instrumental approaches.

ZAPPA'S LEGACY
As a composer who has left a vast legacy of over a thousand diverse works, many featuring the guitar, Frank Zappa's output is unparalleled in the rock world and its compositional sophistication will ensure that it will last as outstanding music.

VIRTUOSO ROCK

Rock shifted gear when Eddie Van Halen exploded onto the guitar scene in 1978, exhibiting a style based on techniques that enabled him to play with a new vocabulary of motifs, melodic lines and phrasing. His flowing velocity revolutionized rock guitar and transformed its horizons.

EDDIE VAN HALEN
Playing with a flamboyant physical abandon and using a home-made guitar with a simple effects set-up, Van Halen's startling talent had a great impact.

TREMOLO
At the end of the 1970s, the much improved and better engineered tremolo unit offered a great move forward, making possible large pitch variations and greater control.

Van Halen took the rock world by surprise, becoming one of the architects of a new style of voluble heavy metal, characterized by fast-paced riffs and searing intensity. With his band Van Halen, propelled by their highly energized rhythm section and his fully developed innovative techniques, Eddie Van Halen (b.1957) invented a style of his own, inspired by Hendrix and Clapton but with affinities to the ideas of Allan Holdsworth (*see pages 116–17*).

THE VAN HALEN REVOLUTION

Van Halen's speciality is virtuoso soloing, using wide stretches in the left hand, hammer-ons and pull-offs and a highly developed technique of tapping notes with a right-hand finger (*see below*). He also pushes tremolo bars to the limit to alter the pitch of notes by wide intervals, creating dramatic drops in pitch as well as upward movements, a manoeuvre known as "dive bombing". His fiery solos, crackling with cascading sheets of notes, original melodic motifs and growling,

turbulent attack, blasted rock guitar forward from its blues-based pentatonic framework. He was undoubtedly influenced by jazz and classical music, and his immediate acclaim and widespread popularity changed the nature of linear improvising in rock, bringing it closer to some jazz approaches.

The highlight on the debut album, *Van Halen* (1978), is "Eruption", an unaccompanied solo on which the fast, seamless phrasing sounds similar to classical keyboards. Pyrotechnic additions and shattering metallic incisiveness can be heard on the group's remake of The Kinks' "You Really Got Me", while on *Van Halen II* (1979), the same linear techniques are used on a nylon-string acoustic guitar, producing the scintillating "Spanish Fly". On "Women In Love", he taps upper-octave and larger compound-interval harmonics. Van Halen continued to produce material of a consistently high quality with albums such as *Fair Warning* (1981), which contains the solos "Dirty Movies" and "Mean Street". "Jump" and "Hot For Teacher" are the highlights on *1984* (1984), which incorporates guitar synthesizers.

TAPPING TECHNIQUE

Eddie Van Halen plays mesmerizing lines by tapping upper notes with a right-hand finger. He glides through fast passages of scales and arpeggios, and creates the kind

of new, inventive lines that had been, until now, virtually impossible to play with standard techniques. Any interval can be added to notes played with the left hand. The developing sextuplets, below, consist of double-triplet repeating motifs.

Opening with C and D in the left hand, F and then G are added with the right-hand finger. Then the left hand moves up to play D and F, and G and A are added, forming a minor arpeggio. (*See pages 234–35 for musical terminology.*)

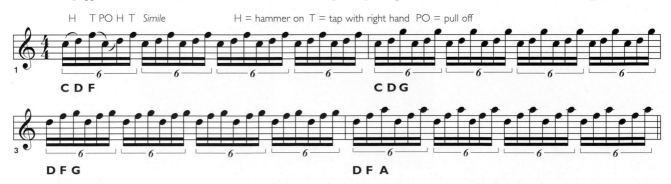

H   T PO H T   *Simile*   H = hammer on   T = tap with right hand   PO = pull off

C D F   **C D G**

D F G   **D F A**

YNGWIE MALMSTEEN

One of the most unusual styles to be developed in this period is the pronounced neo-classicism of Swedish guitarist Malmsteen, who emerged in 1983. He played fast passages by composers such as Paganini and emphasized harmonic minor scales in a heavy-rock context. Among the highlights of his work is the solo "Black Star" (1984).

KIRK HAMMETT

With the flamboyant heavy-metal band Metallica, Kirk Hammett and James Hetfield brought together heavy distorted riffs, fast soloing, high-speed tempos and driving forceful rhythms in a combination that personifies the genre.

VERNON REID

Vernon Reid of Living Colour brings jazz, fusion and inventive funk guitar to heavy rock. On "Cult Of Personality", from the album Vivid *(1988), stop-start rock riffs back Reid's solo, which has an intense, attacking style with shaking sounds, screaming and plunging notes courtesy of the tremolo bar.*

OTHER GUITARISTS

Inspired by innovations, a number of talented, inventive rock soloists started to redefine and expand the rock-guitar vocabulary. Randy Rhoads (b.1956) took progressive blues-rock and incorporated classical phrasing. His outstanding soloing on *Blizzard Of Ozz* (1981) includes the sharp and sinuous "Crazy Train", the surging "Mr. Crowley" and the inventive "Revelation (Mother Earth)".

A player with strong melodic sensibilities, Steve Morse (b.1954) started with fusion group the Dixie Dregs on albums such as *What If* (1978) which showcase his unique, eclectic style, drawing on jazz-rock with blues and country. The accurate definition of Morse's sharply picked lines always stands out, and during the 1980s he also used a guitar synth pick-up to extend his range of textures. His instrumental solo album, *High Tension Wires* (1989), has compositions based around New Age and Celtic folk music. Morse uses multi-layered acoustic and electric guitars in tight arrangements; "Highland Wedding", with its fast passages of embellishment, is an example of his unusual hybrid approach.

Eric Johnson (b.1954) shows more conventional stylistic influences, fusing blues and rock with sensitivity and finesse, and playing well-balanced, lyrical lines with a smooth sustain as on his album *Tones* (1986). On the following album, *Ah Via Musicom* (1990), "Cliffs Of Dover" starts with unaccompanied blues-rock improvising with a pentatonic framework and switches to a rhythmic, violin-like figure. Johnson achieves a creamy, supple upper-register sound and remarkable clarity on a solo that combines classical melodic thinking and blues ideas.

JOE SATRIANI

A gifted individual with versatile techniques and linear scalar ideas, Joe Satriani (b.1956) plays *tour de force* pieces with a modern electric-guitar sound, using effects. Initially inspired by pop and rock, he developed through listening to jazz and classical music, and by studying theory. His compositions often open with heavy metal-style riffs, leading to melodies that themselves preface virtuosic soloing. The emphasis is on modal improvisation, using a technique that seamlessly welds together picked, legato and tapped notes. Phrases often develop motifs with sextuplet and irregular seven-note groupings. On the commercially successful instrumental album, *Surfing With The Alien* (1987), the showcase title track opens with rock riffs and the melody has a muted tone. Satriani breaks into lengthy improvising in sections that modulate between major and harmonic minor tonal centres. Among the variations is the use of a special technique to play fast, high-register trills, finely controlled tremolo-bar pitch variations, harmonics, exaggerated flamboyant bending, double stopping and tapping. "Midnight", with its synthetic-sounding technical reinvention of a fingerstyle sound, is one of the most unusual tracks. This album established Satriani as the leading technician in rock, and in a career that includes writing about playing, he has become one of the most influential and progressive figures in rock guitar, extending the range and technical horizons of the instrument.

STEVE VAI

After playing with Zappa (*see pages 196–97, 205*), Steve Vai (b.1960) released the debut album *Flex-able* (1984) with instrumental tracks featuring very fast soloing and unusual arrangements. His playing style is assured, with long sustain, and uses modes and altered scales, and his solos include ideas from practice exercises and motifs. Vai broadens his palette with all the standard modern rock techniques, including tremolo bar and effects. His album *Passion And Warfare* (1990) shows differing moods and approaches, including a humour that gives his music a refreshing additional dimension. "Erotic Nightmares" uses modern techniques to convey the experience as a soundtrack astonishingly well. On "The Animal", Vai parodies heavy metal and plays a typically over-the-top solo. "For The Love Of God" has a long, contemplative sustained melody and builds up to an intense, passionate improvisation, scales and phrases erupting over the slow-paced drums and arpeggiated backing.

IBANEZ JEM
This type of "Superstrat" incorporates traditional design and modern developments. It has a 24-fret, two-octave scalloped fingerboard, humbucking and single coil pick-ups, and a Floyd Rose tremolo system.

STEVE VAI
A powerful, physical player, Steve Vai has a range of unusual influences, extending from Zappa to jazz-rock fusion. He often builds his solos to a high point with screaming linear pyrotechnics and uses a comprehensive range of techniques.

JOE SATRIANI
With an all-round command of scalar and chordal thinking, together with inventive close voicings, shifting harmonic sequences and interesting modes, Satriani's music is sensuous and lyrical as well as tightly structured and well arranged.

RACK-MOUNTED EFFECTS

In the 1980s, a range of effects previously only available in top studios started to be rack-mounted in modules for musicians to use live and in recording. The TC 2290 digital delay unit adds fractional delays and other effects to thicken notes and create interesting sounds, and the Eventide H3000 SE harmonizer adds an extra part at a fixed interval.

TC Electronic 2290 and Eventide H3000 harmonizer

ROOTS REVIVAL

Guitarists drawing on traditional musical roots emerged during the 1980s. Figures whose approaches ranged from the traditional to the adventurous, recast styles with vibrant rearrangements and built up a receptive audience for the combinations of established styles.

STEVIE RAY VAUGHAN
A figure with a tremendous ability to focus and project his playing, Vaughan combined different strands with a powerful and appealing sound. He infuses the standard vocabulary of the guitar with meaning and vitality.

DANNY GATTON
As a wide-ranging eclectic figure with a complex style, Gatton's acceptance within mainstream rock marks a return to the roots of the type of electric guitar playing that was part of rock 'n' roll in the 1950s, when players brought strong jazz and country as well as blues influences to the genre.

In contrast to the modern, technically advanced rock players, retro stylists such as The Stray Cats with Brian Setzer (b.1959) emerged in the 1980s. Their music, based on 1950s rock 'n' roll, helped to start the "rockabilly" revival, and Setzer creates a satisfying, authentic feel using chords, chord breaks and single lines in a smooth, melodic style. The vocabulary is based on 1950s licks and devices, and he uses echo and a clean sound that sometimes goes to the edge of natural distortion. On "Stray Cat Strut" (1981), he adds shakes and bends with a Bigsby arm to chord breaks and inventive lines. "Rock This Town" (1981) has echo-laden rhythm, chiming fills and a grooving solo.

In a climate increasingly receptive to traditional music, the outstanding figure to emerge was Stevie Ray Vaughan (*see page 61*). After appearing on David Bowie's album *Let's Dance* (1983) and recording the *tour de force* blues album *Texas Flood* (1982), he looked to material with a more modern rock sound on the album *Couldn't Stand The Weather* (1984). The title track features stop-start riffs and funky chords and there is an accomplished recreation of Hendrix's "Voodoo Chile", on which Vaughan simulates the sonic effects and ambience with great skill.

DANNY GATTON

A great all-rounder who defies categorization, Danny Gatton (1945–94) derives his playing from a wide range of music, and his considerable facility enables him to use single lines, double stopping and chords alongside a complex vocabulary taken from almost every major genre. On his album *Unfinished Business* (1987), the zany instrumental "Lappin' It Up" has bright, twangy guitar that is rootsy as well as quirky and characterful. Gatton's breaks sound as if they come from a succession of different guitarists: shifting textures and skipping lines with fast improvisation meld

elements from virtually every major American genre. On his album *88 Elmira Street* (1991), the rocking "Funky Mama" has cutting blues breaks and Gatton takes off with a distinctive, crunching, glassy tone. Surreal rockabilly is conveyed on "Elmira St. Boogie", where he plays with echo and adds unexpected dissonance and a series of almost disconnected passages to traditional material, using effects for a mocking edge.

MODERN POP & ROCK

Modern pop and rock in the United States is represented by a marked divergence between approaches that has led not just to thrash, but to grunge and styles in which music from the 1960s and 1970s has been recombined to form a 1990s hybrid.

In mainstream songwriting, Peter Buck (b.1956) of REM plays with a smooth, understated approach using arpeggiated chords and straightforward rhythms to create a style derived from 1960s and 1970s pop and American folk-rock influences.

The album *Green* (1988) harks back to a 1960s sound with pop-rhythm playing and catchy, melodic figures. The group's popular album *Automatic For The People* (1992) is well-produced and reveals fine songwriting and a measured, balanced maturity. Many of the tracks employ acoustic guitar as a major strand to lend depth and atmosphere. Buck does not use soloing, and electric guitar is only brought in for added touches, as on the atmospheric acoustic "Drive", which has theme-like electric lines, and "Star Me Kitten", on which lilting electric guitar follows the voice.

BOB MOULD

With Hüsker Dü, Bob Mould (b.1960) was playing an alternative, stream-of-consciousness style with a loud, bright intensity and droning, open-string power chords strummed with a chaotic energy sometimes described as thrash.

EXPLOSION OF STYLES

Dozens of talented players with an unprecedented diversity of styles have become established under the generic label, rock. Among the popular figures of the last 20 years are the blues-rock based Richie Sambora (b.1960) of Bon Jovi, Bonnie Raitt (*see page 201*) with her electric slide, and Billy Gibbons (b.1950), the blues-rock boogie guitarist with ZZ Top. There has been a place for virtuoso soloing, with artists such as Paul Gilbert (b.1966), with Mr.Big, and Extreme's Nuno Bettencourt (b.1966) on the album *Pornograffitti* (1991).

The music is in some ways an extension of punk and heavy metal, but clothed in loose, imaginative harmony. On the groundbreaking *Zen Arcade* (1984), Mould uses a wash of high-energy distortion to provide a resounding wall of noise. In spite of the seeming limitations of this style, he uses the guitar to play parts that show considerable variety. The music has surprisingly attractive ringing chords, as on "Broken Home, Broken Heart", and there are adventurous instrumentals such as "Dreams Reoccurring", with its backward soundscape. Typical of his intense sound is "Indecision Time": overdriven chords merge together and there is an insanely fast solo with darting tangential lines; and the surging fast lines on "Pride" accurately invoke a sense of compressed power and mania.

BOB MOULD
A primary architect of a style of playing in which distorted guitar is used to create a resonant, sustaining energy, Mould helped to establish a new approach that has become part of modern rock. His playing conveys excitement and a startling sense of immediacy, and many tracks are short bursts of cathartic expression.

PETER BUCK
Buck uses the guitar to support the song, relying on breaking up chords to provide simple, melodic arpeggios, and using distorted riffs to build the momentum.

KURT COBAIN

One of the major groups of the 1990s, Nirvana with Kurt Cobain played rock with added psychedelic colour, a form that came to be labelled grunge. Cobain's simple and highly expressive playing was musical and direct. He used Fender Jaguars and Mustangs as well as hybrid instruments with effects.

SLASH

Guns 'n' Roses with guitarist Slash (Saul Hudson, b.1965) base their music on blues-rock. Slash plays supple, melodic solos, as heard on tracks such as "November Rain"; one of his most popular pieces, "Sweet Child O' Mine", from Appetite For Destruction *(1987), has an attractive melodic figure.*

SONIC YOUTH

Another adventurous group is Sonic Youth with Thurston Moore (b.1958) and Lee Ranaldo (b.1956) on guitars. Formed in New York in 1981, they use avant-garde sounds and approaches and acknowledge the influence of the experimental composer and guitarist Glenn Branca (*see page 31*). Their music evinces enervating lassitude and they adopt strange tunings and sequences. Guitars are used to make noise, and all sorts of unusual objects – including pieces of wood and screwdrivers – are wielded to give new textures.

The group's experimental album *EVOL* (1986) is a departure within rock, yet fits into a line of development begun by The Velvet Underground. The track "Tom Violence" has a hypnotic character and guitars are used to create passages of unfamiliar sounds and ringing harmonies that have a dark, sombre quality, sounding like the sonic backdrop to a gloomy urban wasteland.

"Met A Stranger On A Train" starts with koto-like harmonics interweaving irregularly with ringing notes over a simple rhythm that creates a disembodied, dream-like feeling. The beginning of "Star Power" is seemingly conventional, until the guitars crash in with buzzing sounds and explosive noises before progressing to a dissonant passage full of what sounds like the clattering of industrial machinery. "Green Light" eschews all trappings of conventional melody and harmony over a stark rhythm. Instead, the guitars play alienating riffs and meandering interludes, with detuning that creates bell and clock-chiming sounds. The group plays extensive dirge-like passages over basic rhythms, the guitars totally rejecting conventional vocabulary in a manner that is both questioning and disturbing.

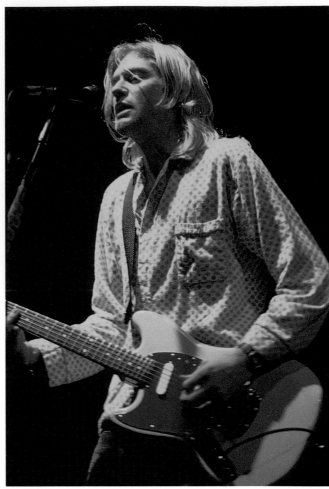

KURT COBAIN

One of the most talented figures of the 1990s, Kurt Cobain (1967–94) demonstrates melodic sensibilities, and his material conveys emotion and frustration. He plays with distortion and effects, holding on to notes to give them a powerful tone. On the album *Nevermind* (1991), "Smells Like Teen Spirit" starts with rough-edged rhythm guitar and builds up

TOM MORELLO

With the Californian rap metal band Rage Against The Machine, Tom Morello (b.1965) is an important innovator. On their eponymous 1992 debut album he redefined the role of the guitar and expanded its range of textures. Playing within visceral funky hip-hop rhythms, he has used the guitar to imitate samples and scratchy turntable interjections in the manner of a DJ. He uses effects including a whammy pedal and techniques such as rapid switching.

THE RED HOT CHILI PEPPERS

A group that combines an intense, funk style with rap and progressive ideas, The Red Hot Chili Peppers have had a shifting personnel on guitar. The album *Blood Sugar Sex Magik* (1991) features John Frusciante (b.1971), who combines funk with rock riffs and drops in zany rock solos and fills. "The Power Of Equality" reveals bright sounds with a metallic edge to the sharp rhythmic parts, and he adds wah wah and blues-influenced breaks. Other tracks often use brittle, funky rhythms. Heavy riffs and screaming solos define "Suck My Kiss" and he uses acoustic guitar on "I Could Have Lied".

THE 1990s

As the 1990s unfolded, a number of figures established themselves on the rock scene. The Smashing Pumpkins, formed in Chicago in 1989 with Billy Corgan (b.1967) and James Iha (b.1968), encapsulate modern trends with their mixture of rock and progressive sounds from the 1960s and 1970s. On the album *Siamese Dream* (1993), "Cherub Rock" opens with a funky sound, with heavy, distorted guitar dominating the song and a skewed rock solo; the energetic "Geek USA" adopts punk rock with riffs and high-register interjections that drop away to a spacey interlude then a fast rock solo. The group build a series of sound pictures in their music. "Quiet" starts with noises that have a mechanical texture, and the song is built around hypnotic riffs. "Hummer" has a floating, mellifluous solo passage at the end, and a dream sequence is created for "Soma", with opening melodic lines that break into rock chords and soloing. On the album *Mellon Collie And The Infinite Sadness* (1995), the group produce a range of material, from the heavy riffing of "Zero" to more reflective sounds.

Prevalent trends mirror recent history in popular music. There is a heavy-metal world of players displaying ferocious physicality and technique, such as Diamond "Dimebag" Darrell with Pantera producing popular guitar solos including "Floods" (1996). the other extreme, songwriter Beck (Beck Hansen, b.1970) has brought together a tremendous range of guitar styles on albums such as *Mellow Gold* (1994) and *Odelay* (1996). His modern, diffused crossover style best uses guitar when it merges into the whole as a modern folk instrument, with a vocabulary that draws on a vibrant heritage.

quickly to heavy distortion. Atmospheric broken colour chords and overdriven sustaining guitar add to the intensity, and the simple guitar solo is based on the vocal line with a processed, effect-laden sound. On other tracks, Cobain uses the guitar in a balanced way to enhance the songs. "Come As You Are" features guitar sounds processed with effects, low broken chords and bright additions with a shimmering solo. "Breed" is typical of Cobain: the guitars are bright and fuzzy, but pushed into the background in a murky, dark mix that rolls along as a backdrop. His energy can be heard on "Territorial Pissings" – driving wild, punk-style guitar with touches of feedback. He also uses acoustic guitar effectively. In his tragically short career, Cobain triumphantly re-established a way of playing in which simple guitar merges with the vocals and does not obscure the songs.

BILLY CORGAN
One of the more imaginative 1990s figures, Billy Corgan with The Smashing Pumpkins draws on progressive rock sounds and plays thick, textured guitar over orchestrated backgrounds with synthesizers and mellotrons.

EARLY 1960s JAGUAR
The original Fender Jaguar series ran from 1962 to 1974. With a short scale neck, tremolo system, string mute and a range of individual controls, they produce a bright, metallic tone. Jaguars were adopted by 1980s pop guitarists, including Kurt Cobain.

213

LATIN & WORLD

Introduced in the 16th century, the guitar flourished in Latin America and has been used to produce a wide range of musical styles. It has also spread all over the world, adapting with ease to highly diverse cultures, drawing on indigenous and popular crosscurrents to produce great music in Africa, the Caribbean, India and other regions.

BADEN POWELL *One of the great acoustic virtuosos, the Brazilian guitarist Baden Powell has had a long, fruitful career, recording vibrant music with tremendous technical skill.*

SPANISH AMERICA

As light, portable instruments, guitars and *vihuelas* were ideal for travel and so were taken to the "New World" by Spanish colonists from the 16th century onward. Over the centuries, a vibrant mix of cultures in Latin America led to the development of distinct forms of music.

EARLY MUSIC BOOKS
Spanish books of music for vihuela, *such as Luis de Narvaez's* Delphin de Musica *(1538), were being sent over to Latin America as early as the 16th century and used in the towns and cities of Mexico and other countries.*

The *vihuela*, a type of large renaissance Spanish guitar, often with six strings, was taken to the Caribbean and Mexico during the early 16th century. A reference from 1509 indicates that the instrument was being used on the island of Hispaniola at that time, and a *vihuela* player named Ortiz accompanied the conquistador Hernán Cortés on one of his expeditions in 1519. With contributions from the indigenous population and imported slaves from Africa, Latin America developed unique cultural crosscurrents. A traveller in Mexico in the first half of the 17th century described South American Indians dancing in a Spanish style accompanied by the guitar, and in the Mexican book *Tablature de Vihuela* (1740), songs and dances of African slaves are written out to be played on a relative of the guitar.

ARGENTINA & URUGUAY

Gauchos helped to establish the guitar in 19th-century Argentina and Uruguay, accompanying Spanish-influenced songs with their *rasgueado* strumming. Precursors of tango groups used

line-ups such as a trio of flute, violin and guitar for dances. The tango evolved in Buenos Aires in the 1920s and 1930s, where one of the first singing stars, Carlos Gardel, used backing guitarists who played with a strummed style. Julio Sagreras (b.1879) took tangos and adapted them for guitar. Another major figure who developed Argentinian music for the guitar was Abel Fleury (1903–58), who produced pieces such as "Ausencia", a *milonga* (an Argentinian dance predating the tango) in 2/4 time that has a sombre melody. In the 1980s, Fleury's music was arranged by classical guitarist Roberto Lara.

CUBA

Spanish, African and French cultural influences have shaped Cuban music, which has developed many styles, including *rhumba* rhythms and *son*, a statement-and-answer form conveyed with powerful intensity.

The singer and guitarist Maria Teresa Vera (b.1895) plays infectious *rhumba* rhythms to provide a full backing on "Buchin El Carpintero" (1916). On the emotional "Cintura De Alambre" (1920), a *son* with a strong Spanish flavour, she sings phrases and answers them with strummed melodic figures.

The *tres*, a guitar with three courses with octave strings, is widely used in Cuba. In the 1920s and 1930s, *tres* player Miguel Matamoros produced music with finely woven parts of catchy melodies and offbeat rhythms.

One of the great *tres* players, Arsenio Rodríguez (1911–72), started playing with *son* groups in the 1920s. He was a tremendous player, composer and bandleader, and his recordings from New York in 1953 are fiery and full of energy: he plays lines with the brass instruments, giving a percussive edge to the music, and adds answering

melodic variants. A piece featuring him, the stunning "Arpeggio Por Arsenio", offers a short, catchy opening figure and Rodríguez improvises with beautifully clear articulation and strong, well-centred rhythmic control, his unusual lines often based on three-note chords with syncopation, with shifting modulation up and down the neck. During the revolutionary turmoil of the 1960s, Silvio Rodríguez, the politically active singer-songwriter and guitarist, emerged as an influential figure. In the modern age, Ry Cooder (*see page 203*) has helped to rediscover figures such as Compay Segundo (b.1907), who plays a small, seven-string guitar.

DIVERSITY

Over the vast area of Latin America, native cultures have had a reciprocal impact on dance, song and rhythms brought in from Spain and Portugal. There are variants on the guitar. The *tiple* with four courses is used in Colombia and Venezuela to accompany dances including the *bambuco*, and in Peru the guitar plays rhythms to accompany the *charango*, a mandolin-like stringed instrument with a back made from armadillo shell. In Mexico, ensembles play a rhythmic accompaniment and melodic fills behind the *huapango*, a fast, complex dance accompanied by heel and toe tapping.

ABEL FLEURY
An important figure in Argentinian guitar history, Abel Fleury took regional folk styles and turned them into polished solo guitar pieces which he recorded and published in Buenos Aires during the 1940s.

AUGUSTIN CARLEVARO
The Paraguayan Augustin Carlevaro, brother of the classical guitarist Abel Carlevaro, has been called the "dean of tango" after devoting himself to the music and making recordings from the 1960s onward, developing traditional material and arranging the compositions of Astor Piazzolla.

STREET BANDS
Latin America is home to many bands playing in all contexts. In Mexico, mariachi bands use a range of guitars of different sizes and registers, including the bass guitarron and the vihuela.

BRAZIL

During the 20th century, a number of great acoustic guitarists have emerged in Brazil. Using classical guitar, they have developed their own distinctive identities, playing music that is often rhythmically dynamic as well as harmonically advanced.

GAROTO
The great early hero in Brazilian guitar, Garoto was a technically versatile player who could work in a range of styles. He integrated Brazilian ideas with outside influences, including swing jazz, developed advanced harmonies and was a prolific writer of beautiful compositions.

By the 19th century, an eclectic blend of Portuguese colonials, European settlers, indigenous cultures and black Africans saw the emergence of ensembles with stringed instruments and percussion playing vibrant rhythmic music loosely based around European dance forms. This was dubbed *choro*, which translates as crying or sobbing. Guitars and *cavaquinhos* are used, producing melodies and harmonies with inventive syncopated rhythmic variations. In the 20th century, jazz influences from America mixed with *choro* and other Brazilian elements to create a sophisticated music that uses distinctive rhythms, including *sambas*.

The great Brazilian guitarist and composer, "Garoto" Anibal Augusto Sardinha (1915–55), came to the fore in the 1930s, playing with many leading bands. In the early 1940s he used electric guitar on recordings such as "Rato-Rato" and "Tico Tico No Fuba", where slide melodies with attractive phrasing and fast, detailed jazz solos meet bright, well-articulated lines.

FUSION PIONEER

Laurindo Almeida (b.1917) played a part in forming the link between Brazilian music and the American jazz scene, recording duos with Garoto in the 1930s. He moved to America in the 1940s and in 1947 worked with Stan Kenton's band, playing nylon-string guitar. His 1950s albums with saxophonist Bud Shank, including *Brazilliance,* were forerunners of the fusion of modern jazz and Brazilian *samba* that came to be termed *bossa nova*. In a long career, he was central in the *bossa nova* movement, and played with Stan Getz in the 1960s.

LAURINDO ALMEIDA
One of the first Brazilian guitarists to become established in America, all-rounder Almeida played classical as well as steel-string guitars.

a sumptuous, harp-like tone with beautiful chord voicings and arpeggiation. In contrast, Bola Sete (Djalma de Andrade, 1923–87) demonstrates a fast, inventive linear jazz style on both acoustic and electric guitar, producing flamboyant solos such as "Copacabana".

BOSSA NOVA

During the 1950s, composer Antonio Carlos "Tom" Jobim was writing songs with rich, modulating harmonies and attractive melodies, while João Gilberto (b.1931) was developing his highly personal style of singing and playing *samba* rhythms with subtle displacements to create a captivating sound. Gilberto's recording of Jobim's "Chega Da Saudade" (1958), paired with his own "Bim-Bom", caused a sensation, and was part of the beginning of the Brazilian *bossa nova,* or new wave. Gilberto's albums *Chega de Saudade* (1959) and *João Gilberto* (1961) combined intimate, seductive vocals, light *samba* rhythms and classical and jazz harmonies in which bass and upper chord voicings alternated, helping to define the new, appealing style.

Outside Brazil, Jobim's "Desafinado" became a hit in Europe and the USA when it was recorded in 1962 by Charlie Byrd (*see page 108*) and saxophonist Stan Getz. Byrd was one of the few established American guitarists to use a classical guitar; on "Desafinado", he plays the harmonies with a subdued understatement and takes a dry, elliptical solo over the rhythm section. The classical guitar *bossa nova* sound was further popularized when Getz and Gilberto recorded the album *Samba Jazz* (1962), and a year later released "The Girl From Ipanema" with Astrud Gilberto on vocals. Gilberto's modulating chord sequence, played with a laconic rhythm style and earthy texture, helped make this track one of the most popular guitar pieces in musical history.

Garoto's multi-faceted musical personality included classical technique, revealed on his recording of intricate acoustic fingerstyle pieces such as "Primavera". He established a strong Brazilian guitar style, and the 1950s saw many following his lead, including Paulinho Noguieira (b.1929) who produced the influential album, *A Voz Do Violão* (1958).

Noguieira recorded instrumental solos on classical guitar in a Brazilian style, achieving

PAULINHO NOGUEIRA
A talented acoustic virtuoso, Noguiera plays entrancing chord melodies with great refinement. He has a classically influenced technique with a bright tone and sustain, and plays a range of material, including pieces by Garoto.

LUIZ BONFÀ
An important composer and guitarist, Luiz Bonfà (b.1922) emerged in the mid-1950s and wrote much important material, including the sound track for the film "Orfeo Negro" ("Black Orpheus", 1959), which became standard repertoire.

JOÃO GILBERTO
In his long career, Gilberto has recorded a tremendous range of material, stamping it with his own inimitable style.

SAMBA STYLES

Samba and *bossa nova* rhythms are written in both 2/4 and 4/4 time. They have rhythmic patterns featuring a series of syncopations with tied notes which often run across bars. *Samba* with jazz harmonies, and bass patterns with repeating bass or root-to-fifth movements, also form the basis of *bossa nova* guitar styles. The five two-bar samba/bossa examples below can all be seen as repeating patterns or excerpts from chord sequences. (*See pages 235–35 for musical terminology.*)

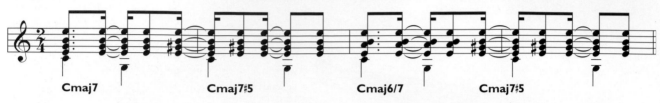

Cmaj7   Cmaj7♯5   Cmaj6/7   Cmaj7♯5

EXAMPLE 1
This has three voicings built on C major 7 with alternating root-to-fifth movement in the bass. The fifth, G above the root, moves up to an augmented fifth, then a sixth, to give a close voicing before moving back down to an augmented fifth.

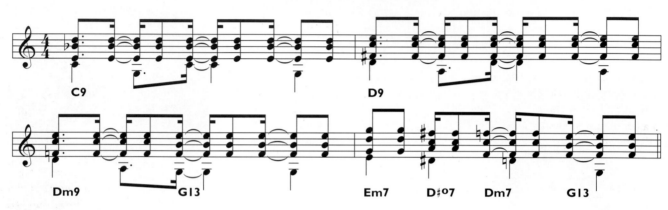

C9   D9

Dm9   G13   Em7   D♯°7   Dm7   G13

EXAMPLES 2 AND 3
In **2**, the C9 chord has an alternating fifth in the bass and moves up to a D9 with the same shape and alternating bass. **3** has Dmin9 with root to fifth moving down to G13, and then a chromatic descent in the bass from Emin7 to D♯ dim7 to Dmin, before returning to G13.

Am9   Bm11   E13♭9 Am9   Am♯9   Am9   Am6/9

EXAMPLE 4
Amin9 with a close voicing moves to Bmin11, retaining the E in the upper voice before moving to an E13♭9 that resolves to Amin9. This proceeds with an internal voice moving through the chord, giving Amin/maj9, Amin9 and Amin6.

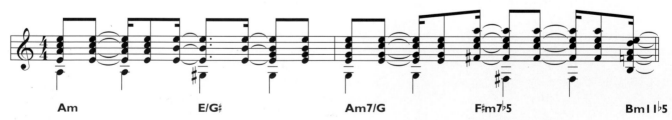

Am   E/G♯   Am7/G   F♯m7♭5   Bm11♭5

EXAMPLE 5
This starts with Amin and has a descending bass, moving in semitones. Amin moves to E/G♯, then Amin/G and F♯ min7♭5 before moving to a Bmin7♭5 chord. The upper note E is retained throughout the sequence.

BADEN POWELL

A brilliant virtuoso, Baden Powell (Roberto Baden Powell de Aquino, b.1937) drew on the innovations of Garoto and Nogueira as well as *bossa nova,* and developed his own dynamic fingerstyle approach characterized by a strong tone and physicality, great technical flair and rhythmic verve. He incorporates rhythmic ideas from percussion instruments and improvises with a succession of fast, plucked chords, often staccato, to form musical sentences. Melodic variations on solos are created using arpeggios and single notes and he incorporates classical flamenco and jazz ideas.

Powell became established in Rio de Janeiro at the end of the 1950s and often worked with a co-writer, producing material such as *Samba Triste* (1959). From the 1960s onward, he recorded prolifically in ensembles and occasionally solo. In the early 1960s, he recorded "Girl From Ipanema" with a group and then reprised the chords and rhythms when he played it as a solo piece. He conveys a sense of momentum with rolling, syncopated rhythm and melody supported by arpeggios, then moves the harmonies with a rhythmic improvisatory style. Powell's compositions often have varied sections. His standard "Berimbau" (1964) features a powerfully hypnotic rhythmic modal figure and a melody with arpeggios before moving to a contrasting section with sentimental chords.

On the album *Tristeza On Guitar* (1966) he plays with flute, bass and percussion. "Tristeza" is bright and sunny, with clean syncopated chords and passages of chord melody soloing. Thelonius Monk's jazz standard "Round Midnight" is played with a measured elegance, using space and conveying emotional depth by the careful deployment of a variety of expressive tones, bluesy bends and flurries of notes on sensitive, inventive lines. On "Sarava", Powell adopts close-voicing chords and incorporates a chord melody soloing over an infectious rhythm with a range of percussion. The hypnotic Afro-samba "Canto De Ossanha" starts with interweaving bass parts and juxtaposes catchy, rhythmic melodies with insistent underlying syncopated chords.

A UNIQUE SOUND
One of the foremost acoustic players of the 20th century, Baden Powell forged his own sound. He improvises with chords and rhythms, as well as arpeggios and single notes, and uses a variety of voicings with a resonant tone and presence. He is shown here in the late 1960s and early 1990s.

POEMS ON GUITAR

In a group context, Powell's ability shines on a wide range of material. On *Poema On Guitar* (1967), "Feitinha Pro Poeta" contrasts dissonant opening chords with a light, dancing melody over a relaxed groove; Powell plays a single line solo with fast passages. "Consolacão" features tangled, low legato passages and the attractive, pensive chords of "Samba Triste" suddenly burst into life with bouncing rhythmic variations. The haunting solo piece "Euridice" conveys a stillness with shimmering chords and "Reza" crackles with flamenco touches. Powell's mastery on "All The Things You Are" creates melodic variations and arpeggios based on the harmonies with a Brazilian and classical flavour linking chords with single-line passages.

GILBERTO GIL

Playing acoustic and electric guitar, Gilberto Gil (b.1942) created his own type of pop fusion. He emerged in the late 1960s and developed a light, positive melodic crossover sound called "Tropicalismo". His album Refazenda *(1975) has funky, samba-rock rhythms on tracks such as "Ela".*

OSCAR CASTRO-NEVES

A guitarist who has developed within the mainstream, Oscar Castro-Neves (b.1940) has a fine controlled classical style.

TONINHO HORTA

A player who developed a progressive fusion sound, Toninho Horta (b.1948) plays acoustic and electric guitar. On the track "Vento" from the album Toninho Horta *(1981) he sings over beautiful, drifting ambiguous voicings and progressions played on electric guitar with a processed sound.*

The album is full of different moods and approaches; "Manha Da Carnaval" is slow and reflective with attractive voicings, "Invenção Em 7½" is like a classical invention, with interweaving upper and lower parts and the guitar playing lower chords and lines, and the guitar on the introspective "Das Rosas" plays a long series of inventive voicings. "O Astronauta" is vibrant and jazzy, with powerful, driving chord figures.

BREAKTHROUGH

Powell visited Europe in 1967, winning wide acclaim and rave reviews. His fantastic power can be heard on the live *Berlin Festival Guitar Workshop* (1967) where he simply overwhelms the rhythm section. "The Girl From Ipanema" bursts with rhythmic invention as Powell rolls through complex syncopations and strumming patterns. "Samba Triste" hums with pulsating electricity, and the solo on "Berimbau", on which strumming cyclical patterns are played with a sparkling agility, is full of rich textures and mesmerising intensity.

His introspective album *Solitude On Guitar* (1971) comprises mainly solo pieces. Highlights include "Introducão Ao Poema Dod Olhos Da Amada", which is a journey through a colourful landscape of pensive moods, the sorrowful "Se Todos Fossem Iguais A Voce", full of lamentation encapsulated by a resonant string sound, and the group piece "Marcia E Tu Amo" which conveys yearning via a flamenco sound and emotional soloing. The atmospheric "Por Causa De Voce" has a melancholic depth and an Oriental sound. Sweet, poignant harmonies on "Solitario" evoke loneliness.

EGBERTO GISMONTI

A visionary composer and guitarist, Egberto Gismonti (b.1947) started with piano and studied composition in Europe with Nadia Boulanger. He became interested in Brazilian music and took up guitar in 1967. Gismonti's

music is shaped by classical compositional thinking and progressive jazz. Drawing on Native South American Indian traditions from the remote parts of Brazil, he has created a music for guitar and piano that has unique depth and colour; his work ranges from reflective pieces imbued with a meditative stillness to compositions that simmer with rhythmic density. By the early 1970s he was using 8-string guitar and one of his early albums, *Danca Dos Cabecas* (1976), demonstrates sensitive, sophisticated playing and interplay with percussion.

Gismonti works with ideas from around the world and experiments with crossover styles, including Indian on "Raga" (1978), that features 8-string guitar with percussion backing. He

creates startling vocal textures, with lines that move from harmonics to a breathtaking range of staccato sounds over a pedal tone, and uses space with great effect, building suspense with repeating motifs and flurries of swirling notes interspersed with passages of silence.

There is a calm intimacy in the weaving arpeggios on "Salvador" (1979), played on 8-string guitar; the unexpected harmonic shifts take listeners on a journey, beguiling them with thoughtful melodic improvisation, rich bass textures and percussive artificial harmonics.

RAFAEL RABELLO

An outstanding prodigy, Rafael Rabello (1962–95) integrated classical flamenco and tango ideas to create his own virtuosic style. On *Rafael Rabello* (1988), he plays 7-string classical guitar. "Lamentos Do Morro" features a recurring tremolo note with chords across it, pulsating rhythms and punchy staccato with tremendous drive. He improvises with a legato linear technique featuring a sensuous string tone and colour. Delicate arpeggiation with doubled notes and altered scales creates a rolling, tangled beauty on "Comovida". "Ainda Me Relondo" weaves inventive, low-bass figures underneath liltingly rhythmic, bouncing chords.

On "Magico" (1980), steel-string arpeggiation with soprano sax and double bass conjure a dreamlike continuum where a gentle, round-toned, nylon-string guitar comes in to play a sensitive solo.

Gismonti's voicings are influenced by piano and he uses 10- and 14-string guitars to create large, wide voicings and fresh sounds. An outstanding album, the concentrated, intense *Danca Dos Escravos* (1989), uses the guitar to imitate percussion instruments. "Trenzinho do Caipira (Verde)" opens with meditative, single-note lines brushed with delicate minute touches and low bass notes, giving way to shimmering sounds with a staccato melody, with earthy notes that are bent out of pitch and staccato chords with dissonance. Notes are mixed with percussive, high-register, artificial harmonics, and Gismonti plays dark, rumbling lower-string figures with buzzing strings and vocal upper answering phrases. Using great dynamic control with quiet passages, he plays with meditative concentration, moving into a landscape of mysterious textures. In contrast, his single-note improvising on "Alegrinho" is full of caprice and inventive turns, performed in a style between jazz and classical music.

HAWAII & INDIA

A curious circular interrelationship links India, Hawaii and slide guitar playing. Hawaiian slide guitar developed during the 19th century, after the slide style was introduced from India; and during the late 20th century, the popularity of the guitar has led to its adoption in India.

SOL HOOPII
One of the great virtuosos on Hawaiian slide guitar, Sol Hoopii is shown here with a small lap steel that has a bakelite guitar-shaped body.

NATIONAL STYLE 3
Ornate, metal-bodied Tri-cone guitars, featuring three resonating cones, were first developed in the 1920s and used by Hawaiian musicians including Sol Hoopii.

Indian musicians have been playing slide style on instruments such as the *vichitra vina* (a kind of sophisticated zither) for hundreds of years. Indian sailors may have introduced slide styles to Hawaii, as there is a description in 1884 mentioning an Indian sailor playing slide-style guitar and attracting keen attention for the way he played. Slide returned to India on the guitar when the Hawaiian player Tau Moe, working in Calcutta in the 1940s, helped to start a fashion that led to middle-class Bengali girls being taught to play *Tagore* songs using the Hawaiian-style guitar.

HAWAIIAN SLIDE

The first Hawaiian slide exponent was Joseph Kekuku, who started recording in 1909. By the mid 1920s, Hawaiian music had became fashionable in America and many recordings feature players using "slack key" open tunings. One of the most talented was Sol Hoopii, born in Honolulu in 1902.

INDIAN SLIDE

The guitar was established during the 1960s as a slide instrument used to improvise and develop traditional phrases within the classical traditions and frameworks that used *raga* scales and *tala* rhythmic cycles. Archtop acoustic guitars are placed on the floor, and the musicians sit beside them, using thumb and fingerpicks on the right hand and playing slide with a bar. Brij Kabra produced ground-breaking recordings such as "Call Of The Valley" (1968), that features astonishingly subtle and expressive slide. Vishwa Mohan Bhatt (b.1952) plays with great depth and uses added drone and sympathetic strings tuned to the *raga*.

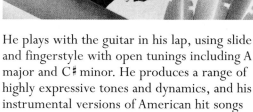

He plays with the guitar in his lap, using slide and fingerstyle with open tunings including A major and C♯ minor. He produces a range of highly expressive tones and dynamics, and his instrumental versions of American hit songs were widely popular. Among his recordings from the late 1920s are "Twelfth Street Rag", on which his tremendous fingerstyle technique is backed by stomping rhythm; he slides and shakes notes, and creates a tremulous sound with exclamatory phrases. "I Ain't Got Nobody" features biting, staccato, stinging lines, ethereal whispering and very effective crying, descending phrases. The popularity of this type of music led the Rickenbacker company to make the "Frying Pan", the first commercial lap steel guitar with a magnetic pick-up, in 1931. In the 1930s Hoopii adopted the electric lap steel slide guitar, which was later taken up by players in country music.

CARIBBEAN & REGGAE

Black music in the Caribbean is a diverse mixture of folk styles and a range of rhythmic styles with African and Latin influences. From the late 1950s onward, Jamaica led the explosion in popular styles, including ska and reggae, with electric guitarists developing unique rhythmic styles.

Many different styles appeared in the Caribbean, from Trinidadian calypso to the acoustic folk style of the Bahamian Joseph Spence (1910–84). Important developments took place in Jamaica, including ska – a medium- and fast-tempo swing rhythm with the guitar playing delayed offbeat chords – which emerged by the early 1960s. The word "ska" is thought to derive from the sound the electric guitar made when playing the chord. Pioneers of ska included the Studio One label, with producer Clement "Coxsone" Dodd, and the guitarist Ernest Ranglin (b.1932) who played with Clue J & The Blues Blasters, recording instrumentals such as "Surfing".

REGGAE & THE WAILERS

The brilliantly talented songwriter Bob Marley (1945–81) was brought up in Kingston, Jamaica, and started recording in 1961. A year later, he teamed up with guitarist Peter Tosh (1944–87) and a rhythm section to form The Wailers, playing music influenced by R&B, soul, gospel and ska. They had an early hit with "Simmer Down" (1964). From around 1968, they developed the distinctive offbeat patterns that came to be known as reggae. The track "Cheer Up" (1969) has a bright, abrasive, scratchy rhythm, and the type

SKA & THE SKATALITES

One of the leading ska groups, the Skatalites, formed in 1963, were a jazzy instrumental brass line-up with the guitarist Jerome "Jah" Jerry Hines (b.1921) playing a minimal rhythm role supporting tracks dominated by melodies, riffs and saxophone solos such as "Lee Harvey Oswald", "Bridge View" and the uptempo "Teach The Ska". In the UK and the USA, there were ska hits with bright guitar rhythm, such as Millie's "My Boy Lollipop" (1964). A slower, rock-steady style with greater emphasis on the rhythm section came in during the mid 1960s, when Jamaican music absorbed ideas from the black soul music of the USA.

ERNEST RANGLIN
With a long career starting in the 1950s, Ernest Ranglin has worked as a fine jazz guitarist and contributed a great deal to Jamaican music as a session musician on many tracks.

REGGAE STYLES

The guitar rhythms and approaches developed in reggae underpin the sound of Bob Marley's successful singles. After Tosh left the group in 1974, Marley used a number of players, including Earl "Chinna" Smith and Donald Kinsey. "Is This Love?" (1978) has catchy linear riffs, and "Three Little Birds" (1980) and "Buffalo Soldier" (1983) have simple rhythms. "Could You Be Loved" (1980) features a funky, muted rhythmic line and short, offbeat chords.

THE WAILERS
Bob Marley and Peter Tosh forged their style of rhythm that contrasts with earlier styles, and uses different offbeat patterns.

BACKBEAT CHOP
One of simplest reggae rhythms is a quickly strummed staccato chord "chink" on the upper strings on the second and fourth backbeats of a bar of 4/4. The chord here is a B♭ major, using the upper four strings. In certain arrangements, this positioning of a chord lifts like an offbeat.

OFFBEAT VARIATIONS
With left-hand muting controlling the sound, the guitar plays repetitive, offbeat patterns and variations. In this example, C minor is played on different offbeat sixteenths (semiquavers), and other parts of the chord are sometimes added. Left-hand muting is also used where the strings are marked with an X.

OTHER RHYTHMS
A lilting, triplet feel also occurs in reggae, and chords can be played on the beats as well. This example shows A minor moving to D minor with a triplet feel; offbeats are also followed by on-beats on the fourth beat of the bar.

PETER TOSH
One of the finest reggae guitarists, Peter Tosh developed his sound and moved toward a rock approach in the 1970s.

of sound which would make the group popular can be heard on "Trenchtown Rock" (1971), driven by an insistent, hypnotic guitar rhythm. "Stir It Up" (1973) has bright, chipped chords and wah-wah fills, and the funky "I Shot The Sheriff "(1973) features inventive liquid rhythms with wah wah.

KING TUBBY & DUB

In the early 1970s, artists such as singer Yabby U (Vivian Jackson), and D.J. U Roy (Ewart Beckford) put out singles on which an

PETER TOSH

After leaving The Wailers in 1974, Peter Tosh became a successful solo artist characterized by an expressive use of reggae rhythms and tempos. "(You Gotta Walk) Don't Look Back" (1978) rolls along in a trotting rhythm, and a laid-back chopping rhythm is put down for "Pick Myself Up" (1978). He uses wah-wah sounds on "Crystal Ball", and "Reggaemylitis" (1981) has a dry sound with echo. His witty and infectious reggae version of "Johnny B. Goode" (1983) has an overdriven, bluesy sustaining guitar solo. The live "Equal Rights-Downpresser Man" (1984) stands out with its catchy upper register, melodic additions and sonic elements.

instrumental version of the A side track with creative studio dubbing produced by King Tubby was put on the B-side. This approach became known as "dub". Sections from session guitarists such as Earl "Chinna" Smith (b.1955) were extensively doctored, using echo, tone and volume variations and other effects to give colourful touches ranging from smooth lines to abrasive, spiky chords. The instrumental album by Yabby U, "King Tubby's Prophecy of Dub" (1976), with guitarists Earl "Chinna" Smith, Albert Griffiths (b.1946) and Ranchie McClean, opens with the floating "Version Dub", on which guitar sounds, including single-note slow trills, slides, octaves and chords, fade away with long, repeating echoes. "Beware Of God" features a rasping sound for the melodic intro and a bluesy solo. A disturbing sonic landscape with descending glissando octaves, short, muted fills, rattling echo and volume level fluctuations is created for "Robber Rock", and on "Rock Vibration", the guitar loses itself in a shimmering landscape, with dragged offbeat effects. Offbeat chords on "Zion Is Here" shift position to give a spatial effect, and "Love And Peace" is textured with echo, fading wah wah, metallic, liquid tones and bluesy improvising. Smoky chords, see-sawing dynamics and bluesy fills can be heard on "Homelessness".

LES PAUL TV
Peter Tosh played a Les Paul TV Special with a limed yellow finish, which first came out with double cutaways and 22 frets clear of the body in 1959.

AFRICA

Myriad cultural crosscurrents and tribal traditions — from music played on indigenous instruments to influences from the Americas and Europe — are reflected in African guitar styles. Today, acoustic and electric guitars are fully established in both rural and urban communities.

KWA MENSAH
Described as the "grandfather of palm-wine highlife", the Ghanaian guitarist Kwa Mensah was taught by his uncle Jacob Sam, also known as Kwame Asare, and during the 1950s released dozens of recordings.

Exploration and early settlements by the Portuguese may have taken the guitar and its relatives to Africa as early as the 16th century, although little physical evidence exists to confirm this. However, there have always been indigenous lutes and harps, and a traveller visiting the Guinea coast in 1669 mentions "a sort of guitar" with six strings which may be a harp-lute. By the 18th century the *ramkie,* a plucked, stringed instrument is mentioned in southern Africa. During the late 19th century, colonial expansion by the British and French, and links with Brazil and the Caribbean, brought the guitar to west Africa. By the late 1920s, the instrument was well established and singers and groups with guitars travelled to London to make recordings.

AFRICAN STYLES

Capos are often used to play guitars with gut and steel strings with standard and unusual open tunings to give higher register open-string positions, and many African guitarists play by plucking with a finger and thumb. Musical forms are often based on indigenous rhythmic approaches; cyclical melodies mixed with basic chords, bass runs and added fills are played with an infectious dancing momentum.

In Ghana, the introduction of the early style known as palm-wine highlife is linked with the traditions of the Kru fishermen and sailors. In 1928, Ghanaian guitarists Kwame Asare (Jacob Sam) and H. E. Biney in the Kumasi Trio can be heard using repeating melodic figures in an eight-beat pattern to support the song "Yaa Amponsah". Kwame Asare's nephew Kwa Mensah took up the guitar and became a prolific recording artist during the 1950s.

With the advent of radio and recordings and the subsequent dissemination of ideas, the developing towns on the west coast of Africa became musical centres, where visiting musicians and recordings of styles ranging from jazz to Brazilian and Cuban music could be heard and assimilated. Church music and styles from across the Atlantic helped to shape the development, and ideas were incorporated from calypso, *rhumba* and *samba* rhythms.

Nigeria, adjacent to Ghana, developed its own version of palm-wine highlife; a hybrid indigenous crossover style termed *juju* appears in the early 1930s in Western Nigeria, centred on Lagos, and is associated with Tunde King (b.1910), who can be heard on "Oba Oyinbo" (1936) playing a clipped, syncopated rhythm on guitar-banjo. Irewolede Denge was a palm-wine guitarist who started recording for Zonophone in 1929. He plays with a rich warmth and his gentle, lilting style with melodic passages answering the vocal line can be heard on "Orin Asape Eko" (1937). He has been called "the grandfather of juju".

ELECTRIC DEVELOPMENTS

In the Congo region from the 1940s onward, a traditional acoustic palm-wine style was being played by figures such as Mwenda Jean Bosco. In cities such as Kinshasa, a contrasting urban music was developing. The legendary player was Franco (Franco Luambo Makiadi, 1938–89), born outside Kinshasa, who started recording in the early 1950s. He took up electric guitar and formed his own group, OK Jazz, in 1956. They developed their own heavily Latin-influenced *rhumba* fusion style. Franco has a bright sound and uses thirds and plays melodic fills figures and countermelodies and chords in songs. On recordings from the late 1950s and early 1960s, he plays unison lines with the saxophone and often uses electric tremolo effects to give a shimmering sound. Tracks such as "Ata Osali Ngai Se Na Ye" and "Ah Nazangi Tata" have a strong Latin and Caribbean flavour.

EARLY HIGHLIFE BANDS

During the 1950s, acoustic groups with guitars playing melodic variations and rhythm parts started to pave the way for guitar groups. In Ghana, highlife was further developed in the 1950s by the guitarist E. K. Nyame (1927–77), who led his own band using a rhythm section with bass and percussion. In Nigeria, a sophisticated sound was being played from the 1950s by trumpet-player and bandleader E. T. Mensah (1919–96), "The King Of Highlife". His brass-dominated group played Latin and African music and, from the end of the 1950s, included electric guitarists playing lines with a tremolo sound.

FRANCO
Called the "sorcerer of the guitar", Franco continually adapted ideas from all types of music and his groups had a tremendous influence on African electric guitar styles. Franco's bands often had large line-ups with guitarists playing rhythms and melodies.

AFRICAN STYLES

There is a vast range of styles across Africa. Rhythmically and harmonically, certain popular styles originated outside Africa but have been transformed by the rhythms and melodies of the powerful indigenous local traditions. There is a tremendous number of variants around three-chord sequences, and eight-beat highlife and irregular, 12-beat bell-pattern rhythms can be heard on acoustic and electric instruments. Fashions spread from west Africa and inspired musicians to develop their own approaches.

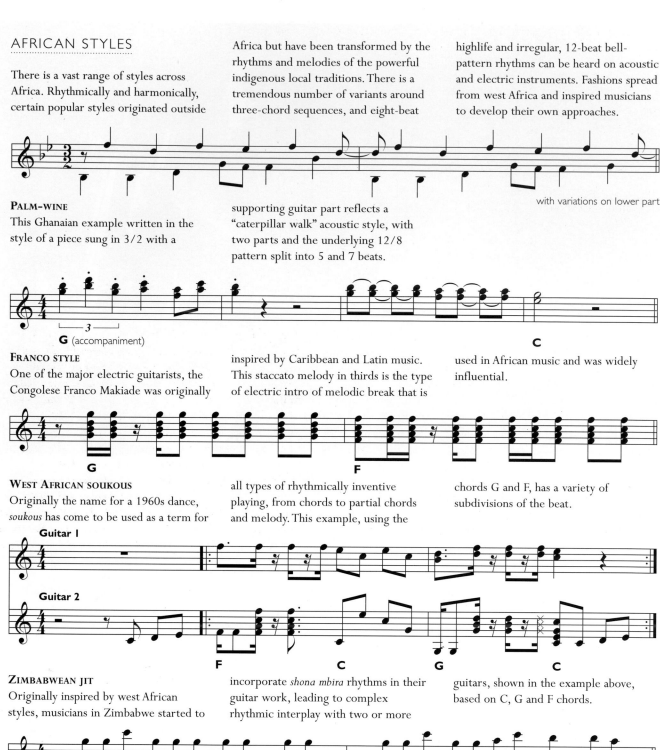

with variations on lower part

PALM-WINE

This Ghanaian example written in the style of a piece sung in 3/2 with a supporting guitar part reflects a "caterpillar walk" acoustic style, with two parts and the underlying 12/8 pattern split into 5 and 7 beats.

G (accompaniment)

FRANCO STYLE

One of the major electric guitarists, the Congolese Franco Makiade was originally inspired by Caribbean and Latin music. This staccato melody in thirds is the type of electric intro of melodic break that is used in African music and was widely influential.

WEST AFRICAN SOUKOUS

Originally the name for a 1960s dance, *soukous* has come to be used as a term for all types of rhythmically inventive playing, from chords to partial chords and melody. This example, using the chords G and F, has a variety of subdivisions of the beat.

Guitar 1

Guitar 2

ZIMBABWEAN JIT

Originally inspired by west African styles, musicians in Zimbabwe started to incorporate *shona mbira* rhythms in their guitar work, leading to complex rhythmic interplay with two or more guitars, shown in the example above, based on C, G and F chords.

KENYAN BENGA

In Kenya there have been parallel developments with two or more guitars playing interlocking melodic rhythms. In the example above, two lines played by separate guitarists work around underlying C, G and F chords.

During the 1960s, Franco moved away from overt outside influences and developed a more African sound. At the beginning of the early 1970s, he can be heard playing acoustic melodic intros and rhythms on "Bomba L'Heure" and "Fungola Ya Mbanda".

Another Congolese guitarist, Dr. Nico (1939–85), played lead guitar in a group with his brother on rhythm guitar, basing their style on that of the indigenous xylophone. Nico's supple, resonant electric style and glistening sound can be heard on "Bilombe Ya Africa" (1962–63), on which he plays chordal melodic fills and solos. In Ghana, the African Brothers Band with Nana Ampadu emerged in 1967,

producing a style that integrated rock and reggae rhythms.

In Nigeria in the 1960s, Ebenezer Obey (b.1942), working with up to 20 musicians in the International Brothers group, developed a jiving, electric *juju* style. Highlife continued in the hands of musicians such as Charles Kofi Mann. During the late 1960s, *soukous* — a *rhumba* variant with an African rhythm — evolved in Congo, and traditional tunes were recorded with *soukous* rhythm. Larger bands were also fashionable, often with three or more guitarists. One played lead, another played rhythm, and a third took a middle part often using an interlocking single note pattern.

Guitars increasingly interacted with percussion and emulated indigenous rhythmic styles. Franco's band had three lead guitarists in the 1970s, and by this time *soukous* had become a term for a wide number of rhythmic styles all over west Africa. In Nigeria, the Kabaka International Band had formed with guitarist Godwin Kabaka Opara, whose jiving, repetitive guitar rhythm with an abrasive sound can be heard on "Onye Mere Ihe Akaya" (1978).

KOO NIMO

Traditional acoustic guitarist Koo Nimo (Daniel Kwabena Amponsah, b.1934), grew up listening to the Kumasi Trio. He uses various scales and modes and palm-wine highlife repeating motifs, often based on an eight-beat pattern, equating with two bars of 4/4. He also uses an irregular, asymmetrical 12/8 rhythmic cycle. Nimo's style is characterized by an intricate thumb and forefinger crossrhythm style called "caterpillar walking", that has affinities with indigenous harp styles. His rhythmic, melody style with lilting rhythms and a touch of classical guitar style can be heard on "Otou Akyeampong" (1976).

NICO MBARGA
Nigerian Prince Nico Mbarga based himself in Cameroon. He developed panko style and had a colossal hit with "Sweet Mother" (1976).

SUNNY ADE
Nigerian guitarist King Sunny Ade (b.1946) developed his own electric juju style that features his cleanly articulated playing.

AROUND AFRICA

The guitar is played all over Africa and both acoustic and electric styles are thriving. In South Africa, the Zulu nation has developed the acoustic *maskanda* style, played with independent patterns that have two and three parts, often based on five- and six-notes scales. The three lower strings represent male voices and three upper strings, women's voices.

In Kenya and Zimbabwe, guitarists were influenced by the styles in west Africa and fused them with their own regional styles. Benga Beat emerged in the 1980s with the Les Kilimambogo Brothers Band. On "Wakumbuke Wazazi", infectious, repeating chords and melodic figures with dry, brittle interlocking fills contrast with minimal fills and sounds created by using a vibrating pick on one note and playing behind the bridge.

Zimbabwe is dominated by the Shona tribe, whose *mbira* thumb piano has influenced guitar playing. In the 1940s, many *mbira* players adapted interlocking *mbira* rhythms for the guitar and this can be heard in the playing of Ngwaru Mapundu. Guitarist Jonah Sithole (b.1952) drew from both Congolese influences and adapted *mbira* ideas to electric guitar. "Zeve Zeve" (1977) opens with a muted, weaving figure and moves into a tremulous melody with glassy rhythm parts shimmering under the vocal. On "Pemberai" (1983), the group developed fast, skittering cyclical rhythmic styles with different guitarists playing crossrhythms.

A further style, *jit,* was developed and played by groups including the Bhundu Boys, who emerged with "Shabini" (1986). An outstanding *jit* group, the Four Brothers, created the bright, layered tapestry of differing rhythms and textures with interweaving melodies and melodic breaks heard on the album *Makorokoto* (1988), which has rasping, dragging figures and snapping rhythms.

Today, Africa is producing some of the most exhilarating guitar styles. Musicians are developing new ideas based on fascinating indigenous instrumental traditions integrated with music styles from all over the world, from blues to jazz.

MALI & GUINEA

In this region, guitar styles are based on folk lutes, the *balafon* (an indigenous xylophone) and the *kora,* a stringed, harp-like instrument. Guitarists such as Papa Diabate and his brother Sékou (who played in the outstanding Benbeya Jazz National Band) and Mory Kante drew on indigenous traditions. In Mali, Ali Farka Toure worked in traditions closer to blues. Today, guitarists play in regional styles, using chords and single-note solos ranging from melodies and countermelodies to flurries of notes supported by pulsating, shifting rhythms. A well-known singer, Salif Keita, joined the guitarist Kante Manfila in Les Ambassadeurs and made great recordings such as "Djata" and "Toubaka" in the early 1980s.

GLOSSARY

altered chord, altered scales A chord or scale in which one or more of the notes is changed to a note not normally associated with that scale.

arpeggio, arpeggiation, arpeggiated Literally, "like a harp", i.e. playing the notes of a chord one after the other rather than together. Also known as a broken chord.

artificial harmonics Harmonics produced by fingering a note on the frets and lightly touching the string a fourth higher.

atonal Not part of the tonal system of major and minor keys, in no key at all.

augmented *see also* **diminished** Intervals increased in size by a semitone are known as augmented intervals. The augmented chord is a major chord with the fifth raised a semitone.

baroque The period in musical history from around 1600 to 1750, characterized by an ornate and dramatic style.

bending *see* **string bending**

blues An African-American hybrid style of music which uses a scale including flattened thirds, fifths and sevenths – "blue notes" – within a predominantly twelve-bar form.

boogie(-woogie) A style of blues and jazz playing with a repetitive rhythmic bass figure derived from early jazz piano-playing.

bop, bebop, hard bop A style of jazz that emerged in the 1940s, using fast melodic lines over adventurous extended harmonies. The terms bop and bebop are interchangeable, and hard bop usually refers to the 1950s blues-influenced variant.

bossa nova A Brazilian rhythmic style of jazz and popular music of the 1950s, widespread in the USA and Europe in the 1960s.

bottleneck A guitar technique using a metal bar or tube rather than the fingers of the left hand to play notes and chords, and to slide from one to another.

break In jazz, a short solo passage without accompaniment that usually occurs at the end of a phrase.

call and response In African-American music, especially early blues, the performance of alternate phrases by different voices or instruments.

chamber music Music for small groups of up to about nine players. The term "chamber jazz" is sometimes used for the more formal style of small combo such as the Modern Jazz Quartet.

changes The sequence of chords used as a basis for improvisation in jazz.

choking Damping the strings of the guitar to give short staccato chords.

chord substitutions In jazz, alternatives to the conventionally used chords in a sequence.

chords, roots, inversions, etc. A chord is any combination of more than one note played together, in tonal music usually based on the triad formed by the first, third and fifth notes of the scale: for example, the chord of C major consists of C (the root of the chord), E, and G. Chords can be in root position, i.e. with the root as the bass note, or various inversions using other notes in the chord as the bass.

chorus *see* **effects**

chromatic Chromatic notes are those that fall outside the notes of the key a piece of music is in. The chromatic scale is a 12-note scale moving in semitones.

Classical The term "classical" is used loosely to describe art music to distinguish it from folk, jazz, rock and pop, etc., but more precisely it refers to the period of music around 1750–1830.

comping Jazz jargon for "accompanying".

compressor, compression, compressed *see* **effects**

counterpoint, contrapuntal The playing of two or more tunes at the same time, within the same harmonic framework. The added tunes are sometimes called "countermelodies".

country (and western) A predominantly white, rural popular music originally from the Southern and Western USA.

DADGAD tuning, etc. *see* **open tuning**

delay *see* **effects**

detuning Intentionally putting one or more of the strings out of tune for a specific effect.

diatonic Using the notes of the major scale.

diminished Intervals decreased in size by a semitone are known as diminished intervals. The diminished chord is based on intervals of a minor third, and the so-called diminished scale consists of alternating tones and semitones.

distortion *see* **effects**

double- (multi-) tracking Recording technique enabling a player to superimpose a number of "takes" of a particular piece.

double stopping Forming a chord by stopping two or more strings with the left hand on the frets.

drone, drone strings Strings not intended to be played with the fingers, but tuned to vibrate in sympathy with the main instrument's strings.

echo *see* **effects**

effects Numerous special effects are possible on the modern electric guitar. They include:

chorus Simulates the effect of more than one instrument playing the same note.

compressor Compression boosts the volume of quieter notes, and reduces that of louder ones, evening out the sound of fast passages.

delay (echo) Mimics the echo effect by playing a delayed copy of the original sound.

distortion Change of tone quality, with a harsh sound achieved by overdriving an amplifier, or the use of a distortion pedal, fuzz box or overdriver.

enhancer Device to improve definition of a sound.

expander The opposite of compressor, increasing the range of volume.

flanger Chorus-type effect, using a delayed signal with a slight pitch variation.

fuzz A form of distortion, operated by a fuzz pedal.

harmonizer A chorus-type effect adding a sound in harmony with the original signal.

Leslie The Leslie cabinet, originally for use with electronic organs, contains a rotating speaker, giving a swirling effect.

octave divider An early form of harmonizer, adding a sound an octave above or below the original signal.

overdriving A form of distortion.

panning Moving the source of the sound within the stereo field.

phasing Playing two identical sounds slightly out-of-phase with one another.

pre-amp The pre-amplifier can be used as a form of tone control, or to boost the signal.

reverb Mimics the echo effect, either by a built-in spring reverb or a digital electronic emulation.

tremolo (tremolo bar) Small and rapid variation in the volume of a note. This effect is often confused with *vibrato,* and the tremolo arm or bar is used to bend the pitch of notes on electric guitars.

Uni-Vibe Swirling effect, similar to Leslie.

vibrato Small and rapid variation in the pitch of a note.

volume pedal Means of altering the volume of sound, useful in creating the "fade-in" effect or as a "swell" pedal.

wah wah The wah-wah pedal controls the relative bass and treble response of a sound. Fully down it has a high treble tone, fully up it emphasises the bass, and the characteristic "wah-wah" sound is achieved by rocking the pedal back and forth.

enhancers *see* **effects**

expander *see* **effects**

fade-up The opposite of fade-out – the sound is brought up gradually by means of a volume control.

feedback The loud whine produced by a microphone or pick-up receiving and amplifying its own signal from a loudspeaker.

fill In jazz and rock, a short melodic figure played by an accompanying instrument between phrases.

flamenco A Spanish style of playing, singing and dancing. Forms of flamenco include *alegrias, bulerias, fandangos, farrucas, ganadinas, malaguenas, seguidillas, siguiriyas, soleas* and *tarantas,* and the guitar often interjects *falsetas* (melodic improvised interludes) into these. Techniques in flamenco guitar-playing include *alzapua* (up and down strokes with the thumbnail), *apagado* (left-hand damping), *golpe* (tapping on the body of the guitar), *picado* (fingerstyle) and *rasgueado* (strumming by unfurling the fingers across the strings).

flanger *see* **effects**

folk The music of rural cultures, usually passed down orally. The word "folk" is also used to describe composed music in the style of true folk music, particularly after the "folk revival" of the 1950s.

free jazz, improv A jazz style of the 1960s which is freely improvised without reference to a specific tune or harmonic sequence.

fusion A hybrid style, generally referring to jazz-rock fusion, but also referring to any form of "crossover" from one style to another.

fuzz, fuzz pedal *see* **effects**

glissando A slide from one note to another.

golpe *see* **flamenco**

grace notes Short notes played just before the main note of a tune as an ornament.

groove A repeated rhythmic pattern in jazz and rock.

habañera A Cuban dance, or its rhythm.

hammer-on, hammering Notes played by hammering the string with the fingers of the left hand, rather than plucked with the right hand.

harmonics Notes with an ethereal tone higher than the pitch of the string, produced by lightly touching the string at certain points.

harmonizer *see* **effects**

head In jazz, the statement of the tune before and after the improvised solos.

interval, intervallic The distance between two notes. For example C to G is a fifth (i.e. five notes of the scale), C to E a third (three notes), and C to C an octave (eight notes).

inversion *see* **chords**

jazz A music of African-American origin, characterized by the use of improvisation, "blue notes" and syncopated rhythms.

Latin Music of Latin-American origin, including dance rhythms such as the habañera, samba, rhumba and bossa nova.

legato Smoothly, not staccato.

Leslie *see* **effects**

licks In jazz and rock, short, almost clichéd, phrases inserted into a solo or used as fills.

microtone Interval of less than a semitone.

MIDI Musical Instrument Digital Interface. This allows musical instruments such as electric guitars and synthesizers to communicate with sequencers, effects boxes, computers, etc.

minimalism A movement in classical music from the 1960s using static harmonies, repeated patterns and a minimum of material.

modes, modal Scales using the notes of the diatonic scale, other than the major and minor scales. The modes, such as Dorian, Phrygian and Aeolian, originated in medieval music, but were adopted by jazz players in the 1950s.

modulate Moving from one key to another.

motif, motivic A short, recognizable melodic phrase.

octave divider *see* **effects**

octave, fifth, third, etc. *see* **interval**

open tuning Tuning the strings of the guitar to a specific chord, rather than the conventional EADGBE. There are also other non-conventional tunings such as DADGAD.

overdriven *see* **effects**

overdubs Parts added to a recording after the original take.

panning *see* **effects**

partial chords Chords not using all the strings of the guitar.

passing chords Chords used "in passing" from one harmony to another, not part of the main harmonic sequence.

pedal note A repeated bass note which supports a sequence of changing harmonies.

pentatonic A scale of five, rather than the more usual seven, notes.

phasing *see* **effects**

pick scrapes Scraping the strings with the pick to give a harsh, grating sound.

pick-up The device on electric guitars that picks up and transmits the sound of the strings to the amplifier.

pickguard A protective plate on the body of the guitar.

pre-amp(lifier) *see* **effects**

pull-off A note played by pulling the string with the fingers of the left hand.

raga A scale used in Indian music. There are hundreds of different ragas, many using microtones.

ragtime An African-American style of mainly piano music, a precursor of jazz.

rasgueado *see* **flamenco**

renaissance The period in music roughly 1300–1600.

reverb *see* **effects**

rhythm and blues African-American pop music originating in the late 1940s, the precursor to rock 'n' roll.

riff In jazz and rock, a short, repeated melodic phrase.

rock, rock 'n' roll Rock 'n' roll evolved in the 1950s from **rhythm and blues,** and in its 1960s form became known simply as "rock".

root, etc. *see* **chords**

rubato Not strictly in tempo – played freely and expressively.

rhumba (rumba) Afro-Cuban dance.

samba Afro-Brazilian dance.

scales, scalar A series of ascending or descending notes in a specific key, the basis for compositions in the tonal system.

segue Moving without a break to the next movement, section or number.

semitone The smallest interval in the diatonic scale – for example, the distance between E and F, or B and C.

serial, 12-tone Avant-garde compositional method using the 12 notes of the chromatic scale in series, without reference to traditional harmony or tonality.

slide A style of guitar-playing using bottleneck, where notes and chords slide from one to another.

staccato Detached. Staccato notes or chords are short and clipped, not smoothly moving to the next.

straight eights, swing In jazz, playing "straight eights" means playing exactly on the beat, whereas "swing" indicates that the rhythm should be interpreted more freely.

string-bending Using the fingers of the left hand to pull a string to one side, "bending" the pitch of the note.

swap fours In jazz, when soloists alternate improvisations with one another every four bars.

swing A style of jazz of the 1940s, mainly for big bands. Also an instruction to play rhythms freely *see also* **straight eights**.

syncopation Shifting the accent of a melody off the main beat of the bar – a characteristic of jazz and much rock and pop music.

tapped notes, tapping Notes produced by tapping on, rather than plucking, the strings.

tempo The underlying speed of a piece of music.

timbre The tone quality of a sound.

tonal, tonality Relating to the system of major and minor keys.

tone (whole tone) An interval of two semitones – for example the distance between C and D, or F and G.

tremolo *see* **effects**

trill Rapid alternation between one note and the note above.

turnaround In jazz, the harmony under the last phrase of a tune taking the music back to the beginning for its repeat.

Uni-Vibe *see* **effects**

unison On exactly the same note. For example, on a 12-string guitar, the pairs of strings are tuned in unison, i.e. to the same note. In jazz, the tune of the head is often played by several instruments in unison.

vamps, vamping Repeated accompanying figure in jazz and popular music.

voicing The spacing of the notes in a chord.

volume pedal *see* **effects**

wah wah *see* **effects**

whole-tone scale A six-note scale formed entirely of intervals of a whole tone, for example C-D-E-F♯-G♯-A♯.

INDEX

ACKNOWLEDGMENTS

AUTHOR'S ACKNOWLEDGMENTS

This book is dedicated to Karen.
I would particularly like to thank the following. My agent Julian Alexander for helping with my synopsis and getting the project off the ground. Carol Chapman for encouraging me to pursue this idea, planning it with me over many years and her invaluable research in every area. She has great perception and musical judgment and without her this book would never have been written. Tim Foster for a tremendous contribution to this book not only as an excellent designer but for an extraordinary amount of work in organising major aspects of the project and adding helpful thoughts on many areas. Without his input this book would never have appeared! Nigel Moyse, a talented friend, for a whole range of high quality transcriptions and written musical examples in rock, pop, blues, jazz, reggae, Brazilian and African music and general help and advice. Rafael for writing the flamenco pieces and advice on flamenco, and Thérèse Wassily Saba for classical and flamenco research. The staff on this book have been good to work with and I thank them for their patience! Christopher Davis for his vision, Susannah Marriott for her passionate enthusiasm for music, all kinds of help and as a positive guiding spirit throughout the project, Jamie Robinson for picture research, Daphne Razazan and Anne-Marie Bulat for important fine tuning and Ann Kramer and Viv Croot for their work as editors and helpful advice. Thanks also to Martin Clayton for letting me read his draft on India for the forthcoming book Guitar Cultures (Berg).

Thanks to all the following for various forms of help: Derek Bailey, Andy Bennett, Eric Clapton, Martin Clayton, Kevin Dawe, Chris Dawkins, Paul Day, Christopher Dean, Lee Dickson, Simon Dinnigan, Jan Fairley, Gerry Farrell, Paul Fischer, Paul Gregory, Fiona Harrison, Vince Hastwell, Lee Hodgson, Nick Hooper, Steve Hoyland, Mike Messer, Richard Padley, Stephen Parker, George Platt, Dominic Raymond-Barker, Gerald Seligman, Andy Simons, Gary Southwell, Joe Staines, Saiichi Sugiyama, Janet Topp-Fargion, Marcus Weekes, David Weston, Jim Westbrook, Martin Wheatley, Andreas Young, Christie's and Incus Records, and to Paul Midgley for advice and the Hank Marvin guitar and equipment.

PUBLISHER'S ACKNOWLEDGMENTS

Dorling Kindersley would like to thank: Maurice Summerfield at Classical Guitar Magazine; Dede Millar and Jon Wilton at Redferns; Andy Seal at Retna Pictures; Dave Booth at Showtime Archives, Toronto; Mike Gavin at Ray's Jazz Shop; Charles Measures at Chandlers; Barry Moorehouse at The Acoustic Centre; Nigel Osborne at Balafon; Dave Brewis, Martin Kelly, Stuart Cumberpatch. Additional picture research by Amaia Allende, Monica Allende, Louise Thomas and Stephen Parker. Also Emily Lightfoot, Salima Hirani, Michael Downey for editorial assistance, Clare Shedden and Rachana Shah for design assistance, Anne Townley for proofreading and Ingrid Lock for the index.

Music
Transcription and composition: Nigel Moyse, except: Rafael 39; Théresa Saba 20, 23.
Permissions: Suzanne Grain. Consultant: Marcus Weeks. Typesetting: Cambridge Notation.
Dorling Kindersley would like to thank the following for their kind permission to reproduce the following musical transcriptions:
20 "Prelude No 1", Villa Lobos Reproduit avec l'autorisation des Editions Max Eschig, Paris, proprietaires de l'oeuvre pour le monde entier.
23 "Chaconne" in D minor, Bach/Segovia GA 14. Reproduced by permission of Schott and Company Ltd, London.
27 "Dreaming" from Nocturnal by Benjamin Britten, Copyright © 1964, 1965 Faber Music Limited. Reprinted by permission of the publishers Faber Music Limited, London.
56 "The Stumble" Music by Freddie King and Sonny Thompson © 1962 Fort Knox Music Co Inc & Trio Music Co Inc Copyright Renewed, All Rights Reserved Reproduced by kind permission of Lark Music Ltd (Carlin), London NW1 8BD/Copyright © 1962 Hal Leonard Corporation.
102 "Solo Flight" by Charlie Christian. Copyright © Mautoglade Music Limited, London.
111 "West Coast Blues" by John L. (Wes) Montgomery © 1960 by Taggie Music Co., a division of Gopam Enterprises, Inc. Renewed. All rights reserved. Used by permission.
131 "Yesterday" and "Day Tripper" Words and Music by John Lennon & Paul McCartney © Copyright 1966 Northern Songs. Used by permission of Music Sales Ltd. All Rights Reserved. International Copyright Secured/Copyright © 1966 Hal Leonard Corporation.
139 "And Your Bird Can Sing" Words and Music by John Lennon & Paul McCartney © Copyright 1965 Northern Songs. Used by permission of Music Sales Ltd. All Rights Reserved. International Copyright Secured/Copyright © 1965 Hal Leonard Corporation.
144 "Crossroads" by Robert Johnson, arranged by Eric Clapton © 1990 world copyright Delta Haze Corporation, USA Exclusive UK licensee: Interstate Music Ltd/Paul Rodriguez Music Ltd
149 "Something" Words and Music by George Harrison. Copyright © Hal Leonard Corporation.
156 "Stairway To Heaven" Words and Music by Jimmy Page and Robert Plant © 1971 Superhype Music Limited, London W6 8BS Reproduced by permission of International Music Publications Ltd.
164 "Goodbye Pork Pie Hat" by Charles Mingus, arranged by Jeff Beck. Reproduced by permission of Complete Music Ltd, London.

Picture Credits
Key to pictures: a = above, b = below/bottom, c = centre, l = left, r = right, t = top
The publisher thanks the following for their kind permission to reproduce the photographs:
Jacket Jazz Index: T. Harvey Collection front cover c; Redferns: back cover bl, Keith Morris front cover tl, David Redfern back cover br, Tony Russell back cover r; Retna Pictures Ltd: Joel Axelrad front cover cl; Rex Features: front cover cr, Albert Ferreira front cover br, spine.
Introduction Christie's Images Ltd: endpapers, 3; London Features International Ltd: Paul Canty 5br; Redferns: William P. Gottlieb/Library of Congress 1, David Redfern 2; Rex Features: Albert Ferreira 6; Val Wilmer: 5t.
Classical Ashmolean Museum, Oxford: 14cl; Bridgeman Art Library, London/New York: The court of Alfonso X 'the Wise', King of Castile and Leon, miniature from the 'Cantigas de Santa Maria' (manuscript) Biblioteca Monasterio del Escorial, Madrid, Spain/Index 10; British Museum, London: 11; Courtesy: Classical Guitar Magazine: 12bc, 13b, 17t, cl, cr, 18br, 19br, 22, 23, 24bc, cl, 26tl, 28b, 30b, 31t, b; Corbis UK Ltd: Archivo Iconografico, S.A. 8, Hulton-Deutsch Collection 20; The English Heritage Photo Library: The Iveagh Bequest, Kenwood 14tr; Hulton Getty: Erich Auerbach 21b; Institut de France – Musée Jacquemart-André. Paris. France: 12l; Libreria del Prado: 18c; The Metropolitan Museum

of Art: Gift of Emilita Segovia, Marquessa of Salobrena, 1986. (1986.353.1) Photograph © 1987 The Metropolitan Museum of Art 21cl; Popperfoto: 25; Redferns: Peter Cronin 30tl, David Redfern 26br, 28tl; Réunion Des Musées Nationaux Agence Photographique: R.G. Ojeda/© Succession Picasso/DACS 2000 19cl; Rex Features: 29cl; The Royal College of Music, London: 13tc, tcl; Jim Westbrook: 15, 18bl.
Flamenco Agencia Efe, S.A.: 38tr, 42br; Bridgeman Art Library, London/New York: El Jaleo, 1882 (oil on canvas) by John Singer Sargent (1856–1925) Isabella Stewart Gardner Museum, Boston, Massachusetts, USA 35; Courtesy: Classical Guitar Magazine: 34, 38cl; Corbis UK Ltd: Elke Stolzenberg 42bc; Libreria del Prado: 36ac, 37, 40cl, 42cl; Redferns: Keith Morris 40br; Rex Features: Michael Holder 43t; Frank Spooner Pictures: Philippe Renault 32, 41, Stills/Banjee 43b.
Blues Balafon Music Books: 47cr; Blues Unlimited: 53; Christie's Images Ltd: 54c; Geoff Dann: 51bcl; Frank Driggs Collection: Ray Flerlage 55cr; Michael Ochs Archives/Venice, CA: F.R.D. 51bcr; Sylvia Pitcher Photo Library: 57bl, 59br, Tony Mottram 61tl, Brian Smith 60b; Redferns: 49bl, Dave Ellis 60cr, Robert Knight 61cr, Elliott Landy 59tl, Michael Ochs Archives/Venice, CA 56, 57tr, 48br, 50, 54b, David Redfern 58br, Brian Shuel 58c; Courtesy of Showtime Archives (Toronto): 51tl, tr, 52, Colin Escott 44, Colin Escott/Ernest C. Withers 54tr; Soldier Myer's Bop House: 48tl; V&A Picture Library: Harry Hammond Collection 55b; Val Wilmer: 46, 47tl.
Country Balafon Music Books: 73bc; Courtesy of Country Music Hall of Fame and Museum: 62, 64cr, 71cr, 73c; Michael Ochs Archives/Venice, CA: 69, 71b, 74bl, Jon Sievert 76tr; Redferns: 65bc, Patrick Ford 77cb, Beth Gwinn 77cr, Michael Ochs Archives/Venice, CA 68bc, 72cl, David Redfern 77ca; Repfoto: Robert Ellis 75b; Retna Pictures Ltd: Robert Altman 75c; Tony Russell: 66-67; Courtesy of Showtime Archives (Toronto): 65tl, 67tl, 70c, 74cl, 76bl, Colin Escott/R. Bennett 68cl, Buck Owens Production Co. Inc. 74cr.
Folk Pierre Bensusan – DADGAD Music: Lebeolinski 90cl; Collections: Brian Shuel 83cr, 84tr, b; Folk Roots Magazine: Ian Anderson 89ca; Courtesy of the Woody Guthrie Archives: 80cl; London Features International Ltd: 84cl, 86br; Angela Lubrano: 91tl; Michael Ochs Archives/Venice, CA: 81tl, 82, John Sievert 87ca; Dave Peabody: 89br; Pictorial Press Ltd: 91cr; Redferns: Pete Cronin 91b, Michael Ochs Archives/Venice, CA 86 cl, Dave Peabody 88t, br, Andrew Putler 87b, David Redfern 81bc, 85t, 88c, Ebet Roberts 78, Tony Russell 86cr, Brian Shuel 83b; Repfoto: Robert Ellis 85cr; Retna Pictures Ltd: John-Christian Jacques 90cr; Southern Folklife Collection: Norman Varshay 80b.
Jazz Richard Chapman: 106bc; Dat's Jazz Picture Library: Derick A. Thomas 122cl; Frank Driggs Collection: 95tr, 97cr, 103t, 104cl, 106cl, 107bl, 118br, Dunc Butler 96tr, Steve La Vere 118cl, John W. Miner 104br, Charles B. Nadell 103c, Popsie Randolph 105bc; Jazz Index: T. Cryer 108br, Christian Him 117bl, 120c, 121t, 123cl, br, Jak Kilby 113cr, cl, Peter Vacher Collection 110br, F. Winham 111; Max Jones Archive: 105tc, 107tr; London Features International Ltd: 114bc, 121b; Redferns: Richie Aaron 120br, William P. Gottlieb/Library of Congress 101, Max Jones Archive 94, 98-99, 102, Michael Ochs Archive/Venice, CA 95tl, 100, 108cl, Andrew Putler 115b, David Redfern 109tr, 112, 115c, t, 116c, 119, 122tr; Retna Pictures Ltd: Michael Putland 116br; Gérard Rouy: 117r; Courtesy Duncan Schiedt Collection: 98cl, Chas Peterson 95b; John Smith: 110cl; Star File, Inc.: Steve Joester 117tl; Val Wilmer: 92, Peter Tanner 96bc.
UK Rock & Pop Apple Corps Ltd: 138 background, 140 background, John Kelly 147, 148bc, cr; Balafon Music Books: 145cb, 149, 154c; Bowstir Ltd: Gered Mankowitz 132–133; Christie's Images Ltd: 126cl, 153b, 170br, 172bl; Corbis UK Ltd: 170bl; DK Picture Library: Apple Corps Ltd 138t, 140t, Courtesy of EMI Records Ltd 161cr; EMI Music Archives: Apple Corps Ltd 129t; Jill Furmanovsky: 165; London Features International Ltd: 134b, 137cb, 141tr, 145c, Griffin 168c, Imperial Press 160b, 166cl, Geoff Swaine 172ac; Angela Lubrano: 173tc; Not Fade Away: 136t, 142, 143tl; Collection of Yoko Ono Lennon: David Behl © 1999 Yoko Ono Lennon. Used by Permission/All Rights Reserved 130cl, 148tl; People in Pictures: Apple Corps Ltd 128bl; Phillips London: Osiris Agency Ltd 141tc; Pictorial Press Ltd: 146, 163tr, M. Sharratt 136b; Player Magazine: 144c; Barry Plummer: 161t, 169tl; Redferns: Richie Aaron 162c, 167c, Balafon Archive 130bl, Chuck Boyd 154cr, Peter Cronin 171t, Mick Hutson 172bc, Bob King 133c, Brian Leggett 166br, Graham Lowe 152cl, Steve Morley 159, Andrew Putler 153c, David Redfern 124, 132c, 134c, 135, 151cr, 155, Ebet Roberts 170cl, Peter Sanders 151tl; Repfoto: Barrie Wentzell 158cr; Retna Pictures Ltd: Michael Putland 162cl, 167tc; Rex Features: 127cr, 139, 152bc, 158bl, Dezo Hoffman 144t, 141bl, Miki Slingsby: 163c; Star File, Inc.: Bob Gruen 157, Jeffrey Mayer 173cr, Jurgen Vollmer 128cr; V&A Picture Library: Harry Hammond Collection 126bc; Val Wilmer: 150.
USA Rock & Pop Balafon Music Books: 186cl; David Brewis: 191cl; Bridgeman Art Library, London/New York: Rock concert poster for The Grateful Dead and others at the Fillmore, San Francisco, 1966 by Wes Wilson (20th century) Private Collection 188cl; Bill Carner: 189b; Christie's Images Ltd: 177b, 181c; Corbis UK Ltd: UPI 182t; DK Picture Library: Rykodisc 197tl; Jill Furmanovsky: 201b; Jean-Pierre Leloir: 191cl; London Features International Ltd: 181t, 187t, Paul Canty 197b, George DeSota 212tr, Sam Hain 208t; Barry Plummer: 188–189; Redferns: Chuck Boyd 187b, 195, Fin Costello 198b, Grant Davis 208c, Mick Hutson 212bl, Elliott Landy 194, Michael Ochs Archives/Venice, CA176, 180cl, 181b, 182br, 184bc, R.B. 185, David Redfern 178, 179, 186c, b, Ebet Roberts 202br, 205cr, 207, 209cr, t, S&G 183t, Chuck Stewart 177t, Michael Uhll 11c; Repfoto: Liza Leeds 213cr; Retna Pictures Ltd: Joel Axelrad 192, Steve Granitz 208b, G. Hanekroot/Sunshine 203c, Photofest 174, Michael Putland 201t, 203t; Rex Features: 190; Dezo Hoffman 200b; Courtesy of Showtime Archives (Toronto): Colin Escott 183b; Courtesy of Sotheby's Picture Library, London: 193bl; Frank Spooner Pictures: J. Marshall/Liaison 198c; Star File, Inc.: Jim Cummins 199bl, Bob Gruen 205b, Laurens van Houten 202cl, Jeff Mayer 211br, Chuck Pulin 204b, 210c, Amalie Rothschild 200t, David Seelig 210b, Barrie Wentzell 196; Topham Picturepoint: 184cl; Val Wilmer: 193tr.
Latin & World Biblioteca Nacional, Madrid: 216; Courtesy: Classical Guitar Magazine: 217tc, cr, 218cr, 219tl, cr; Frank Driggs Collection: 219bl, 224cr; Graeme Ewens: 231b, F. Collins 228; Jazz Index: Christian Him 217b, 221tr; Jak Kilby: 225br, 229, 231tr; Palm Pictures: 225bc; Redferns: Geoff Dann 227cr, William P. Gottlieb/Library of Congress 218b, Tim Hall 232, Mick Hutson 223t, David Redfern 221c, 222cl, tr, 223cr; Retna Pictures Ltd: Adrian Boot 227t; Rex Features: 226; Jack Vartoogian: 214, 222br, 233.

Commissioned Photography: Steve Gorton, except Garth Blore 127.
Additional pictures: Matthew Chattle, Paul Goff, Garth Blore, Andy Crawford, Tim Ridley.